UNCLE ELMER'S

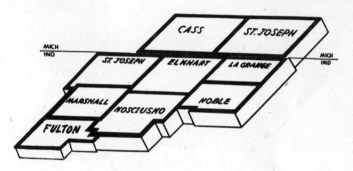

FARM

FAMILY STORIES

Original Manuscripts by:
Elmer Lehman
Published by:
Uncle Elmer's Farm Family Stories
Goshen, Indiana 46526
September, 1974

ELMER E. LEHMAN

DEDICATION

To my countless friends in Michiana, who have egged me on to attempt this for many years; and especially to Aunt Lita, who has sat out in the car waiting for from two to five hours for the story to be wormed out over the kitchen table, in patience and with a knowing twinkle in her eye, when I finally emerge.

Uncle Elmer

PREFATORY

The purpose of this book is manifold.

In the first place it is our hope these stories will serve as a recognition of farm families for the many, long, hard days in the field and over the hot pressure cooker in the kitchen, as well as the hey-days and the heart-breaking days.

Secondly, that the success of these many families, with great odds against them in some cases, will be an encouragement to others to plug on patiently knowing that perseverance is bound to pay off.

Thirdly that we may help glorify Farm Life a bit, for, many hold to this day, that the farm is the best place in the world to live, to bring up a family, and to enjoy a rich life - privation, notwithstanding. For where else may one find, independence, fresh air, unspoiled environment, beauty of nature and the great country cookin', not to mention the unmatched friendly and helpful neighbors.

The Agricultural Agents, extension staffs, Vo. Ag. teachers, as well as many government agency personnel, and Agri-business people have contributed beyond measure. They all know it takes 3 things for a farm family to get their story in this book.

1. A line of forebears who were farmers.
2. Successful family and farming operations story.
3. The family or someone in the family must have made some definite contribution to Michiana Agriculture. For example, Bill and Frances Phillips, and now their son Charles, have never gone big in farming, but who is to measure their contribution to Agriculture for their irrigation water in a dry summer like this?

Uncle Elmer

OSCAR E. ACKERSON — Agronomist

Nels A. Ackerson, born 1857, Marie Olson, born 1859 came to America from Sweden on the same ship in 1886. They landed in Chicago, where it was so hot a team of horses drawing a street car, succumbed on the street. They had both worked in Denmark, he on a horse farm, and she as a milk maid on a dairy farm. They were married in September 1887. They then rented the Thomas Heckerson farm of 80 acres, at Penfield, Illinois, which they farmed for 5 years. Oscar E. was born here in 1890. Four other children born in Illinois, were Alice, Harry, Esther and Ralph. They next rented the Cherry farm of 200 acres, for $1200. cash rent. This farm was not ditched, and due to a wet year, the crops failed and he had to sell out at auction to meet his obligations. In this depression year (Cleveland Panic) a team of horses sold for $2350. Then they rented the 80 acre Bradley farm for 5 years, and then the 220 acre Grant Swearington farm for 7 years. The profit on these 2 farms, gave them enough money, that he could buy a 152 acre farm 3 miles west of Westfield, Indiana. He paid $78.50 per acre for this farm, and they moved there in the Spring of 1906. Oscar finished high school there in 1909 and then went to I.U. to take Teacher Training so he could teach and earn enough money to finish college. He taught a year at Eagleton, and a year at Westfield, and then transferred his credits from I.U. to Purdue and secured his B.S. degree there in Agronomy in 1915.

His first job was teaching Soils and Crops, in the Summer School at the University of Iowa, Iowa City. He then taught Vo. Ag. at Monticello, Indiana for 2 years. In 1917 he became County Agricultural Agent of Greene County, at Bloomfield, Indiana. In the Spring of '18 the draft of World War I took him overseas, after which he studied at Rothamstead experimental station for a while, the oldest one in the woeld.

On his return to the U.S. he became County Ag. Agent in Montgomery County at Crawfordsville, Indiana, for 3 years. Here in 1921 he was married to Edith A. Vancleave, Sec'y in the County Agents office.

He then became Farm Advisor (same as Co. Agt. in Ind.) of Rock Island County, Rock Island, Illinois for 2 years. Following that he took a job as a farm manager of 3,100 acres of river bottom land, owned by a Chicago millionaire. He rode herd on horseback super-

7

vising the farming of 19 tenants. This was at Eldred, Illinois.

Following this he was for 4 years a Field Representative of a German Potash Company, known as the N.V. Potash Export Co., with headquarters in New York. He worked out of Danville, Illinois, conducting field tests on Indiana and Illinois soils. He next worked for the Metropolitan Life Insurance Company, managing many of their foreclosed farms, out of the Indianapolis office. This was during the depression after the Stock Crash and the Metropolitan and the Northwestern Life companies, had to take back many, many, farms.

Then the rainbow touched down for them when he connected with the Soils Conservation Department in 1935. They started him out as a project manager at Bedford, Indiana. These were the years of the W.P.A. (Works Progress Administration) and C.C.C. (Civilian Conservation Corps). Unemployed persons in a camp assigned to do some conservation project under technical experts like Oscar, who by this time knew his stuff. Foresters had them harvesting mature trees and other woodland management practices. Engineers had them laying out terraces to establish contour farming. C.C.C. labor also worked the quarries crushing limestone for liming the soil. The Agronomist developed soil conserving crop rotations and soil building and crop rotation programs, 80 people in camp.

In 1940 Ackerson was transferred to Logansport, where he worked on Agronomy programs for several soil Districts, and the next year he went to Goshen, where he was stationed at the S.C.S. office. It was at this time that the District was formed and an office was authorized, under Don Smith, District Conservationist. Cal Doniphan was the technician. Oscar worked on state wide Agronomy and Minimum Tillage programs, under the direction of the State office at Indianapolis.

Minimum Tillage became a major project to conserve soil and water. Minimum Tillage may be described as a method of making the fewest possible trips over the field with farm machinery to get a good seed bed and grow a successful crop. Excessive tillage operations, pack the soil, impair its physical condition, and retard rainfall absorption. These conditions increase rainfall run-off and increase soil loss by erosion. Extra trips also increase the cost of production. Many meetings were held over the state to explain the idea, and numerous tillage field demonstrations were conducted state wide to prove that the method would work.

Farm Implement companies designed their machinery to do minimum tillage. At the demonstrations, each dealer would be assigned a strip of the field 8 corn rows wide to demonstrate his machinery. In the Fall the strips would be harvested and the yield determined.

One farmer at Decatur, Indiana, achieved the ultimate in Minimum Tillage. He hitched his corn planter to the plow in such a way that plowed and planted the field by making just one trip over the field.

Oscar and Edith had 5 children, Mary, Cedric, Thelma, Ina and Norma, all have college degrees, and Edith died in 1950 at 210 East Monroe in Goshen, not 100 yeards from our front door. The children are now all married and well established, most of them in our Presbyterian Church. Cedric is next in line to be president of Salem Bank. Mary is in Palo Alto, California, married to a M.D. Thelma's Myron has taught for ages, Ina has inherited several farms, and Norma is still our Granddaughter's best friend. Their family visited us in Englewood, Florida, 2 years ago, we nearly got lost in Rattlesnake country.

After 44 years of Public Service, Oscar retired in 1960, wanted to travel while he was still young and needed a companion, so Katie M. Kring and Oscar teamed up in the second marriage and toured the world and spent winters in Florida.

ALBION PRODUCTION CREDIT — Goshen Branch

After the stock market crash of 1929 and the many innovations of President Roosevelt, by Presidential Decree he authorized the establishment of Production Credit Unions to help farmers with farm finances and that was a life saver for many farmers. This happened in 1933, and following the experience of the Federal Land Banks in 1916, the production Credit Unions mushroomed all over the Country.

In Albion it was very easy, as a Credit Union already there and in some difficulty, furnished many anxious potential members automatically, so overnight it was there. Many people, including Mr. Glen Bowman deserve a lot of credit for the easy and effective transition.

Later a branch was set up in Goshen just west of Main Street on Lincoln, over the shoe store. Noble Hollar of New Paris became the manager. John B. Smith became a member in 1935, in connection with his Registered Brown Swiss herd, and having held a dispersal sale the next year, began to take a special interest in the Elkhart County group, and was manager of the office from 1942 to 1950.

Edwin Andrews then took it over from 1950 to 1967. The present office man is Phil Mishler. Don Beer is chairman of the Board of Directors. The members of the Board must be re-elected to continue to serve for an additional 3 years, and after serving 9 years must drop out for at least one year, for the good of the cause. Loans in reasonable amounts to farmers are made at competitive rates for from 5 to 7 years, for any purpose approved by the board. A total of 310 people have become borrowers, and per se, members. Of these and over 200 are still active accounts.

Phil being the present Manager, perhaps we might give a little of his background, so here goes:

Phil Mishler was born in 1929, son of George Mishler, of New Paris, graduated from New Paris High School in 1947, married Marjorie Mishler, daughter of Charles Mishler in 1951.

They leased his Dad's farm and the Mishler (now Bob Martin's Project farm) across the way, total 140 acres and grain-farmed that for a year, then in 1954 bought the 160 where they now live on County Road 50. In 1960 they rented the Peters farm, 360 acres in addition, and went into Beef Cattle, feeding about 200 steers until he accepted the job with Albion Production Credit, in March 1967.

Son Rick, age 22, graduated now from North Manchester, will go to Purdue and take Medicine; John, 19, graduated from Northwood went to take a short course at Purdue, and is taking over the farm, the farmer of the family, and Kathy, 15, will be a sophomore at Northwood.

Marge was in Lita's Latin class at New Paris. Any teacher knows that the smartest and the nicest students elect Latin, catch?

Production Credit belongs in this book for the great contribution they have made to MICHIANA AGRICULTURE through the years.

THE A.S.C. PROGRAM

The A.A.A. wheat program went into effect in 1933, and the corn-hog program in 1934.

The first County Committee was made up of 3 people, W.W. Oesch, Ezra Lovejoy and James Dunmire. Mr. A.T. Marvel was the County Agent to whom the Committee was responsible. They operated at first in the Court House, from 1933 to 1938, then went to the Shoots building until 1952, then into the Spohn building until 1958, after which they landed in their present location at 106 E. Middlebury Street.

The original purpose of the program was to control prices, by controlling crop production and offering cash payment to those farmers who would sign up for the program.

The Supreme court ended the A.A.A. program in 1936 by denying power of the President to regulate production, and the work was continued in a modified form under a new name, A.S.C.

Albert Groff, Herbert Stroup, Irvin Eby, Clayton Enders, Herbert Caton and Bob Snoberger and also Clint Zollinger, no doubt served the most years. The present Committee, is Dale Inbody, Albert Groff and John Cripe. Erdeen Moyer was office Secretary from 1934 to 1969, 35 years of service. Our hat is off to her! Others who worked in the office were, Fred Kluth, Francis Dunmire, Dorothy Green, Janet Stoner and Rosevelyn Wantz. Noel Murphy will long be remembered.

THE BEERS AND THE BEES

Otto Beer Sr. started the bee business more than 50 years ago. He worked as a barn builder living in Milford for many years. As an avocation he swarmed a few hives of bees. Later he moved onto a 30 acre farm, 2½ miles west of Milford and continued the bee business. In 1941 he bought 80 acres on the south side of U.S. 6, 1½ miles west of Indiana 15, so he could have the advantage of a more accessible location. By 1947 he was full time in the bee business on a commercial basis.

At that time right after the war, honey was quite high in price like 35 ¢ to 50¢ per pound. He built a honey house and put in all the necessary equipment. They supplied both comb and extract honey. Many customers came right up the lane to the honey house to make purchases.

At one time the hives numbered 1200 and now about 600 would catch the figure. They have hives in about 30 locations in 4 counties, Elkhart, Kosciusko, LaGrange and Noble. The keepers of the bees are given honey for the courtesy of allowing the bees to work there.

Otto Beer Sr. died October 1968 and after his death, his son Bill took over the bee business.

Otto Beer Jr., who lives in dad's old house, still does most of the farming although Bill has a few beef cattle. Bill lives in the new house. The widow, mother Beer, lives down the road a bit in the house Otto Sr. had in 1963. When Bill had bought Otto's second house at the time he was married.

Since agriculture has changed, more row crops and less clover, besides the use of more pesticides has brought problems. Those problems plus a greater demand for honey as a food has resulted in a higher price for honey.

The Beer's sell retail and wholesale. Honey is now 45¢ to 50¢ per pound wholesale, and the stores sell it at 75¢ and up.

Otto Beer Junior is a pastor of a non-denominational church in Nappanee. Bill's family attends there too. Junior Beer has 4 children and Bill, three.

The Beers have always been the finest of people. They have also contributed much to know-how in bees and therefore deserve recognition in this book.

HAROLD BEMILLER — Jersey Breeder

Phillip BeMiller was born in 1849, married Margaret Morris in 1868 and started housekeeping on the northwest corner of County Road 28 and State Road 19. His father George had owned all 4 corners of the intersection, and had come from Germany to Ohio and then from Ohio to Indiana in 1837. His wife was a Berringer and they had 4 children, including for our purpose, Phillip.

When Phillip took over his corner, the place was all woods, they cleared a few stretches and had a cow for milk, and folklore has it that Margaret would go out to fetch or find the cow, she would take off her apron and deposit the baby on it, while she looked for the cow.

Phillip developed a Jersey herd through the years, but from the beginning he was crazy about fast driving horses. They had 6 children from 1871 to 1886, and for our purpose, including Albert, born 1879. Later he was married to Phoebe Stauffer in 1900 and they bought the 62 acres on County Road 30 just east of Indiana 19, on the south side of the road, and set up a Jersey dairy herd. They had 2 children, one who died in infancy and Harold, born in 1907, who at school age went to Jonesville to school. It was not long until he and his uncle Irvin were showing registered Jersey cattle at local and State fairs, and they also showed Berkshire hogs at the International in Chicago. They had about 35 Jerseys, and milked around 20. Phoebe was busy churning cream into butter and she herself established a butter route in Elkhart.

Harold was married to Frances Housand in 1931 and they rented a house south of Elkhart and he hauled milk for the Wambaugh dairy in Elkhart, picking up 10 gallon milk cans for farmers. Kenneth was born in 1932, and Max in 1936. In 1934 Margaret had died, and then in 1937 they bought the 80 acre BeMiller homestead from her estate.

They started out with Jerseys, as was the choice of past generations, like less than a dozen cows and heifers the first year. He bought his first registered bull from Ann Arbor, Michigan. Then a son, Albert, came in 1941, another son, Tim, in 1951, and by 1946, Kenny and Max were showing Yorkshire pigs at the Elkhart County Fair, as well as Jersey cattle at the State Fair.

About this time Harold was elected a Director of the Elkhart County Jersey Breeders Association, and later became President of District I of the State Association. At the present time he is President of the Elkhart County Dairy Association.

After Wambaugh closed, they sold milk to Eby's. The younger boys also went into 4-H and won their share of ribbons. All the boys did the full 10 years.

Harold and Frances are in Jimtown Methodist and the others are in the Missionary Church. Harold's father died in 1868, and his mother the next year and then Harold being the only heir, inherited the 62 acres on Road 30, and Max lives there now.

Kenneth is married to Ruth Barnes, does 4 to 500 acres on Oakland Avenue road, owns and operates 3 semi milk trucks, hauling to County Line Cheese, has 3 children, Kent married to Lynette Geil, with a daughter age 1, Ronda, 19, at Ball State, a Sophomore, and Renay, age 10; Max is married to Sharon Wiest, they live on Harold's other farm, he is with Nibco, and has 2 children, Debi, who is married to Monte Holdeman, a mechanic in Elkhart; Albert is married to Mary Qualls, they live on State 19 across from Max (used to be David Yoder's farm) and they have 2 boys, Brian, age 13, and Darin age 9; Tim is married to Donna Wadell, they bought the Olive church parsonage, and they have taken over Harold's cows. They have 3 children, Lisa, 5, Chris, 4, and Linett, 2.

Harold and Frances say "we are proud of our 4 boys and owe a lot to our Jersey cattle". Good for the high test Jersey milk!!!

SIMON BONTRAGER — Clinton Center Mill

Jacob Bontrager, Simon's father, was married in 1908 and Simon was born November 29, 1909. Later Jacob bought the Aaron Martin farm (90 acres) east of the intersection of Indiana 13 and Indiana 4 (in 1915). Simon had started to school at the old Brown School. In 1920 they bought the Bob Moss farm one mile south of the mill (120 acres). Simon then attended the old Clinton Community Center School. His hardest days were plowing with an old fashioned walking plow. Coming of Amish parentage he was able to attend high school at Millersburg only 10 weeks, when he turned 16.

He stayed home working with his folks until he was 21 (1930). He worked for Len Pletcher, the race horseman's father, just one summer. The next year, 1932, Simon started working for Elmer Hostetter, owner of the Clinton Mill, for wages of $20 per month, 66¢ per day. He worked there three years.

In July, 1935 he leased the mill from Mr. Hostetter until he bought it later that same year for $4,500, including mill, all buildings, and the house itself.

In 1936 he was married to Elizabeth Miller, daughter of Harry and Sarah Miller (maiden name Lambright).

They mixed the feed by hand, as no electricity was available until 1939. The first mixer was run by an old Dodge motor.

After electricity was obtained (about 1940) a larger mixer was bought. In the 1940's the house was remodelled and refurbished and many changes made in the mill.

The first son was born April, 1937, and as soon as he was 16 he started driving a delivery truck for the mill. There were eight children, six boys all of whom worked in the mill until they went into volunteer service. At present, there are three boys in the mill. Simon's business is with his loyal customers and friends within five or six miles of the mill. Although in the 50's they became Broiler Kings, before they realized, importing over 1,000,000 chicks in one year.

In September, 1961, the mill burned out completely and was rebuilt. The one thing of sentimental value which burned was a 1924 Model "T" Ford.

In recent years the problems of the business have changed. Simon has a host of friends many of whom have said, "Simon must be in the book". He has been a CROP sponsor for years.

THE BORKHOLDER STORY

John Borkholder homesteaded 160 acres across from the Borkholder school on the Plymouth Road at Beechroad about 1840. John the 2nd took over next, followed by John 3rd. He had 4 children, including Daniel Borkholder who now owns 80 acres on which is located one of the last virgin forests in Northern Indiana. The writer has taken many groups on field trips in this beautiful forest. The family established a very sizable maple sugar business, over 1000 trees being tapped in a single year.

He married Emma Coblenz from Stark County, Ohio and they had 7 children and for our purpose, including Freeman D. Borkholder who was the first born (Oct. 11, 1932). Freeman attended the Borkholder school down the road. He worked on the farm with his folks until he was 19, then he went into voluntary service during the Korean War and was located in Ball Memorial Hospital at Muncie. On returning he was married to Margaret Hershberger, daughter of Ezra and Laura Hershberger of Nappanee. He now has 5 children and the Borkholder dream is described as it came true:

Freeman D. Borkholder started working for Coppes, a kitchen manufacturer, in 1955 as an assembler and machine operator. While employed at Coppes, he married Margaret Hershberger. In 1960, he began working evenings installing storm windows for a friend. Some time later, his friend moved to another city and Mr. Borkholder took over the storm window business.

As demand grew for wall siding, he expanded his business to include the selling of Aluminum siding; hiring applicators for installation. Within two years, the business had grown to such an extent, he resigned from Coppes, built a work shop and display room and devoted full-time to running his business.

One day a farmer asked Mr. Borkholder to build him a Post Farm Building. He was content with his current business success, so he thought he would bid high on the building. To his great surprise, he was awarded the contract. Thus did Freeman D. Borkholder enter the Post Building Industry.

News of the Post Building soon got around and one day a salesman from a competitive Post Building company confronted Mr. Borkholder to confirm the price of the Post Building. He was amazed that Mr. Borkholder could build such a fine building for such a low price and offered to sell all the buildings Freeman could build.

Soon Borkholder's operations expanded along with his reputation. Across northern Indiana, he built buildings of all types, concentrating on low cost, low maintenance construction. His relentless search for quality never stopped. He added new buildings to his operational facilities - and a new design department. He acquired the finest materials and employed the most knowledgeable craftsmen available to constantly improve the quality of his products.

The main office of F.D. Borkholder & Co., Inc. is located four miles west of Nappanee, Indiana on U.S. 6. There are branch offices located in Kokomo, Fort Wayne, and Columbus, Indiana and in Lawrence and Coopersville, Michigan.

F.D. Borkholder & Co., Inc. will do approximately $11,000,000 in sales this year in Indiana, Michigan, Ohio, Illinois, Pennsylvania, Delaware and Maryland.

Freeman is on the Board of Directors of the South Bend Rescue Mission and the Bremen Community Hospital. He is past president of the National Frame Builder's Association. He is a member of the International Platform Association, non-partisan organization of distinquished, dedicated people from 55 nations. He developed the Industrial Park. He is a member of the Bethel Conservative Mennonite Church and all his effort is based upon Christian dealing with the public according to the Golden Rule. WHAT A STORY!

THE BROWNS OF WAKARUSA

Ira Brown was born in 1874, went to Holdeman school, 1 mile west of Wakarusa, and when he grew up he married Anna L. Flickinger, the daughter of Cyrus Flickinger, farm just west of the schools south side. The old Bauge Creek cuts the farm in two, one of the 150 Centennial farms of the county, and one of the oldest at that.

They had 9 children. Joe was the first at the turn of the century, (1901). He, too, went to the old Holdeman school, and at recess and noon always wanted to be a fielder, as he had such long legs. When he came "of age" he worked for neighboring farmers for 3 years, then worked for the Layer Brother grist mill. At that time he was married to Nellie Martin, bought a bread route and sold bread for Hossicks in Elkhart.

In 1931 he rented his grandfathers farm in St. Joe County, 80 acres, and farmed there 15 years. At age 45 he bought the Henry Martin farm, in the lane on the north side of the road, ½ mile west of Wakarusa. It was 80 acres, and they started in the Holstein dairy business, 12 to 15 cows, and sold milk to Litchfield's of Warsaw. A few years later he took on the Wenger farm and has farmed it for C.J. now for 25 years (80 acres). He was on the Mennonite Disaster Committee for 13 years, and has been on the C.R.O.P. canvassing and farm operating committee longer than that. They are members of Salem Mennonite south of Foraker. They have 45 to 50 Holsteins and milk 20 to 25. Joe says, - "Boy, it keeps me humpin' the way things are these days".

Abner was born in 1910, and I was thru with College by the time he started in Holdemans school. (Warren Holdeman was his first teacher). Abner graduated from Waky high in 1927 and worked from then on until he was 21 years old for his dad, Ira.

Then in 1935 he married Vivien Weldy, and 7 children came from 1937 to 1957. They started in Holsteins, bought the old Holderbaum cider mill, to make room for hogs, but lately has pushed the dairy more. They rented the quarter section for 20 years, and bought it in 1956. They now have around 60 Holsteins and milk about 30. They also have some 500 laying pullets. They are Holdeman Mennonite, work hard on Mennonite Relief and Mennonite Disaster as well as C.R.O.P. Many of my friends say "He is the hardest working fellow around". This I know, he is doing a good job on the Project

17

Committee for the Elkhart County Agricultural Society.

Another brother Lemuel was born in 1911, married Marie Truex, and they have really gone big with Brown and Brown in Wakarusa, they have done many, many large school projects and other public buildings such as the Goshen City Hall. Both Greencroft and the Greencroft Nursing Home are to their credit. Last week, Marie tells me they paid 40 employees. Lemuel was injured years ago when a horse he was riding rammed him between 2 buildings. Too much sitting in the wheel chair gets him in trouble. When Milton was with him they were a team. Milton then took over the Walters Lumber Co., and now semi-retired is in with Bob Ehret.

Lowell, another brother has hauled milk for 35 years for the Mishawaka Farmers Dairy (born 1914, married to Christene Weaver). Roscoe died, just recently, his last days at Abner's.

THE BROWNS — Waterford-New Paris

Rufus Melvin Brown was born 1871 on the Rohrer farm, sect. 16, Harrison Township.

He was married June 9, 1897 to Mertie Mease. They set up housekeeping on his fathers farm then bought 80 acres of the Rarick family in section 1 of Union Township, 2 miles east of Foraker (Road 146). Three sons were born there and for our purpose including J. Howard Brown in 1900.

In 1903, he bought what is now known as the Brown farm just west of the big bridge over the Elkhart River near Waterford.

It seems the first cash income was firewood, the cutting organized by his brother, George, and the work done by laborers from Waterford across the river, anyone who needed work. Rufus and George also had a reputation of breaking in and selling western horses. Corn, oats, wheat, clover and or timothy hay. At that time loose timothy hay was delivered to barns back of city homes for horses as a cash crop. Later it was baled and shipped east.

In 1905 and 1906 the barn was built mostly from native timber. Rufus and William Christner got out the logs and William and Irvin Stiver of New Paris sawed up the timber right on the farm and the building was done by Jacob Culp and crew from Wakarusa.

Five years later the process was repeated for the present house but the logs were sawed out at Baintertown by Tom Harriman at his big water powered mill.

Horse farming remained the chief method in his generation.

Now with an adequate barn he went to raising Belgian horses and moved from Durham cattle to Holsteins (dairy).

Tractor farming was to come with his oldest son Carlyle operating.

At this time J. Howard's mother was a popular speaker in Farmer's Institutes in Indiana and Ohio.

J. Howard graduated from Purdue in 1922 and in 1923 after teaching in Ohio 1 year, he bought the 40 acres south of the Brown farm, then he taught Vocational Agriculture in New Paris 3 years, in New Mexico two years and in Goshen High School 8 years and then taught one year at Purdue. Then he married Thyra Nell Collins of an Oklahoma pioneer family.

At this time Purdue recommended him to the Elkhart Co. Extension Committee and he was named County Agricultural Agent serving from 1937 to 1943. He then bought 40 acres more and had a farm management service.

Later in 1948 J. Howard bought the 120 acres known as the Neff Farm south of New Paris where they developed an Ayrshire herd and by this time Beverly and Jarvis came along and were winning prizes in 4-H including a fine Ayrshire heifer won in a National contest by Beverly, subject "Why the Ayrshire is the breed for me". Jarvis took up agriculture and is now associate professor of Agronomy in Bozeman, Montana State University.

J. Howard and Thyra Nell switched to Black Angus with 15 breeding cows and the money from the calf crop helps to send the semi-retired couple to Florida each winter, and returning in March to look after the calving and the sugar camp.

Howard has sold part of the farm and moved toward an easier schedule, and built a beautiful home on 72 acres he retained adjacent to the post office on the old state road. Every other August they go to Oklahoma to attend the wife's reunion.

The Browns are one of the 5 families in the county to have a Tree Farm which they have retained. On a tree farm the cooperator signs up with the Indiana Tree Farm Association agreeing to many things, including fencing the woods, not pasturing, treating for insects and disease, and marketing trees as they mature.

GLEN BYLER

In 1936 Glen's Parents moved to the County and bought the old Hoke farm (80 acres) when Glen was eleven years old. They did general farming but with seven children, Tom had to work some in town, started the Parkside Grocery in 1939 where he won hundreds of student friends, including the writer. Glen worked the farm until he was 21 in 1946 and then married Lois Garber whom Glen met in evening classes at Goshen College. They settled down on the Dale Hess farm on County Road 21. That is where Glen started in the Hampshire hog business.

Lois's father, Joe Garber, from Low Point, Illinois, gave them a registered bred Hampshire sow and also a registered Hereford cow and calf. Tom had given them the increase in Holstein heifer calves. Lucky for the Bylers they were able to save seven gilts from the first litter and the third year Glen had his first bred gilt sale at the Fair Ground.

This success encouraged Glen, and he went into the Hampshire business in earnest. He bought the 100 acre farm where Gerald Weybright now lives and staked his future on about 20 registered sows.

Glen has had many sales, some of his own, some with Lamar Loucks and many with the Elkhart County Breeders Association.

For the last 25 years he has shown Hampshires at local and state fairs and for 20 years has been showing at the National Hampshire Conference. He had one of the first certified litters in the State of Indiana, based on carcass cut out.

From 1954 to 1960, Glen's Hampshires had a lot of influence in switching the breed from lard to meat type hogs. In this respect there are few Hampshire breeders in Central U.S. who have contributed more to agriculture than he.

A few weeks ago he paid $1600 for a beautiful Hamp Boar who gained 220 pounds in 148 days. In 1973 at the annual Hampshire Sale he consigned 43 boars and gilts; average sale $200.

WILLIAM H. CABLE — Weybright Seed Service

Charles Weybright and Nettie Culler were married on Easter Sunday, 1909, used their savings and with a farm loan bought their 100 acre farm. Charles and his father had looked over farms in several townships and chose the homestead because it was sandy loam and partly cleared. The family cleared the rest of the farm (90 tillable acres). Nettie recalled she had worn out all her new aprons carrying in wood for the kitchen stove when she would bring in the cows to milk.

In 1911 George Weybright was born, in 1915 another son who soon died, and later Miriam, a daughter, arrived. These were the happy years; broad interests in church and community, Camp Mack, Mission work, founding of the Seminary Hospital in Chicago, the Church of the Brethren College at North Manchester, brought hundreds of guests to the farmstead, many staying for weeks at a time. The family was very active in Solomons Creek church until it was closed, then they switched to Rock Run on County Road 38. Many times the family would attend National Church conference as delegates and often at their own expense.

They were registered Guernsey breeders and alfalfa seed producers and worked closely with Purdue and made many trips there. They were instrumental in securing the first County Agricultural Agent and Home Economics Supervisor. Nettie was the organizer of the Elkhart County Home Demonstration Clubs. She and Miriam headed 4-H clubs from 1934 to 1939. Miriam was in the county 4-H Guernsey calf club.

When Hybrid Seed corn was first being developed, Charles had already been furnishing the best years of his Yellow Dent Open-pollinated corn to his heighbors for seed, so immediately they attended group meetings at Purdue to learn about the technique. In 1934 they grew a few rows in the garden, Miriam detassled, hand picked ears for the nail racks for drying. When dry they shelled the tips in one bucket, butts into another, and the center grains in a Basket; this to allow the neighbors planter plates to work easier.

The second year they did a half acre and the next year 2 acres, and in 1937 erected a drying and grading building on advice from Purdue specialists. THUS WAS STARTED THE WEYBRIGHT SEED SERVICE. Charles did his own selling and delivering of seed corn.

In August 1936 the original house burned down. The family

21

was at camp Mack, the neighbors took out what furniture they could, but could not get the big desk through the door, nor did anyone grab the papers out of the desk, so with the fire went all the registry records for the herd. The next year the house was replaced by a new one, and George and his wife asked to take over the homestead farm and did, January 1st, 1937.

Soon thereafter Charles and Nettie built a new home on the north side of the road next to the seed corn plant and moved there.

At a church conference at LaVerne, California, Mildred and Bill met, both ushering for a youth service and singing in the choir. The next year they married. Bill was in the Service by that time and Miriam worked in the hospital and taught school in Tacoma, Washington until their first baby, Charles, was born (1944).

On January 1st, 1946, Bill started working for father Weybright. He had only one full seed corn season to learn the business, before the corn Pioneer dies of Thrombosis. The widow then sold the 80 acre farm to the Cables in 1948 and also sold the business to them in 1953. Nettie, the widow, lived in her beautiful home with all the rich memories and a host of friends for 4 more years until she passed on in 1957.

Bill set out to master the seed business, study, reading, and extension meetings. The seed barn was remodelled, with some small steel bins being installed for small grains. In 1968 a 60' high steel building was erected for grading corn, improvements in drying facilities for drying and storage.

In Charles Weybright's time, field work was done with horses, seed was hand picked to prevent damage, coal furnace used for drying and he was always glad to get through by Thanksgiving time.

Now the Cables use a picker for ear corn, picker-sheller for pollen rows, and gas for drying, and cobs are ground and sold for bedding. But the seed is still dried slowly, always at a low temperature, usually 3 to 6 days. One conservation practice consistently used has been Rye Grass sown with a cyclone seeder at the last cultivation in June. This also gives foundation for tractor wheels in wet fields, with minimal damage, where otherwise it would be impossible.

In 1949 Bill became a Supervisor of Elkhart County SWCD, served as its chairman, and also of N.E. Indiana SWCD until 1963 when the 5 sons required more of his time at home. The lawn of the

Cable home has hosted many SWCD groups.

In 1958 he became a Trustee of the Bethany Brethren Hospital in Chicago, and now that it is combined with the Garfield Park Community Hospital, he is chairman of the 2 joint Boards, assets of the joint arrangement, five million. You may guess, he has to tithe his time.

They have hosted 4 Trainees for Farmers Union, been on Extension and advisory board most of the last 20 years, Farm Bureau 20 years, named Outstanding Farm Family by the Ag. Society in 1958, Director of Land Bank '63 to '73, named Master Farmer by the Prairie Farmer in 1970. Miriam was 2 years President of The Elkhart County Homemakers Clubs. Many, many, responsibilities and honors cannot be mentioned here. No wonder the story ends as it does with the last sentence.

Now for the children. We know them all and love and respect each one for what they are, what they have done and what they stand for. All 5 boys completed 10 years in 4-H totalling 336 projects and each was a corn king in 4-H. They won the award 13 of the last 16 years.

Miriam had to name the firstborn after her dad of course. Charles is a county hospital assistant administrator in Phoenix, Arizona, Alan and his wife have two little girls. He is working toward his Certified Medical Technicians Certificate at Evanston, Illinois Hospital, Bruce is a certified public accountant in LaVerne, California; Lowell, an agronomist is working with the seed Service at home; and Edwin was made an Eagle Scout right before our very eyes, in the park pavilion at New Paris last November. What a night! 150 admiring friends there to applaud.

You will notice the names of the boys names in the right order; C-Charles, A-Alan, B-Bruce, L-Lowell, E-Edwin, so the initials spell CABLE.

Surely this family is a hard working, Committed Family. Bill and Mildred say, "God, first; Others, second; and ourselves third."

THE ADRIAN CARPENTER FAMILY

Arch Carpenter was born on his parent's farm, 2 miles east of Topeka, Indiana in 1876.

They rented 2 other farms and farmed 400 acres which at that time was a large acreage, also some cattle, hogs, and chickens.

They had 9 children, and for our purpose, including Adrian, born 1897. At school age, Beech school was it, just exactly two miles east of town. Although all of Adrian's children made it through high school, Adrian never did. He was needed too badly on the farm. In those days, in the winter, the days were so short that the morning chores would run right into the evening chores, and as a result a fellow would be around the barn all day long, except for a few minutes break at noon for a snack.

Adrian worked for his folks until he was 20 and then was married to Elizabeth Burns, whose father was a minister of the Church of the Brethren in Wakarusa, and was called by the Topeka congregation. That church is no longer in existence, as membership dropped and the group was finally dissolved, the members joining other churches, and the building sold as a blacksmith shop.

Adrian kept working for his father, and 3 children came there, Josephine in 1917, Treva, in 1920, and Dorothy in 1921. Later in 1922 for 6 years they rented 100 acres and farmed another 200, and that is when Willis was born in 1923, Mary in 1924, and Don in 1927.

They also farmed the Waters farm, working by the month from 1928 to 1933, and that is when Roy came in 1929. He was a depression baby and things were real tough. They farmed there until 1933.

At this time Mrs. Amasa Hoovens had 4 farms east of Goshen to furnish milk for their dairy, and Adrian was offered farm No. 4 to be herdsman, so they moved there for 4 years. There Joy was born 1935.

By 1937 Elizabeth's mother wanted them to farm the 53 acres east of Wakarusa 1½ miles (south side of road in the lane) and they wanted them to come back to Wakarusa, which they did and also rented the Charles Husband farm on County Road 7, south of Morningstar's School.

They farmed there 4 years, and 2 of the children came there, Sarah, in 1938, and Ruth in 1940. By this time the children were getting big enough to help with the work, and some of them even getting married.

The Ox-cart was over the hill and by that time prices were a little better.

Then in the Spring of 1941 a Fred Stiver who had inherited a farm east of Benton, and Marty Bassett in the Federal Loan Bank of Goshen sold them the farm as Mr. Stiver wanted to give it up.

They closed the deal moved there and within 30 days after the shift, the last child, Carol was born.

Most of the children were in school in Millersburg, and the boys were in my Vo. Ag. classes there in 1946 and 1947. Roy was a "whiz" on the basketball floor, and he is the lad who dubbed me "Uncle Elmer".

All of these children went through high school, Mary had 2 years at North Manchester, and Treva graduated there in 1944 and later received her Masters in Missouri.

The last one was married in 1963, and so NOW:

Josephine is married to Manford Detwile across from Rock Run, they do several hundred acres, and feed, like a hundred feeder cattle a year. They have 3 children. Treva is married to Dr. Kintner a Vet teacher and she teaches foods, both in Missouri State University. They have 2 children. Dorothy was married to John Huber. Their 5 children are all married. Willis is married to Roberta Whitehead, Merle's daughter, he is co-owner of the Benton Mill with Roy. They have 4 children. Mary is married to Gerald Leer, they have several hundred acres, milk 50 Holsteins, have 6 children. Don married Lena Shidler, new home across from the folks, worked in mill, and has 4 children. Roy is married to Dorothy Hoshaw, he is co-owner of the Benton Mill, and they have the old Tim Blosser farm. They have 3 children.

The Boys bought the Benton Mill from Martins, Inc. and have gone big. Joy is married to Ebert Yoder, works in Travel Equipment office, have a cottage at Fish Lake, live in Goshen, and have 2 sons. Sarah is married to Charles Nulf, draftsman for Condair out west, and has 2 boys. Ruth is married to John Myers, is body-man for Eby-Ford, in Goshen, and has 3 children; and Carol, the baby, is married to David Garber, they have bought the old Ed Bartholomew farm on County Road 31 and they have five children.

There is a lot of "Brain" in this family, also a lot of "Brawn". There is also a lot of "integrity" and Moral Fiber.

Maybe Adrian and Elizabeth had something to do with this. The old couple still goes to Rock Run church of the Brethren. Adrian is just back from the Goshen Hospital, and his tractors and other tools are waiting for him in the barn till he gets straightened out, as he is still the farmer and boss at 77.

Adrian and Elizabeth say, "There are those who are urging us to build a nice new house for our retirement years, but we don't owe a soul in the world and would like to keep things just the way they are."

RILEY L. CASE — Farmer, Vo. Ag. Teacher, County Agent

Zopher Case, Riley's grandfather, had 1,000 acres in Johnson and Milford townships, south of LaGrange, with the homestead house on the corner of 400 South and 600 East. They did general farming with a lot of livestock. He was married twice, his second wife being Anna Smith, a school teacher from Noble County, both wives bearing him 16 children, and for our purpose, including Riley C. Case, who first saw the light of day in 1869. In 1891 he homesteaded in Oregon, near Albany, then came back to Indiana to get his wife, Mary Eshelman, and took her to Oregon, where Riley L. was born in 1896.

When Zopher died, Riley C. inherited some of the holdings on 600 East (200 acres) and came back and went to general farming. Later he built that up to 500 acres. Riley's sister was born in 1898, and he in 1896.

They attended Woodruff grade school and Riley had three years of high school in Woodruff, sister Gay only one. Both completed high school in Wolcottville. Riley graduated from Wolcottville high school in 1914 and from Purdue University in 1918, farmed with his father 2 years, and then began his teaching in Grafton, North Dakota. After that he accepted the challenge to organize a Vo. Ag. Department in Shipshewana High School, the first in LaGrange County, became Principal from 1922 to 1926, and then went to St. Joe, Dekalb Co in the same capacity. At this time he took off a year to get his M.S. degree at I.U., and thereafter returned to Shipshewana, and there married Edna Burkhalter in 1931. Riley B. was born here in 1933.

They went to Millersburg in 1935 to serve as school principal and vocational agriculture instructor.

Then in 1937 he was made LaGrange County Agricultural Agent and served there until he retired in 1964. There Ann Louise was born in 1938 and Mary Sue in 1940.

As an agriculturist Riley was a promoter of 4-H club work. This was true the many years between Jim Kline's term as County Agent and the time Riley took over. There was no County Agent and Riley became the promoter. In 1931 he had organized the County Corn Club as well as the county Girls' Sewing Club. Exhibits were made at the County Corn School. A County Pig Club and a County Baking Club for girls were soon added. Riley was the pusher to establish the 4-H fairgrounds out of LaGrange, and at the same time kept helping the Corn Show which had lost the 4-H.

He pushed National 4-H club Congress trips, built up the Junior leaders group and carried out many demonstrations, plowing contests, and established the Tri-State horse and pony shows at the new fairground.

Riley's goal was to have LaGrange County 4-H represented in every event. A series of awards were instituted, whereby any 4-H boy or girl had an achievable goal, beginning with a 4-H camp trip, an 8 year trip to the International, and culminating in a TEN YEAR RING.

He promoted Hybrid corn, Lamb tour and dinner, husking contests, Draft-horse pulling contests, and Gold Medal Calf club.

After World War II lamb feeding was switched to dairying and soon LaGrange County had the most dairy cows, per mile, of all the Indiana counties.

The County Conservation District was organized in 1951, and Riley was a pusher. His Counsel and advice is sought to this day.

The Cases are at 711 Hawpatch, active in church and Community, a Rotarian, and still busy supervising their two farms. Riley says, "Extension was always enjoyable to me, because I have always loved helping people. The many meetings and events promoted as a County Agent were my life."

V.V. CLARK — Elkhart County

Mr. Clark from Johnson County, Indiana, graduated from Purdue, and became County Agent in Marshall County from 1919-1921. He was married while there to Erma Cressner. In 1922 he moved south of Bristol as manager of the Bristol Orchards Co., 2 to 300 acres, (known at that time as the Milborn Fruit Farm.)

He had extensive plantings of peaches, apples, and cherries. Ed

Judson says he was the best peach grower ever in the area. He was President of the Indiana Horticultural Society. He was The Fruit Authority of Northern Indiana. He did a great deal to promote the interests of the Elkhart County Horticultural Society. When anyone in Indiana would inquire of Purdue about some special problem in horticulture, he would usually be told, "You should go up to Bristol and talk with V.V. Clark, he is the most experienced person in Indiana on fruit."

The yellows in peaches came into the area just before V.V. came to Bristol and brother Clark soon conquered that disease. He had a keen mind and an artful hand. They built large sheds for sorting tables where the fruit would be sorted and the apples rolling down the feeder was a sight. With the whole gamut of machinery sprayers, tanks, and ladders neatly hung on the racks, as soon as you arrived to the top of the hill, right then you knew you were in apple country. He sneered at the improved Ben Davis saying, "the only thing they are good for is as a late keeper in the spring."

Virgil was never too busy to participate and every meeting of any kind which had anything to do with fruit, you would see V.V. right up in the front row right in the center of the problem.

V.V. Clark made a great contribution to horticulture in the Middle States and especially in Michiana.

Virgil is gone but Erma is in a nursing home near her daughter in Virginia. Since this story we got word Erma died this spring.

COLLEGES — Bethel College-Mishawaka

The site for Bethel College was selected by a committee of 18 ministers of the Missionary Church and laymen selected from the Ohio, Indiana, and Michigan Conferences in 1946.

As soon as the site was selected many farmers of the surrounding Missionary churches showed up on a set day with their tractors, plows, and grading equipment. I remember calling at the John Ummel home north of Bethel church near Wakarusa, and was told he was over in Mishawaka helping prepare the grounds to build a college for the Missionary churches. It seems like yesterday.

The college is right on U.S. 20 right at the west line of Mishawaka and when you step west across Logan street, you are in South Bend.

Through the summer of 1947 buildings were built to house 75 students, and 5 faculty members, office, library, classrooms, the laundry rooms, kitchen and dining room. Rev. Woodrow Goodman was chosen as the first President, and he went to work on enrollment on June 1st, 1947. In 1948 the science building was built and in 1950 the Administration went up from the already established basement floor. It is a lovely brick building.

The first faculty consisted of Woodrow Goodman, A.B., B.S., M.A., and others.

The college has had a steady growth, and other buildings have been built. The large Goodman Auditorium, and the mens and womens dormitories. In 1959 Rev. Pannabecker became President and served for 15 years until he resigned. In 1971 the school was accredited, and this was a great accomplishment for Rev. Pannabecker.

In 1974 Albert Butler became the 3rd President, son of Jacob Butler who was a seventh grader, when I graduated from the Holdeman country school a mile west of Wakarusa in 1907. When Jake hit the ball square at recess, he could knock it over the fence every time.

The school has grown from the first 75 to 500 in these 27 years, and 71 Seniors received the A.B. degree this June. There are many ministers, wives, missionaries and school teachers who have been equipped at Bethel. Many students secure part-time employment at the shopping center across the street to help earn expenses.

The Missionary churches own and support the college, and our hearts are with them.

COLLEGES — Goshen

Goshen College began as the Elkhart Institute of Science, Industry and the Arts in 1894 when it was founded by Dr. Henry A. Mumaw, an Elkhart physician and member of the Prairie Street Mennonite Church, Elkhart.

Four students were in the first class, offered evenings at the Institute. Tuition rates at the school's beginning were low. In the academic and Bible departments, one term of ten weeks payable in advance was eight dollars.

During the first years in Elkhart, the highest paid faculty member during the summer school received $75 for eight weeks.

The Institute's move to Goshen in 1903 was largely a result of the efforts of Wilbur L. Stonex, of Goshen. By the time the college moved to Goshen it had come under the control of the Mennonite Church, as it is today.

At Goshen, the Mennonite Board of Education purchased ten acres of land for the campus and 140 city lots adjoining the campus. Although the original campus site was a wheat field, excavation of the school's first building began in June 1903, as soon as the wheat was harvested and while it was in shocks.

During 1903-04 school year 273 students were enrolled, and by 1906-07, 380 students were enrolled and 11 faculty members were on the College staff.

By 1974, 80 years after its founding, the Goshen College campus has 17 buildings and owns over 135 acres. Over 1,200 students are enrolled throughout the school year and there are 57 full-time and 49 part-time teaching faculty.

Today, Goshen College offers 28 majors and degrees in bachelor of arts and bachelor of science in nursing. The college library has 90,000 volumes and is growing. The college has an endowment of $507,000 as of June, 1974.

Students come from over 35 states and 22 foreign countries. The college is accredited by six national associations and in 1974 there are over 14,000 living Goshen College alumni.

COLLEGES — Manchester College

The roots of Manchester College, lie in the little town of Roanoke, to the east a half hours ride. That was the site of the Roanoke Classical Seminary, then operated by the United Brethren Church.

In the Spring of 1889, plans were made to move the seminary, and Manchester being the first to raise the necessary money, acquired the school. The cornerstone of what is now the administration building, was laid August 1st, 1889, and that fall, Manchester enrolled 160 students. The first 2 buildings cost $25,000, while today the buildings and grounds are valued at $12,000,000, the total assets at 17 million and there are 1200 students enrolled. At first there were a few teachers, now a faculty of around 100. The history of the early days of Manchester is the story of Otho Winger. He gave his life to raising money for and guiding the college through the tough days and years. He was President for 30 years until 1941. The college was accredited in March 1932. That same year the little college in Illinois at Mount Morris was merged with Manchester. Vernon Schwalm then became President in 1941, and while Manchester as well as other colleges suffered a loss of enrollment during World War II, Manchester came back strong in the fifties, with greater support from the Alumni.

A. Blair Helman became President in 1956, and since that time Manchester has been "in the black".

The College has served Michiana Agriculture well, in that the hundreds of the children and grandchildren of the 150 Farm Families have received their education there as well as a lot of religious training and MORAL FIBER. When at Goshen College our teams debated with Mount Morris and Manchester. Who won? Sure we both won! May God continue to bless the small Denominational School!

THE COOKS — Jimtown

William Delbert Cook after renting several farms for a few years, south of Jimtown, bought the Chris Holdeman farm, southeast of Jimtown 1½ miles, which had been owned by Ed Martin (120 acres).

Del, as he was called, was married to Martha (Mattie) Holdeman. They had 8 children, 3 boys, and for our purpose including Earl, Warren, and Bert.

Earl was married at age 22 to Elenore Shaum, September 2, 1916. Then he rented the Paulus farm (now called Ralph Eby farm) for 2 years and then bought the Myron BeMiller farm. At that time he was milking 10 cows. His next step was to sell all his grade cattle at the Wakarusa Sale Barn (Abe Baver, auctioneer), and to build a registered herd. He bought his first registered cow from Mr. Byerly in Elkhart about 1924, then bought another from Mr. Laidlaw, south of Mishawaka. Later Earl showed cattle at the Clee Hibschman farm near Syracuse, and later at the Elkhart County and LaPorte County Fairs.

In 1938 he sold out the cattle again and started hauling milk for the Boyd Stauffer Dairy in Elkhart and later for the South Bend City Dairy. In the meantime, he had bought the grandfathers farm from the John Cook estate, and rented it for several years to Eddie Hoover. When Earl's son, Glen, had graduated from High School, they were milking 20 to 25 cows, living where Earl now lives.

By the time Glen was married in 1951, the barn had been modernized and the Cook dairy herd was on the road.

For a number of years Glen and Earl have had the highest type classification average in the area. At one time Glen had the All-American Holstein at Chicago and Madison Shows and she was later sold to 4 buyers for $10,000. The herd now has a full sister to try for the honors again. Earl has now sold the farm to Glen on contract.

In the meantime, Bert and Warren had been starting in. At first they farmed the Del Cook farm for a few years, after which Warren set up the "Cows for sale" Dairy farm west of Jimtown on the old Del Pletcher melon farm.

He bought and sold cows and heifers and would offer to sell any cow in his barn to anyone who came along. He helped many a farmer to add another cow or two and would know where to go to find good cows for sale to again fill the empty stalls. He was known as the "cow trader" of Northern Indiana. You could depend on a "shorty" Cook cow being what was represented.

Bert and Zelma teamed up to carry out a dream of success. Through the ensuing years 10 children came to take part in this dream. Bert, in a short time became a director of the South Bend City Dairy. He served 25 years. His mind was on scientific feeding and production. It has for years been observed he would turn the world over to plan to get the loose hay made without its getting wet. He knew when to cut, when to wilt and when to haul. As a result he always fed the leafiest hay in the area. Bert and Zelma were very well liked and many were happy when in 1958 at a large annual banquet at Goshen College dining hall, the Elkhart County Agricultural Society, named the Bert Cook family as the 1st "Outstanding Farm Family of the Year" in the county. Every one of the 10 children were present to see Bert receive the $50 award check.

A few years after this mountain-top experience, the Palm Sunday Tornado wiped out the dairy barn and buildings and not having the heart to rebuild, Bert sold out to his son Dale, who rebuilt, and now has his own dream going.

THE HISTORY OF THE ELKHART COUNTY FAIR

The Elkhart County Commissioners had passed a resolution to publicize a notice, asking for the farmers to assemble in the Court House at a given date to "Organize an Agricultural Society for the purpose of promoting Agriculture in the county, and especially to set in motion plans to put on County Fairs." The history books at the Goshen Library record that the meeting was held in 1837, and officers elected naming the society, the Elkhart County Agricultural Society.

Fairs were finally begun, the first one in 1851, on the grounds of the County Court house, with nothing but scrub livestock and some other exhibits in tents. The Fairs continued for several years and then the Society bought some ground on East Madison Street around ninth street, held Fairs several years, and then bought 10 acres on South Main, south of the College, and continued Fairs there for a few years, and then the Civil War became a damper, and the Fairs were dropped until in 1874, John Lesh and a group of men bought 20 acres, now the Fidler Woods, built a beautiful race track and that was the first big successful Fair held in the county. That is why the Fair Board called the 1973 Fair the 100th Anniversary. They rented the tract to the Society and Fairs were held and improved until 1893, when the Cleveland Panic became another damper and the Fairs were dropped for about 15 years. The Society disbanded temporarily, and was not reactivated until 1954.

In 1908 then, the son of John Lesh, Joe, a race horse enthusiast with a 40 acre farm, with some financial help sold the farm to the new group, The Elkhart County Fair Association. In the group of Stockholders, were John Abshire, Sam Spohn, George Hay, Charles Method, and Frank Gardner. Others later bought stock. This time the race track was par-excellence, built up with proper mixture of sand and clay, 2 feet deep, one of the finest half mile race tracks in the United States.

The success of the Fair was unbelievable until the farmers depression of 1921 and 1922, put a kink in the attendance and support. Mr. Victor V. Swartz, Herb's father, wore out shoe leather travelling over the county to keep up the interest, but it went down and down, and in 1929 really hit bottom, and for years afterward the association barely survived.

The American Legion then bought the 40 acres and tried until 1955 but they were handicapped because 4-H had moved away from the grounds and showed for years at Rice Field in Elkhart. 4-H leaving in 1943 was a blow from which the Legion could not recover.

At this time the Elkhart County Agricultural Society was reactivated by 40 leaders of the County, Farm Organizations, Government Agencies, and Agri-business people, and after electing officers, they were in the act of buying the grounds, when the City of Goshen stepped in the limelight and claimed the City should own it, used the funds of the City Power and Light, and bought it.

Some people swung back of the City, Uncle Elmer for instance, organized more than 100 farmers, many of them from Millersburg, and in one day they reroofed almost all the buildings with the city hauling out the roofing material. But it was up hill all the way, and through Frank Snider, and Marty Basset, two early presidents of the reorganized society, Mr. Roscoe Stangland was able to bring the 4-H people back to the Goshen Fair, and then the 4-H parents pitched in. The deed was drawn and recorded in 1960 to the 4-H and Agricultural Exposition, and from then on the road was downhill.

Dorothy Kercher has been with the Fair for a generation and her great kindness and generosity are two of the main reasons for the tremendous spirit of today, so from here on the language is hers.

Today everybody is interested because they feel it is their own Fair. This has been accomplished by getting more people and groups of people involved.

The Fair Board is representative of seventeen agricultural and business organizations. In addition, the president and/or executive committee may appoint seventeen additional members with special interest or expertise in Fair operations. One of the special areas has been liaison with the news media. Special effort has been made to report activities and create good public relations.

With the involvement of many people, it was decided to bring in the best entertainment possible on the budget available and make the grandstand free. Income is derived from parking and gate admission for this support.

Food concessions have always strived to prepare and serve the best available in their specialty. This brought involvement of many service clubs, livestock organizations and sororities; as well as, private concessionaires.

The prime moving force for Fair is competition in exhibition and exhibition facilities for 4-Hers, home and family arts and livestock participants. Still another involvement is the drive of special interest groups to build their own facilities in cooperation with the Fair Board. The first to start was the 4-H Saddle Club; followed by the Beef Club, Dairy Association, Swine Club, Sheep Club, 4-H Corporation and Dog Club. Buildings have gone up like mushrooms over the past several years including the finest and most practical livestock show arena on county fairgrounds.

Several years ago the board expressed an interest in competing in the Fair contest sponsored by the Indiana Association of County and District Fairs. After several years of placing in the winners group, the Fair was judged grand champion in 1968 and 1971. The Elkhart County 4-H Fair was the first to win the Grand Champion Fair award a second time and they will continue to compete.

Other involvement includes Boy Scouts, sorority and service clubs in handling parking, admission ticket sales and gate admission. Through all this; an increasing number of commercial exhibitors have participated and the Fair has truly had something for everyone.

DALE CULP — National Champion Sheep-Shearer

Walter Culp farmed in Harrison Twp, East of Wakarusa. Dale was born there in 1933.

Walter farmed several places, one near Dell's School House, where Dale went to school, then in 1950 they landed on the Hay Farm, which Walter's father had bought around 1922, and rented it on shares, 50-50 Share rental, and grain-farmed it for a number of years. Being in Harrison Twp., and in the Wakarusa school district, he went to the Wakarusa school and was in the writer's Vo. Ag. classes in 1949 and 1950, but was in Mina Ganger's 4-H club at Model School.

In 1954 he was married to Stella Saal, daughter of Russell and Gertrude Saal of Goshen and Dale and Stella rented 100 acres east of Wakarusa, and there Kathleen was born in 1953 and the twins, Terry and Gary in 1957. They continued farming there for several years, then moved on Ed Raber's place, and then is when he started in earnest in the sheep-shearing business.

He had been shearing some sheep before this time for 50¢ per head, and soon was shearing 50 to 70 per day, about six or seven thousand sheep each Spring, March, April and May. In 1959 the price went to 70¢ per head and the score for the year was 13,000 fleeces.

By 1960 he became interested in sheep shearing contests. While today he is the best in the world, he says that he had much to learn in the early contests.

In 1962, he won the Indiana State contest and received the money and a trophy. The next week he got up the spunk to buy the 80 acre Russell Stutzman farm on County Road 30, just ¼ mile west of the Basher school.

At first on this farm he had 30 Registered Brown Swiss cattle, milking around 15, but that made too many chores which got in the way of the shearing, so he put out the cows with young farmers just getting started, and he gets all the calves for his profit. Now he has cows with 5 different farmers.

Then he bought 40 acres of land (no buildings) across the road from Joe Gorsuch, and now the boys are big enough to do all the farming

Dale had started some years before auctioneering with the Jonas Miller sale barn at Wakarusa. He had also been helping Argel McDowell with his farm and Household Goods sales so he was also becoming an auctioneer.

In 1965 he was second place in the International Sheep-Shearing Contest at Toronto, Canada, with money and medal. By that time, he was shearing over 100 sheep per day, and in 1966 and 1967 he won the same International, two years in a row.

On September 7th, 1970, he hit the big one at Indianapolis, THE UNITED STATES NATIONAL SHEEP-SHEARING CONTEST, the one they all try to win; and in late October he did 263 sheep in 10 hours, catching his own sheep, and tied up his own wool for Morris Klein, of Hicksville, Ohio. (Dale had won the District contest in Des Moines, Iowa)

About that time the Sale barn at Wakarusa closed and Dale associated himself with the Goshen Livestock Auction. There he auctions off calves, lambs, and butcher hogs.

In 1971 and 1972, he won the Sweepstakes at Detroit and the Little Brown Jug at Delaware, Ohio. Gary is now in the swing, having won the Junior Division of the Indiana State contest. Little Kelly came in 1973, and the shearing price goes to 85¢ and the score (annually) up to 17,000. Last year Dale won the Champion of Champions at Columbus, and repeated the Little Brown Jug at Delaware. Kathleen is now at Ball State, the twins will be seniors at Northwood, Gary a wrestler and Terry shooting baskets Dale says, "Sheep-shearing is hard work but a lot of fun". THE WORLD'S CHAMPION RIGHT IN OUR BACK YARD!!!

CULP'S DUTCH BELTED DAIRY CATTLE

Elwood Culp is Public Relations at the Salem Bank. He is married to Martha Card, and they have a son Jerry, who is a sensation with his Dutch Belted. The young lad bought an 80 acre farm in 1973 on County Road 43, and people are watching.

Mr. Vern Marquardt, artificial breeding specialist, with ABS, is working with Jerry, doing some cross-breeding, and they have found already that the dominant characteristics of milk production is 100 when a Dutch Belted bull is used on another breed. Jerry just sold a Belted Bull to a Nebraska rancher with 1,000 heifers.

At the moment Jerry is batching, not having found the girl yet, but he is still looking.

They have some 25 animals, and Jerry is shooting for a goal of 30 "cows in milk".

The Breed came into United States in 1838, and Jerry is already a member of the National Association of Dutch Belted Cattle Breeders. He also rents another 100 acres near his farm.

OWEN CUSTER — Columbia Sheep

Fred Custer was born in 1892, went to the little school, Eberhard, to the north. Later took over and bought his father's farm of 128 acres, on Custer Road, just east of the church on North Burr Oak Road. He was later married right there to Hazel Sindlinger from Bronson in 1914.

Owen was the first and only child born in 1920 at the start of the Farmers Depression. At school age he, too, attended Eberhard for 5 years, and on consolidation was transferred to Colon, 3 miles to the north. He graduated there in 1932, and then up and married Florence Wall a gal from Sturgis, and they rented a farm at Burr Oak for 3 years, and then rented 190 acres near Colon for 12 years. They bought the Ware farm in '47 and at the same time rented his dad's farm. This is 3 miles north of Burr Oak. This went on for 17 more years, and during this time Gordon was born, 1950, and Virginia came in 1956. Gordon graduated from Colon, and Virginia from Burr Oak. During their school years they were both in Columbia sheep (4-H) for the full 10 years. Virginia won the champion ewe, champion ram, and later the State 4-H Service award in sheep. (in his day, Owen had shown Oxford sheep at Centerville). Florence was a 4-H leader of the Colon "Ever-Ready" Club for many years.

Owen has been to many sheep sales to buy Columbia sheep, and now has 80 registered Columbia Ewes. To help buy the sheep, Florence drove a school bus at Burr Oak for years. Fred died in 1971, and Owen, being the only heir, inherited the 80 east of the church. They now own 250 acres, rent another 80 and farm 330 acres. Gordon died a few years ago, and this June their house burned to the ground from a stroke of lightning, so Owen lost father, son, and home in a short space of time. But they are a strong couple, moved into the house to the south, will pull in a trailer for a few months, and re-build. Owen has contributed a lot to Michiana Sheep "Know-How". Owen says, "I can sit down and talk and rest as long as I want and if tomorrow doesn't come, it won't make any difference, anyhow". Good Philosophy, eh?

OTIS DAVIDHIZER — St. Joseph County, Indiana

Enos Davidhizer was born in 1864 on the Davidhizer Centennial farm two miles west of Wakarusa, the son of John and Barbara Davidhizer. (160 acres with several acres sold to the Wabash for right-of-way.) John in his day did general farming, and Enos, likewise. Enos had gone to the Holdeman school before the Loucks school was built. They had lots of hogs. Money from the hogs enabled them to buy another 160 acres, the Francis Longenecker farm.

Otis was born in 1909, went to the Loucks school, then went to the Wakarusa High School for one year, and when Madison High was built in 1914, transferred there and graduated in 1927, worked for his dad 2 years for spending money, and then up and married Miss Mary Enders, daughter of Albert and Ellen Eby Enders in 1929, and worked for Enos several years at $20. per month plus the free rent of the tenent house back of the big Brick spacious home.

Then Otis and Henry rented the place on shares in the thirties, 50-50 for several years, when Otis bought Henry's share and became the sole tenant. At this time they began to replace the old wood-stave silos with cement and increased the herd of cattle.

Imogene had come in 1929, Eleanor in 1931, James in 1934, and Nancy in 1938. For some time there had been room for 24 Holsteins, but now they built another 12 stanchions. They sold milk to the City Dairy in South Bend.

About 1942 Otis and Mary rented a stall (booth) in the South Bend Farmers' market, offering dressed poultry and eggs, in order to supplement their income, 4 children coming up. Later they bought the booth and ran it until two years ago when they turned it over to Nancy and her husband who now live in the tenant house.

By 1944 James and Eleanor had joined 4-H dairy calf club and Otis bought the 1st 2 registered Holstein Junior calves to start them out. Nancy started in 1946, and then the fun began. The writer remembers his grand-daughter Judy showing against Nancy at the Indiana State Fair. Encouraged by the interest of the children, Otis decided to go into the purebred business. He first started with Curtis Candy, but wanting production rather than conformation he swung to the A.B.S. out of Mt. Carmel. The increase from the registered calves soon loaded Otis up with the record keeping and he has been "keeping at it" for the past 30 years.

They now have 60 registered Holsteins, milking 34, and sell milk to the Dean Milk Co. at Rochester.

Imogene is home, Eleanor teaches at Fullmer, James is in Christian Service, and Nancy and her husband, Donald Parcell run the market, and help week ends at home. They live in the tenant house.

Otis has been in Pure Milk Association and AMPI for 35 years, and presently he is President of the Dairy Council for Northern Indiana.

They are all Holdeman Mennonites. James and Nancy have shown cattle at the International in Chicago, but generally speaking, they have not gone for show, or for expensive "ultra-modern equipment", trying just for production and still keeping up the records.

Otis says "I am on a farm because I don't know anything else. I have never worked off the farm, except to go to market, it's hard work but I like it, for diversion we look forward every year to a 2 weeks vacation when we go to Pinecraft Mennonite Settlement, at the Southeast edge of Sarasota, Florida, 1 mile east of the Sears Roebuck store on U.S. 41."

Note: The writer was born just 2½ miles from the Davidhizer Centennial farm. Great folks!

HENRY DETWILER

Joseph R. Detwiler was a blacksmith on what was later known as the Shank farm at Harrison Center, west of Goshen. Henry was born there on April 27, 1892.

Later Joseph traded his blacksmith shop for a farm north of Zion Church in Washington Township, where the 4 brothers did the farm work and Henry became the cook and housekeeper.

Henry was married to Stella Fisher in 1915. Then Henry lived there and farmed the home farm until 1926.

Having bought 100 acres onCounty Road 104 north of Bristol he moved there in 1926 and went into the Jersey Dairy farm business, calling the setup "The Twin Pine Farm". He began to keep records and register the calves. He developed a herd of about 30 cattle, milking about an average of 10. They sold cream to the Constantine Co-Operative Creamery on the basis of 25¢ to 35¢ per pound of butterfat, starting with a Sharpless Cream Separator and ending up with a DeLaval. He exhibited cattle at many different local fairs.

He had his share of champions and grand champions. He has held every office in the Jersey Breeders Association.

Henry and Stella had 5 children, every one of which went through the 4-H years of the Jersey Dairy Club. Henry was a 4-H leader 43 years.

One September night in 1943, lightning struck their barn and burned all the buildings but the house to the ground. They lost 4 head of cattle including 2 champions in the fire.

Henry had fitted many of his own cattle for show and through a friend, who taught him Bovine Beautification work, took up special training, and decided to go on the road fitting cattle.

His first sale after that was to fit 50 Guernseys for the Hardware man, Harold Hodgson, on the farm now called Romayne Sherman's Farm No. 1

He has followed the line ever since that time, working each sale herd from 8 days to 5 weeks, fitting each animal from the nose to the tail switch, polishing the horns and trimming the feet. His largest job was fitting 265 animals taking 5 weeks.

Stella passed away December 31, 1971. Henry says we should say "She always did her part". The writer adds "Neither one will ever be forgotten".

TOBE EASH AND HIS BOYS

In 1907 Tobe Eash married Anna Bontreger and bought his father-in-law's farm a year later (120 acres) located three miles south of Middlebury on State Road 13. They have five living children: Mabel, Sanford, Kathryn, Linus and Ellen.

Tobe soon began to feed out beef cattle that had been shipped in from the West. He continued this for about fifteen years. The cattle were driven on foot from the stockyards in Middlebury to the farm and then back again to Middlebury or Millersburg and shipped to commission merchants in Chicago or Buffalo, N.Y. In the early twenties he took an interest in purebred Jersey cattle; he also started feeding out 300 to 600 western feeding lambs during the winter. In the late twenties and early thirties 20 to 25 Jersey cows were milked along with the lamb feeding. The milk was separated and the cream was sold to the Middlebury Co-op Creamery for 25 to 35 cents a pound of butterfat. The skimmed milk was fed to the hogs.

As a Vocational Agriculture project in high school in 1928, Sanford started broilers in a 10x12 brooder. This business grew in the Eash family for about fifteen years. A.T. Marvel was Vo. Ag. instructor in Middlebury at that time and was a strong influence on the boys for better farming methods. Mr. Marvel always found Tobe ready to accomodate the Vo. Ag. classes on field trips and demonstrations, even though he was an ardent member of the conservative Griner Mennonite Church, ½ mile down the road. He was always strong for education, agressive in trying new things and always enthusiastic about his work. Even though the early thirties were hard times, Tobe always had confidence times would change.

Tobe bought another farm in 1929, 159 acres in Clinton Township on County Road 37, what was then known as the Pletcher Farm. Sanford was married to Orpha Kauffman in 1935, moved on this farm, working for his father for two years and renting the farm for two years, then bought it in 1939.

Linus attended Middlebury High School and by that time Tobe was producing as many as 30,000 broilers yearly and started raising turkeys in the early forties. Linus took over the home farm on shares in 1950. Tobe continued in broilers and turkeys in a broiler house on the big Middlebury hill. He sold this in 1958. Tobe died in 1960 at the age of 77.

Linus married Susan Yoder in 1950 and kept on with turkeys a few years and broilers about 10 years. They milked cows for only one year then went into beef and hogs. In 1957 Linus bought the home place. He started out in the beef business by buying about 40 head of light western cattle and has now increased to 150 head. These finished steers are sold to special eastern buyers and are trucked directly to their markets. Linus is known for his ability to buy quality western calves and feed out prime cattle.

Linus also feeds out about 500 feeder pigs yearly, which he buys as weaning pigs from neighborhood farms in Elkhart and LaGrange Counties. The pigs are fed a complete ration mixed by a local feed mill. Most of the hogs go to either Goshen or Topeka hog buyers.

He also sells seed corn and does some custom work along with farming. Linus always has nice-looking crops.

Linus and Susan have four children: Carolyn Jane, Alta Fern, David Lynn and Linda Faye. The family takes a vacation at least once a year. The last few years Linus has given about ten percent of his time for construction work in disaster areas, working usually with Mennonite Disaster Service or other agencies needing construction help. The family belongs to the Griner Mennonite Church.

Mabel and Kathryn live in Middlebury. Ellen is married to Rev. Albert H. Miller. They have four children: Eldon, Leon, Gary and Karen. He is the bishop of the Griner Mennonite Church.

Eldon and Leon have done two years of service work in South and Central America, graduated from Eastern Mennonite College and are now teaching in church high schools.

Gary married Anna Horst and they have a daughter, Kendra. They live in Red Lake, Ontario, where he did his service work and is now employed by a private firm as an airplane mechanic. Karen recently graduated from High School and is still at home.

Sanford and Orpha's family of four boys, Dale, Galen, Marvin and Loren, and one girl, Nancy, all were born in the late thirties and early forties. During this time the broiler business contributed a real part of the financial gain made at that time.

Dairy cows always were steady sources of income, working up to 80 head in the sixties, but Sanford never considered himself an outstanding dairyman. Turkeys were raised from 1946 to 1971. In 1970 when Loren decided to go to college, the dairy cows were sold and the family started buying Holstein bull calves, starting them and feeding them out as steers. Today 700 to 1,000 steers are fed out annually. The cattle are on a high corn silage feeding program. In 1974 a hog feeding setup was installed and they are feeding out 800 head of feeder pigs.

In 1957 Sanford purchased a 120 acre farm on County Road 38; in 1967, 159 acres on State Road 13. In 1974 another 94 acres on County Road 35 west of the home farm were added. At present the family rents an additional 300 acres.

In 1965 the Sanford Eash family was the Elkhart County Farm Family of the Year. In 1970 the family farm was incorporated and all five children and the parents own stock. Orpha has been active through the years in planning and decision-making, and both parents are still active today in various capacities.

Dale did his service work in North Africa, attended college and worked at Salem Bank a few years, then came back to the farm. He married Judith Schrock, a Registered Laboratory Technician. They live on County Road 38. Dale is secretary-treasurer of the organization and is in charge of cattle feeding.

Galen is a medical doctor with a good general practice in the Red River Valley of North Dakota. He married Marlene Grabill and they have two daughters, Kristine and Lori.

Marvin graduated from Goshen College and spent three years in Peace Corps and two years in the Office of Economic Opportunity. He then moved back to the home farm. He married Pamela Miller, R.N. They have two children, Christopher and Elana. He is in charge of calf starting and hog feeding. Dale and Marvin share the crop work.

After college Nancy spent two years teaching English in Japan, returned home and got a masters degree in education, at North Western. She married Victor Myers, who has a Ph.D. in chemistry. They have a daughter, Joanna, born during a three-year teaching assignment at the University of Zaire, Africa.

Loren did his service work in Nigeria in connection with a British agricultural mission. He came back and milked cows a few years, then went to Purdue University where he majored in international agriculture and graduated in 1974. He married Frances Irizarry; they have a daughter Leslie Maria. They will be going to Africa as agricultural missionaries.

Both Sanford and Orpha spent many years as Sunday School teachers in the Clinton Frame Mennonite Church. They have been involved in many of the church's outreach, educational and building programs. Sanford is an elder at present.

Sanford and Orpha built a new home on State Road 13 in 1971. They have a farm pond as part of the setting there, and the whole family enjoys the fishing and swimming.

MERVIN EBY FAMILY

He was born 1886, on the Jacob Eby homestead. The name of his wife was Goldie BeMiller. They were married in 1907 and in 1908 he bought the old Johnson farm, 4 miles north of Wakarusa.

In 1908 they drove a team of horses and surrey to Rochester where Merv paid $65 for a registered calf not yet weaned, laid the calf in the rumble box and Goldie cried all the way home to their farm over spending so much.

But the calf became the foundation cow in the herd Mervin had dreamed of. The herd grew and 10 years later they had a reduction sale and one of the animals was auctioned off for $1000, which was an unheard of price at that time. In 1924 Mervin and his family started bottling Guernsey milk, in the basement of their house and started delivery routes in Elkhart. Out of this humble beginning grew both the Eby's Guernsey Dairy and the Lookwell Guernsey Dairy of Elkhart. In 1935 the 120A Cocanower farm, across the road, was purchased. This new purchase enabled the Guernsey herd and milk business both to be enlarged. In 1941 the Cocanower farm was sold to their son and daughter-in-law, Everett and Anna Eby. A father and son partnership was formed and the herd was enlarged to 50 milk cows. The Lookwell Guernseys were tested for milk production and showed at many of the leading Dairy Shows throughout the Mid-

West. The two greatest highlights that the Eby's had in the Guernsey business were the caring for and milking the first Guernsey cow to make 1000 lbs. of butterfat in Indiana; and breeding, raising and showing two daughters of a cow that were voted Reserve All-American Produce of Dam.

By 1951, Everett and Anna were the proud parents of 3 boys and 3 girls, therefore as a little sideline they started raising 5000 turkeys a year. In the spring of 1958, Mervin and his wife, Goldie, decided to retire and sold the farm that they purchased in 1908 to Everett and Anna and moved off of the farm that they moved on 50 years before. In 1959, there was a new milk house put up and in 1960 there was an addition built on to the dairy barn so as to accomodate 60 milk cows with the young cattle. As Everett's boys grew older, a 120A farm, ½ mile north was purchased and in 1965 a 40 x 300 turkey brooding building was erected. The following year another 30A farm was purchased and the turkey project grew to top of 80,000 turkeys a year. In 1969 the Elkhart County Agri-Society picked the Everett Eby family as the Outstanding Farm Family of Elkhart County.

These accomplishments are most graciously credited to a never dying faith in a great, kind and loving God, plus a great family cooperation and effort.

At the present time, Everett and Rolland are 50-50 partners. On the old Elcona farm No. 1, which Everett and boys bought, they stable as many as 500 dairy replacement calves (mostly Holsteins).

In two years time the business has grown to where they handle 1500 to 2000 calves per week.

EBY'S PINES

Harry Eby's father bought the Eby farm at the turn of the century (160 acres) and had two sons, Harry and Frank. It was on Elkhart County Road number 29 near the Michigan line, west of Vistula.

Harry married Inez Lee in 1926 and took over the farm. From the first he was interested in legumes, soil drainage and fertilizing the soil. For two years he was president of the Indiana Soil and Water Conservation District. Also he was appointed by Gov. Craig as chairman of the State Soil Committee and served four years. He was Trustee of Washington Township eight years.

Harry had run the Vistula store for eight years where he learned a great deal about human nature.

He bought 75 acres on Indiana 120 in 1948 and started pine seedlings which were to become Christmas trees someday.

Then he built the roller skating rink in 1953 and it became a great recreational center for young and old in Michiana.

In 1958 Harry and Inez built the beautiful home west of the skating rink and moved there when it was finished and then Frank quit the Vistula store and moved back on the old farm.

The Eby's have three girls: Doris, Helen, and Carol. Doris is associated with the restaurant which they built in 1963. They can serve 600 people and have the help to do it.

Later he established the camp grounds on 80 acres across the road along the stream "Little Elkhart".

They now own 600 acres, about 400 of it in Christmas tree production.

Harry was elected to the Elkhart County Governmental Board and is now serving his third year.

He says his desire from the beginning had been "to leave the country better than when I came, serving the community first, and accepting for pay whatever comes there from."

LEO ECCLES-Portage View Farm — St. Joseph County Michigan

Leo lived near Girard, Illinois and for many years sold yellow page listing and advertising. He married a young lady from Chicago, who had come from St. Joe, Missouri.

All their married life they were devoted fishermen and finally concluded their happiness lay in finding a farm on some lake where they could fish anytime.

In 1942 they found where the rainbow touched down and bought from Mrs. Utley 75 acres, a part of the Hallam land on County Road 120 with long lake frontage on Portage Lake in St. Joseph County Michigan. They stocked up with grade sheep, went into registered Hampshires and then changed to registered Corriedale, a dual-purpose breed for both mutton and wool.

One purpose of this story is to show how a family in town can move on a farm and make a success if you have it in your heart.

They have 40 sheep, 23 breeding ewes. Also they breed and train Border Collie sheep dogs.

Leo has been a market lamb 4-H leader in the county for 11 years, and is considered an expert on sheep, as well as sheep dogs. He does not believe in breeding the ewe lambs until they are 18 months old.

He supplements orphan lambs with goat milk which is very nourishing. He gets $50 and up for both ewe and ram lambs.

He has won many firsts, reserve champion, and champion, and grand champion awards at the Centreville St. Joseph County Fair.

They sold 5 ewe lambs recently which went to Mexico under the Heifer Project, a self-help program.

One of the handicaps the Sheep Breeders Association has is to fight the wild sheep dogs.

If you can drench a sheep without choking her to death, you know your stuff. Here is a very popular and happy sheep family.

Even the Home Economics leader of the county living in Mendon bought one of their young sheep dogs.

EDD'S SUPPLIES

In 1967, 5 boys formed a corporation, Edd's Supplies, 1 mile west of Shipshewana to furnish mainly plant food including liquid fertilizer. They manufacture their own fertilizer by running water in the mixing tank, adding the necessary potash, phosphate and nitrogen in that order to produce the desired formula. It can be stored indefinitely in stationary or truck tanks.

Ed Swartzendruber, President; Franklin Heign, Vice President; Ellsworth Fanning, Secretary-Treasurer, Jerry Mast, and Lonnie Hostetler. Most of the customers are within 30 miles radius of Shipshewana.

Liquid fertilizer has made much in the bulk fertilizer business in recently offering plow down application, in the row and top dressing for small grain.

Ellsworth Fanning being a vocational agricultural instructor for years at Shipshewana and a Purdue graduate has "the know how" to build public relations and Ed Swartzendruber with high record corn production and wide acquaintance in Michiana is the man back of sales and promotion, and the technician for the plant.

The plant has considerable storage facility at Edd's complex south of Goshen. The efficiency of liquid fertilizer in crop produc-

47

tion has contributed much to Michiana Agriculture, and this outfit is to be commended for their wide services.

Ed Swartzendruber's spread is on Road 27, around 160 acres of corn average 150 bushels per acre and 50,000 roasters to occupy his spare time.

ROBERT EHRET — Undertaker

Jacob Ehret, Olive Township, set up undertaking on his farm (now known as the Clem Hunsberger farm). He was assisted by his sons Cornelius, Fred and Albert. He was a farmer, undertaker and general contractor. So he built his own caskets. One of the buildings he contracted was the Zion Evangelical Church on New Road. In those days (late 1800's) a casket would cost $15 to $40. He had built coffins in the carpenter shop of the U.S. Army in 1865 during the Civil War.

Henry Culp, (Elmer's grandfather), had the same background in Harrison Township, on the Merritt Loucks farm, later, at the southwest corner of Wakarusa square.

Edward Lienhart (Wakarusa) bought out the two pioneer undertakers and merged the two farms in the 1890's and called it the Lienhart and Weaver Funeral Home and after one year it was changed to the Edward Lienhart Funeral Home. Edward operated the business with his sons, Calvin and Dewey, and later Cal's son-in-law, Tully Obenhoff (Lois's husband).

In 1891 Henry Culp backed his son Ephraim to open the Culp Funeral Home on Sixth and Clinton in Goshen (southwest corner) and after several moves landed at 311 South Main Street in 1924 (commonly known as the Culp Funeral Home).

Later in 1964 the Culp Funeral Home in Goshen was closed after Elmer's and Floyd's death and a new corporation was formed by Don Rieth and Wallace Rohrer and Robert Ehret to buy the Culp Funeral Home location, opening the new business immediately.

In 1967, after Tully died, the Lienhart Funeral Home was bought by the Rieth, Rohrer and Ehret Funeral Home in Goshen, thus keeping it in the Ehret family. The firm now has facilities in Goshen, New Paris and Wakarusa.

In the meantime Dwight Ehret and son Robert had operated a funeral home in Puerto Rico for about 18 years, 1946-1964, where they introduced embalming within reach of the general public for burial in the Island. So it should be noted there were four generations of Ehret families in the undertaking business.

ELKHART COUNTY CO-OP

The Co-op was established in Elkhart County in 1925. James Dunmire of Jimtown was the leading promoter. Harvey Stahly, from Nappanee, was employed as manager in 1929 at $30 per week. The Incorporation was set upon June 14, 1927. Ernie Smoker became the new manager March 31, 1930.

At first feeds were bought out of Chicago, Arcady Feed Co. (now out of business). Petroleum was purchased in carload lots.

In the beginning feed and gas and oil was the chief operation. The departments added since then were lumber, fertilizer and seed (1903) and implements (1941). Charles Speicher was the first manager of the implement department, followed by Dale Love in 1959, and then the present manager, Lester Hummel, in 1966.

Nappanee and Bristol branches were established in 1941. The Bristol Mill burned in 1968, but the Nappanee branch has prospered the last 31 years with Bill Hostetler as manager.

1948 was the year of expansion and the new hatchery building and the processing plant south of New Paris were built. The processing plant did not pay out and it was later sold to Pringle and Roth (Land 'O Goshen) who later sold it to Polo Foods, of Chicago, about 1965. The community room over the hatchery was used for many years for schools and meetings but the hatchery was later closed down as it did not pay out, and now the general offices are established upstairs.

In 1954 the large elevator was constructed on the old F.E.C. Hawks site, the purchase of which was partly engineered by DeMain Warner, the President of the Board of Directors at the time; it was purchased in 1937 from Mrs. Dan Spohn, a granddaughter of Frank Hawks. Ernest Smoker after serving as manager for 25 years, resigned and Woodrow Risser served until 1962 when the present manager, Mr. Don Metzger, took his place, to whom the writer is very much indebted for his patience in digging up this information.

THE ELLER CENTENNIAL FARM — St. Joseph County, Indiana

Elam Eller was born during the early part of the 19th Century, in 1826, and established the Eller farm on Basswood road, just off the Dragoon Trail to the north. The Peppermint still stands there to this day to help identify the old homestead. The name CLARK is on the big mail box. (East side of the road).

Elam married in 1847 and they had 2 children, Warren, 1849; Robert, later who died young. Some of the large sales of imported Belgian Horses were held in their big red barn. When Warren grew up he became interested in the Belgian horses and helped the Elkhart County Agricultural Society with their importations and sales. Many of these Belgian horses from these sales were the horses which pulled the logs out of the thick woods in Olive, Bauge, and Madison townships, and some of them it is reported helped build the Corduroy road from Wakarusa to Wyatt. In wet weather, the horses would sink down in the clay and dark soil in mud, so far that they themselves had to be pulled out with large ropes.

Elam and Warren had 200 acres to farm, then they bought 80 acres on the south side of Dragoon Trail, first farm east of Cedar Road. Warren went to Vesey school and had a mechanical mind.

When Warren grew up he was married to Laura Fuller, just after the civil war, took over all the farming operations, and Elam moved to Osceola to retire, where he lived until he died in 1910.

Warren and Laura followed in Elam's footsteps, and continued to farm the Eller farms, Peppermint on the old homestead and general farming on Dragoon Trail. Also they got interested in the Belgian horses and always had a scad of horses around. Warren was "in for new things", and had the first automobile in the area, a "Jackson".

Warren and Laura had 3 children Lucius, 1884, Clinton 1887, and Jay 1892. Two years after Jay, Laura became ill, contracted tuberculosis, and died at an early age, 34, in 1894.

As teen-agers, Clint and Jay teamed up on projects of their own and soon found themselves working together. Lucius married Elsie Cook in 1905, they moved on the 80 on Dragoon and farmed there 7 years.

Later, in 1920 Clinton married Hazel Proudfit, and Jay married her sister, Grace. The double wedding was held at the home of the Proudfits, farther to the east. Then Clint moved on the old homestead, and Warren moved to Osceola and retired. Jay moved onto the 80 acres after the house was burned and rebuilt. Lucius then bought the Weston Snider farm on Dragoon by Ash Road.

Soon after Clint and Hazel were married Warren J. was born and Max came in the Jay and Grace home.

About 5 years later, 1925, Clint and Jay who had been farming together bought the George Moon farm (201 acres) on the south side of Dragoon Trail just east of the 80 acres, and then Clint moved there.

Clint and Jay kept working together, and built up their holdings to 600 acres and in 1942 both died of heart attacks, 6 months apart, Jay being age 50 and Clint, age 55. Since then Warren J. has taken over Clint's interest and gone big in Dairying, and Max, Jay's only son has taken over his interests and has also developed quite a spread.

Lucius died in 1957, Elsie sold the farm, and is now in the Rudgedale nursing home in South Bend. They had 7 children and for our purpose including Warren E. Eller who bought the Frank Watkins farm on Potawotomi Trail, west of Jimtown, and is now retired. He is married to Helen Null.

THE FEDERAL LAND BANK

At a meeting of interested persons held April 14, 1917 in the office of the County Superintendent of Schools for Elkhart County, Mr. Robert W. Elliot was made temporary chairman and ten directors were selected including Robert N. Elliot, Fred M. Eby, J.N. Teal, S.L. Morse, W.W. Oesch, Frank W. Watkins, George Bostwich, and Ralph Kline. Loan committee was Eby, Marty and William H. Spaulding.

On April 21, 1917 the group met and elected Mr. Harry Vernon, attorney, as secretary-treasurer. He was to keep the minutes, keep the records, take loan applications, prepare abstracts, deeds and mortgages, get them approved by Louisville Federal Land Bank, headquarters for Indiana, Kentucky, Ohio, and Tennessee, secure the check for the loan from Louisville, arrange a closing appointment, deliver the check and record the deed and mortgage. All this was done in Mr. Vernon's office which became the headquarters during the early years for the Federal Land Bank Business.

Martin Bassett was born 1904 in Shelby County, attended Purdue University, married Catherine Watson and taught vocational agriculture at Greencastle High School until 1930, when he was made manager of the Goshen office and moved onto a farm north of Goshen. He arranged for countless loans and for years helped people who could buy a farm with a 50% loan at a very low rate of interest, 4 to 4½%. He built a beautiful new headquarters building on W. Lincoln in 1961. He served exceeding well for 35 years and then needing assistance brought Larry Penrod into the business. Larry was born west of Wakarusa in St. Joseph County July 1, 1939. He attended Madison Township School 12 years, went to Purdue, B.S. degree in 1961, married Monta Johnson, a Junior 4-H leader from Penn Township and then taught vocational agriculture at Millersburg High School from 1961 to 1965, when he received his M.S. degree from Purdue working summers. Larry was made a field assistant for Mr. Basset in 1965 for 1 year, then was made assistant manager for two years. He built a new home on County Road 40 and then took over the Bank when Marty retired August 1, 1969. Larry bought the 58 acre farm from Mrs. John Inbody and moved there for his home. They have two daughters Karen and Pam.

Since then he bought 80 acres on County Road 43 north of County Road 38, next farm south of Elwood Kauffman.

Both Marty and Larry won their way into the hearts of Elkhart County farmers. Marty is retired and lives in a beautiful home on South 7th in Goshen. Larry is pushing the loan business hard, but finds time to teach a Sunday School class at St. Mark's Methodist Church in Goshen.

Long live the Federal Land Bank!!!

HOWARD FERM — Broiler King

Howard's father farmed 152 acres near the Sailor School northwest of LaGrange where Howard and the neighbor children rode to school on a bob-sled in the winter and the school hack in the spring and fall.

Howard was born July 6, 1906. When he was age 13, his folks bought a farm north of Elkhart near Kissington, Michigan, where Howard finished his schooling and started raising broilers in what had been a woodshed, using muskrat and skunk money with $20 he had borrowed from his sister. He walked three miles to buy Buff Orpington eggs. The hatch yielded over 100 chickens and he sold them at twelve weeks, weighing two pounds, for $100 to the Christiana Country Club.

Howard worked some in Elkhart and was married in 1929. By the next year his father had bought an 80 acre farm two miles west of Middlebury on County Road 14. After the stock market crash, Howard moved there and took over his father's farm on a share basis. He sold hogs for two and a half cents per pound and broilers for six and a half cents per pound.

In 1937 Howard bought 40 acres north of Lake Grange on County Road 131 and went exclusively into the broiler business. He fitted the farm for broiler production. Then he built a two-story building especially for broilers. By 1940 he had a capacity of 16,000 broilers. In the late 40's he bought 35 acres and built a broiler house 50 x 250 and so he increased his capacity to 31,000 broilers.

In the meantime, in 1944, Howard Ferm called a meeting of all broiler people in the area in the gymnasium of the Middlebury School to organize a group to promote better marketing; then made an investigation of marketing conditions in the other areas of the country. It was finally arrived at to build a processing plant to serve the area. Stock was issued and sold for that purpose. They were then confronted by the Farm Bureau and this whole marketing condition was discussed. It was voted to merge interests with the Farm Bureau and they proceeded to build the processing plant south of New Paris. Since the marketing association was dissolved, it was Mr. Ferm's feeling that a new broiler association should be formed for the objective of public relations, merchandising, marketing at the retail level, and to associate ourselves with the poultry and egg national board. This new association was formed in 1947. The officers and Board of Directors were President, Howard Ferm; Vice-president, Joe Ladd; Secretary-Treasurer, Gerald Kreider; and nine others present were made Directors. Mr. Ferm was then elected by the state organization to serve as chairman of the Broiler Department of the State Poultry Association, dealing with all the problems connected with the broiler industry. Howard proceeded to initiate the movement in this respect.

A meeting was called in Chicago, Illinois, in early spring of 1953 with delegates from the half-dozen areas in the country, and there a national organization was formed and called the National Broiler Association. Howard was elected to serve as its first president. Later the National Broiler Council was established and eventually the two merged. Here is Mr. Ferm's summary statement after all the past 52 years:

Howard says, "Looking back over the last 52 years I have been associated with the broiler industry there have been great changes and advancements. The broiler business has grown from a few million to a few billion. It is all integrated and independence has disappeared; practically all production being on a contract basis. It is therefore all operated on a large syndicate basis. I am hoping that other segments of agriculture will not fall into this pattern, for I cannot believe this to be a healthy condition to exist."

Howard was instrumental in curbing some of the evil through changes in credit loans in the millions by the National Commodity Production Credit Corporation.

THE FISHERS SOUTH OF WAKARUSA

Elias Fisher was born on a farm in Morrow County, Ohio, in 1842. As a lad he lived and worked on the farm, and made many trips with his father to Upper Sandusky and Mansfield. Then in 1851 when but a lad nine years old, his folks moved to Locke Township, Elkhart County, Indiana. He had very little chance for school. He attended a few terms in an old log school house on Morland Albin's farm. He learned the carpenter trade working with Joseph Strohm. He then built the Lockwood school house on a contract. Elias and John his brother engaged in the lumber business, setting up a sawmill in the old Amish settlement, near the Amish or Weldy school on a farm owned by Anthony Culp. Just after they got it in operation, it burned down, and as they were in debt for it, there followed quite a struggle. A few faithful friends came to their help, and soon they were offering their lumber again. They bought an 80 acre farm east of Oak Grove, built a mill on it, and cut the timber, sawed the lumber, and made enough out of it that they had the land for their profit. They sold that land and then bought the old David McCoy farm then owned by Joseph Denby, cut the timber sold the lumber to Studebaker of South Bend, and Lesh in Goshen, and then bought the Fisher homestead and after that went out of partnership. Elias got 80 acres of the old McCoy place and 40 of the old homestead, and John got the remaining 120 acres. This was in 1879. Then they both became farmers.

Elias was married to Matilda Ann Ferguson, granddaughter of one of the earliest settlers, in 1865. The 3 first children died in infancy and those who survived were; Elias Edward (Ed as we knew him), John Lewis born 1874, Joseph, born 1878, Mary Viola, 1889, George, 1884, Harley, 1888. Later Elias bought 40 acres of Mrs. Madlem and that is the farm he later sold to Joe west of the homestead. Then Elias bought 50 acres of the McMain farm, later an additional 50 acres from his son-in-law Bill Overholser and this made for him 220 acres in the two farms.

Besides being a carpenter, millright, and farmer, he was the Locke Township Assessor, and Justice-of-the-Peace, and served for three years on the board of County Commissioners. The large bank barn erected on his farm in 1888 was 40 x 100, hewing all the timber for this big barn himself, however John Hoover with his crew did the carpenter work. Matilda Anna his wife died in 1904, and Elias died in 1927.

Joe married Grace Letherman in 1915. He became a minister in the Christian church and served many years, Kimmell, Miriam, Waterford, and became quite an influence in the church. They had 8 children, and for our purpose including Wendell, who now farms the homestead, married Lorene Pippenger and they have 4 children, Beverly, 17, Randall, 16, Connie 11, and Jane 9.

They own the homestead, now 120 acres, rent 400 acres, total farmed 520 acres. They have some beef and some sows besides.

Their church is the Bible Baptist in Wakarusa, and he has been active in the community for years, Lord's acre, is CROP Chairman of Locke township for CROP and on the SWCD committee for the county.

I remember him in my Vo. Ag. classes in Wakarusa in 1949 and 1950. He ran a liquid fertilizer service for years and his word is his Bond. A nice Happy Family!

CHRISTOPHER J. GERBER

C.J. was from Canada, and his father and he both homesteaded in Alberta early in the century. He and his brother Paul both attended Goshen College. He was from the beginning an athlete.

In the winter of 1917 he married Florence Wenger of Wakarusa, and Lita and Elmer helped them celebrate their "Honeymoon", in the Morrison Hotel in Chicago on New Year's Eve.

He first went into the book business contracting students at the University of Wisconsin at Madison. After training 250 students at the University, the World War I came and drafted every man but one, a Mr. Storbraaten, and he was our only hope to go out and make a sales record for us to use in promotion, but, lo, and behold he spoke a broken English, was thrown in jail as a suspected German Spy, and there went our hopes. Elmer had worked out a correspondence course in Agriculture, based on the 4 volume set of Rural Efficiency Guide but we, ourselves were then drafted for service, and we both took our losses.

On return from service, I secured a position teaching Vocational Agriculture in Las Cruces, New Mexico, and when C.J. returned to Wakarusa and we heard they were back, we wired for him to come out there and coach and teach Science in the High School. After a few years there, C.J. taught in Nebraska, later Principal at Lakeville Indiana, until his love of horses led him to accept the job as Principal of the high school at Wakarusa, where he could train his Quarter horses on their own farm. He also farmed, had the extension award for champion alfalfa field and silver production Holstein dairy herd award, neighbor Brown, the herdsman. Later he took off a year and earned the M.A. degree at Columbia University in New York. He retired from teaching in 1938, having taught 35 years.

An active man like C.J. could not sit down in a rocking chair, so he secured a contract with STATE FARM and in these 36 years has built up a fortune; always leader of the huge company.

While he is over 80 he is young of mind and heart, and can hold his own, and usually win in most any rodeo. When not a single man in the Rodeo could ride the bronco or bull, C.J. would step up and show them how to do it. The writer remembers when he taught Vo. Ag. in Wakarusa, and C.J. was the Principal, sometimes he had to drink some coffee in order to be able to finish the day out, but through careful control and activity, he has whipped it and now can ice or dance late at night without stopping. He says jogging has done it for him. The hardest thing for him to do today, is to sit down at a banquet table for hours without moving. He has made thousands upon thousands of friends.

To get written up in this book, a man must have a farm family background, must be a man of outstanding success, and last but not least, he must have made a definite contribution to the business of Agriculture in Michiana. Well, certainly, with too many farmers falling from strokes and heart attacks, C.J. has taught us how to conquer a heart impairment.

I will be very much surprised not to see C.J. hale and hearty at 100. C.J. says, "Keep on the go, don't sit down in the rocking chair". More power to you, C.J.!!!

NELSON GONGWER'S GOLDEN BROWN

Albert Gongwer lived on County Road 3, south of Olive Church, and was married to Salome Yoder, and they had 6 children, Maurice, Vernon, Walter and Willis and 2 daughters. Maurice was married to Olive Stauffer, and moved in with Ed Martin, a year, lived in a home west of the Baugo bridge by Olive, where Nelson was born in 1916, then moved on the Paulus farm across from the homestead for 5 years, then they farmed the Layer farm 6 years, where Floyd Cripe now lives, and there Ivan and Grace were born.

In 1926 they landed on the homestead, southwest corner of County Road 42 at State Rd 19, with 73 acres. They had a huge orchard, a big truck patch and a garden out of this world. They lived there 32 years.

They were Holdeman Mennonites, and he was a church trustee. Dale was born there, and now owns the farm and rents it out.

Nelson the Barbecue Chicken was married to Eva Bixler, and had 2 children, Dean and Janet. Nelson was with Lehman Packing Co. for many years, mostly dressed poultry, and while there became interested in the problem of Barbecuing chicken over barrels, saw the need for a labor saving device of more efficiency, and invented the Cater-Car, in 1967. This took him to many, many fairs around the country and he became famous with his "Golden Brown", which melts in your mouth.

On the phone last night, he said he was just back from the Indiana State Fair where he did over 7,000 lbs of Pork Chops and Sausages serving such famous people as The Governor, Lawrence Welk, and Dale Evans.

Nelson and Dean have been doing Golden Brown for our Annual meeting of our Ag Society for years, and about 400 tickets go like hot cakes. The Gongwers say,"It keeps us Humpin". Oliver died 1974.

JOSEPH GORSUCH — Holsteins

Joe was born December 6, 1901. He attended Bashor School and graduated from the Goshen High School in 1919.

He was married to Nora Loucks in 1927. He was the son of David Gorsuch who established the Gorsuch farm of 145 acres, 3 miles west of Goshen on Berkey Road.

David Gorsuch, Joe's father bought his first registered Holstein calf from Mr. W.D. Ward, Willoughby, Ohio in 1907 and the farm built up a herd and has maintained a registered herd continuously after that time. When Mr. E.B. Williamson was Livestock Supt. of the Elkhart Co. Fair Association in the 1920's, Joe showed cattle from time to time at the Elkhart County Fair and many times Joe was first in his class.

For some time he was Sec'y-Treas. of the Elkhart Co. Holstein Breeders Association.

For many years Joe has consigned cattle to the annual Holstein Breeders Consignment Sale as well as to the 4-H sale to enable 4-H Holstein club members to get a good start in Holsteins with outstanding claves.

He modernized his farm, constructed a silo and modernized his milk house. In 1950, a calf from his herd was run up to $325, the highest price ever paid at any 4-H sale. It was bought by the writer for his granddaughter, won 2nd in the 4-H Holstein senior yearling and ranked in the top 10 at the State Fair.

Later Joe bought the heifer back for $525 and in the second year lactation period had more than paid for the purchase price and keep.

Joe gained the reputation of selling some of the finest bull and heifer calves to other breeders in the area.

He modernized his beautiful brick home and he and his son,

Richard, are now partners and continue with one of the finest dairy farms in the area. Joe is known as a man of high integrity and it is said of him, "His word is as good as his bond."

GOSHEN IMPLEMENT COMPANY

Charles Gardner and Waldo Wolf bought the International Harvester store in 1944, where it is still located, and secured the franchise to represent the company. A year later, Mr. Paul Kirkpatrick bought out the Wolf share of the partnership. At that time they handled both International trucks and farm equipment. Machinery was hard to come by because of the conditions following World War II. One of the frustrations was too many customers for the machinery procurable. Their largest M tractor sold for $1700. The Farmall B was around $700. Any implement available was instantly saleable. Their annual sales were around $100,000 - 6 men on the staff. They took on the New Idea and the Gehl lines and found they were in great demand. The entire plant burned in 1958, and Paul and Charles split up, Paul taking the truck agency, K & K Truck Sales on U.S. 33 West, and Charles, rebuilding the plant and taking in his brother Frank the following year. In the meantime the firm entered into demonstrations on the Orla and Eugene farm doing a 20 acre field of hay grass into a pile of grass silage on the ground, 400 farmers looking on. The silage was fed to the dairy cattle, all but two loads around the edge which the cattle would not eat and hauled to the field the next spring in the manure spreader. Influenced by the demonstration seven farmers in LaGrange County did piles of grass silage on the ground. Purdue said it was the first large pile-on-the-ground grass silage demonstration in the state.

The Implement Dealers Association was formed in 1955, with Charles from the beginning, one of the officers and directors. Then the implement dealers began to set up exhibits at the Elkhart County Fair. Goshen Implement has always been active in supporting 4-H.

Beginning in 1950 they sponsored the Corn Show (4-H) holding the exhibit right in the plant.

In the beginning an achievement meeting was held in the plant, drinks and eats were served. Later banquets were set up and members of the families invited. Many prizes, including the Annual Corn King Trophy, feature the festive occasion. The Gardners have contributed much to Michiana agriculture and have built up a large trade.

GOSHEN MILK CONDENSING COMPANY

Four men incorporated under the name "The Goshen Milk Condensing Co." in 1908 along the Big 4 railroad track in Goshen, Indiana.

They were John M. Yoder, President and General Manager; A.R. Zook, E.K. Greenawalt, and Lee S. Nafsiger. They built a two story brick building and set in the milk machinery, boiler room and necessary equipment and they sold the condensed milk to bakers, confectioners and ice cream manufacturers; shipping principally to Chicago, Pittsburg, Cleveland, and Detroit.

They established milk routes hauling milk from local dairymen in wagons, some of the haulers were Fred Jessup's father, Martin Lehman from Nappanee, Sam Nagel, and Sam C. Miller of Middlebury, being paid by the hundred pounds. $1.50 per hundred was a good price to the farmers for the milk in the early days. Aaron, Ward and Joe Martin hauled 27 years at $2.50 per day.

They bought some unsalted sweet butter from Freese Brothers in Nappanee and in summer when cream was short, mixed it with milk and homogenized it for ice cream makers.

During the First World War they made evaporated milk and sold it to the government, also pint cans for grocery trade and gallon cans for the ice cream trade.

Business was hard during the depression years, following the 1929 stock market crash, but the plant never shut down a day.

George, who had started with the firm in 1909, served with the company for 41 years.

Frank Ebersole became bookkeeper and after John M. died, became President in 1932. Later Floyd Byers was manager for many years.

In the early forties they merged with the Orville, Ohio Milk Company, and later all was sold to the Farmer's Milk Co-operative of Cleveland, Ohio. Mel Yoder was the first field man, followed by Kenton Garman and Dan Clem.

The years of service of the many people in the firm has served the area well.

THE GRADYS — Kosciusko County

John Markley homesteaded the Grady farm south of Syracuse on Indiana Road 8 and had a daughter who was later married to Isaac Grady.

Isaac had three children and for our purpose including Jesse Grady.

Glen was their son, born in 1907. Glen was married to Zelma Zimmerman and they continued feeding beef cattle as was done by their forbearers, for four generations.

When Jerry their son was married to Jane Godshalk in 1955 they were feeding around 400 steers per year.

They built feeding troughs around the feed lot, bought a Gehl automatic unloading tank wagon and two large bunker silos. They drive the tank of silage under the hose tank and run into the load of silage a mixture of molasses and urea and add the vegetable supplement, then unload into the feeding troughs. They now feed about 1,000 steers a year.

They buy the light feeding steers in West Virginia, Tennesee and Kentucky.

Every boy and girl on the farm looks at the job.

They now own 500 acres of land, rent an additional 500 acres and farm the 1000 acres. In 1973 they have 750 acres in corn and soybeans.

Glen is 66 years this year and, with some youngsters, operates the side delivery feed truck. He resides in a beautiful large trailer in the side yard. Here efficiency is the watchword.

THE GROFFS OF CLINTON TOWNSHIP

Jacob W. Groff, Sr., bought the 80 acre farm, two miles north and one mile east of Millersburg, March 25, 1872, from J.D. Gamett (now the Mark Pfiester farm).

The brick for the house was hauled by him and his neighbors by horses and wagons from Ligonier. The cost of the spacious brick home was right at $1500, that is, the complete house and all the materials in it.

The barn was later built out of native timber, mostly poplar, with oldfashioned shingle roof. He stocked the farm with some shorthorn cattle and a few milkers.

When Jacob Groff, Jr. took over after the Cleveland Panic of 1892, he bought a pure bred Shorthorn bull from a Mr. Smith near Middlebury and developed a graded up Shorthorn herd for a number of years, but later gave up keeping records. Also he acquired 300 acres across the road, what is now known as the Albert G. Groff farm. Richard Groff now owns it.

From the beginning every family was a thresherman, Jacob, Sr., Jacob, Jr. and Albert, until the time the combine came and the threshing machine (separator) was stored in the shed to stay or sold for junk. At this time the Groffs were stabling 20 to 26 work horses.

Albert attended the Cooper school (south to the end of the road) and went two years to Millersburg.

Albert took over the 380 acres on a 50-50 share basis during the 1922 Farmer's Depression. He started feeding beef cattle. The first purchase of feeders, he remembers, was 30 Angus heifers bought at four cents per pound live weight and sold at the same price. The profit came from the increase in weight. Feeders would be bought about every fall and fed out and ready for late summer sale.

It has been said that Albert had one of the first Allis-Chalmers Combines, quit threshing and even did some custom combining.

He bought fertilizer ingredients separately, nitrogen in 200 pound sacks and mixed the phosphorus and potash with a shovel on a flat hay rack, fertilizing mostly wheat at first.

Julia was born in 1928 and five children were born before the Second World War. All the children had 4-H beef calves and all graduated from the Millersburg High School.

About this time W.W. Oesch and A.T. Marvel interested Albert in the corn-hog program. He served on the Township Committee from then on. Later the name was changed to the A.S.C. (Agricultural Stabilization Conservation.) Albert was made County chairman in 1958 and still serves in that capacity.

In 1954 James and Richard took over the spread for one year and then James bought the Harvey Rogers farm and set up beef feeding facilities.

Richard bought 200 acres of the original farm, another 190 and rented still another 120 acres and is feeding 200 steers and feeding out 750 hogs per year.

The Groffs get a lot of fun out of life. They are wonderful neighbors and well liked.

62

THE ROGER HAHN FAMILY — Elkhart County

Roger married Virginia Mishler, and they started out on her mothers 115 acre farm, west of Union Center school 1½ miles.

At first they went strong on Registered Hampshires, sold many boars to Breeders and some gilts to 4-H and F.F.A. boys and girls.

Later they changed the emphasis to a registered Holstein dairy herd, and the family became an influence in the dairy field and also in the show ring at County and State Fairs. They built the herd up to 130 animals, and have sold their milking herd 5 times in the last 27 years. He has been a Director of the County Assoc. 20 years.

Now they own 275 acres of level heavy ground. They have 5 children Phil, David, Holly, Tim, and Todd. Every one of them have won high stakes in Dairy, Swine, and Showmanship.

In 1965 Roger packed his bag and went to Kansas City to the Auction School. He has gone big because of his knowledge of values and his farm background. His son Phil, joined him in 1971 and now they are both busy, full time in the Auctioneer and Real Estate business.

Roger still has a sizeable herd of Holsteins rented out and may bring the herd back to the homestead and let one of the boys take it over.

So far the family has had 4 IFYE boys from Africa, Norway, India, and New Zealand, and their daughter, Holly, has spent a summer in Japan. Roger and Virginia say, "Life has been real good for their family".

HOWARD HARPER'S SHEEP RANCH — Noble County

Ed Harper had a farm on 550 North, 3 miles west of U.S. 33, was married to Cora Bachtel, had 4 children, Frank, Jesse, Hazel and Ruth. He also bought a farm on U.S. 6, and by the time that Frank was grown he was married to Esta Snyder, and the folks moved over to the farm on U.S. 6 and left the home place for Frank and Esta. They took over the place, and the next 7 years 4 children were born, Howard in 1912, Harmon in 1914, Robert in 1916, and Mildred in 1919. All the children went to school in Cromwell, in Howard's day, the buss was pulled by horses, on corduroy roads, with many stick-in-the-muds. All finished high school, all went to college, and the 3 boys graduated. Of course, all 4 were also in 4-H and Howard was a member of the first lamb club in the county.

More than that, Howard was one of the first Junior leaders in the United States, with the illustrious Earl Butz, Raymond Stump, Curtis Gerren, and Paul Schermerhorn. He first had a dairy project and later the sheep. When he went to Purdue, he was first on the livestock judging team and when the team went to the International in Chicago, he ranked 8th in the Nation. When he finished Purdue in 1934, he secured a position with Armour & Co in Chicago, $18.75 take home pay per week as a trainee. He bought calves in Chicago, Milwaukee, and East St. Louis, and then met Betty Carter in 1936, a stenographer for 4 commission firms, and they were married the next year. They continued their connections, and in 1938 a son Harold came, and then he swung over with Kinghan's of Indianapolis in 1939. Being a reserve officer in ROTC he was later called into the service for 4 years, on release came back with Kinghans a year, and then bought a 379 acre farm near Worthington, Indiana, mostly pasture land, so a good livestock farm.

That was when Harold got started in 4-H, Forestry, Swine, Sheep Club, Crop, and Beef Calf Club. He went through the 11 years, Junior Leader and all. On the farm they had 1200 head of sheep and one of the Sheep Field Days was held on their ranch.

Harold entered Purdue in 1956, and when he was a sophomore, the family moved back to Noble County, and began farming with his father.

Harold became interested in sheep shearing and practically put himself through college shearing. He won the National Sheep shearing contest in Indianapolis in the Junior Division. In the Purdue Livestock judging contest he was also high man and 6th in the Nation at the International in 1959. He received his B.S. from Purdue in 1960. Then married Judy Augsburger from Cromwell, and settled down in Waterloo, Iowa, buying lambs for Roth Packing Co., there. Later he was employed by Wilson and Co. at Omaha, and moved there. Later he was transferred to Denver in 1968. They have 3 children, Jackie, Mike, and Diane.

At home they have pushed the sheep business for years. Frank died in 1966 and left them the farm and now they have 300 ewes, quite a few lambs, and 12 rams.

In 1973 they bought the Truelove farm south of Albion, and

there they have 30 Registered Angus cows, and besides feed out about 250 feeders. He does most of his own Vet. work, and is known as an expert with sheep. After 51 years with sheep, Howard says, "we love them, every one".

WAYNE HARTER

Earl Harter was born in Olive Twp, Elkhart County in 1897, and lived within 5 miles of Wakarusa all his life.

He attended the Mitchell school, and when he became older, worked for near by farmers.

Bertha Weldy was born in 1900 to J.I. and Rhoda (Landis) Weldy on the farm 1½ miles south of Wakarusa, on County Road 3, where, by the way, she spent the latter part of her married life. She had 4 brothers, Arthur, the singer, no better tenor, Eldon, Myron and Dwight.

In 1919 Earl and Bertha were marched up the church aisle together and then took over the home Weldy place, later farmed several other farms, moved back on the home farm in 1941, and then bought it for themselves. They just did general farming, kept chickens, hogs, and 15 to 20 milk cows.

To this union were born Miriam in 1920; now Mrs. Willis Nunemaker: Violet, 1922, now Mrs. Ed Schrock of Walkerton; Letha, 1924, now Mrs. Dale Nafziger, of Wakarusa, and yours truly, Mr. Wayne Harter, 1932.

Wayne began his schooling at Madison township and finished in the Wakarusa High School, a senior in my Vocational Agriculture Department in 1950. We attended a sale together and Wayne bid off three Heifer calves for a foundation of the herd of Ayrshires he planned to build. And he did, and What a herd!!!

At first he farmed with his dad on the usual father-son arrangement, 1/3 to the boy. In 1951 he was married to Helen Pletcher and in 1953 Coleen came and the next year Wanda.

Then disaster struck and Helen was killed accidentally and that was a blow. (December 11, 1954).

The next summer at the Fair, Wayne won his first Premier Breeders Award, and he felt better. He also found the right person to help him, and married Barbara Detwiler of Pryor, Oklahoma in August 1955.

65

The next year he bought the 80 acres from his folks, and then business started to boom. Jim was born in 1957, and more Ayrshires.

Records don't lie, and now Wayne has been a 4-H calf club leader for 20 years. My, how the years do roll!!

Wayne was the Outstanding Young Farmer for the J.C.s in 1966, and he has been active in the milk outfits for years, now Pure Milk, Inc. of Cleveland.

By now Wayne has some pretty classy individuals in the herd. Wanda won Grandchampion Ayrshire Female at the State 4-H show and she was Reserve in the open class.

On the home farm now they have 150 of the beauties, and milk 80. They have just put in a new Herringbone Milking Parlor, with new facilities and will put the herd up to 100 milkers.

The set-up includes provision for liquid manure, an underground tank, seems to me 30,000 cu. ft. Sanitation authorities say farm dairies will have to come to it.

In 1973 he bought a 145 acre dairy farm in Marshall County and has it rented out 50-50, 90 milk cows there. Jim is now graduating from Bethany Christian and is a partner. Wayne and Jim say, "We like the business, and love to show our cattle". Wayne is a Trustee and Wanda, Chorister at Locust Grove south of Elkhart.

GEORGE W. HAY, JR.

Joseph Hay was born in New Lebanon, Ohio, in 1836 and in 1855 he and his brother, John, came to Elkhart County Indiana, saw a farm he liked west of Goshen (Southeast corner of Indiana 119 and County Road 19,) went back to Ohio, married Hettie Ehrbaugh, returned to Indiana in 1857 and bought the farm (80 acres). There he did general farming and they had 4 children, including for our purpose, George W. Hay, born in 1860 just before the Civil War.

At school age, he attended the Michael country school, which stood, at that time, on the southwest corner of County Road 19 and 36 (located on the Cripe farm, now owned by Fernlee Runchey).

After that he graduated from Goshen High School and then worked for his father on the farm until he was married to Miss Ella Miltenberger, west on Kercher Road, and they started housekeeping with the money he had saved working on the father-son deal with his father, and buying the 10 acres with buildings where Lloyd Hostetler

66

now owns. (the teacher)

He farmed there and in winter would buy hardwood timber for the John Lesh Lumber Company, and later bought stock in the company, ending up with stock holders, Lesh, Abbot, Prouty, Hay, Sanders, and Egbert. At that time Clever was born in 1890. A daughter was also born in 1896, but died in infancy from Typhoid Fever.

George W. Hay was the ONE; he could walk casually through the timber and make a quick estimate. They built saw mills for 75 miles around in Indiana and Michigan, and he even bought walnut as far away as West Virginia and Iowa.

Handier to be located in Goshen, he sold the 10 acres and moved to 301 South Fifth St., (the Masonic temple now stands there). George Jr. was born there in 1902.

In 1908 George Sr. bought the Valentine Berkey farm on Berkey Road (120 acres), his heart still on farming.

At school age George Jr. went to the South Fifth Street school, at Pearl and 5th, where the library now stands. After that he was graduated from the Culver Military Academy at Culver, Indiana.

At that time he became a buyer for the Egbert-Hay-Fobes Co., the successors to the Sanders Egbert outfit. Then, in 1926, he was married to Ruby McMahon a very pretty Goshen girl, and they started housekeeping at 919 South Seventh, later George III was born there and John was born there in 1929. Their next move was to the old Tom Davis house at 205 South Sixth, and Helen was born there in 1934. Stephen came there in 1943. In 1931 George Jr. had bought the Oil Business from Castetter and Yoder and started into the business. With 6 competitors he has held his own. He built up quite a retail gas business and also delivers fuel oil and gasoline in bulk tank in Goshen and surrounding territory. In 1962 George bought the 370 acre Sanders farm from his uncle.

George Hay Sr. had bought 419 South 5th St. in 1926 and maintained a beautiful home there. He died in 1936 and mother Hay was a gracious neighbor for many years. She walked across the street one day to commend me when we were doing some fixin' up, and there was always a string of people going to her door to please her in her later days. She passed away 1958 and surely missed by many. At that time George became my neighbor. Now George III has 2 children and is with Starcraft; John has 3 and is an Oil Geologist in South

America; Helen married Robert Wheeler, an Insurance Adjuster and 3 children, and Stephen is a City Appraiser in Cleveland. George says, "Live and Let Live". His farm tenants love him.

CARLYSLE AND TOM HERALD

Henry Herald came from around Wooster Ohio, as a young man, about 1860, and bought a quarter section of land, having been married to Elizabeth Brown of Pennsylvania. The Centennial farm is northwest of Ligonier, 1 mile north of Perry school and ½ mile west, the old house stands to the north on the west side of the road. Three children came, Elmer, Salina, and Clara.

Henry died young, at age 50, the widow rented the farm, and took the children back to Pennsylvania for several years, then returned, rented out the fields, and it is said the going was tough.

When Elmer grew up he married Maude Willets, and the first baby was Howard, but when he was nine months old his mother died. Later Elmer re-married (Elva Leopard) and set up a hardware store in Topeka, which he operated for a number of years. The farm was on its own for a while and neglected. In 1916 Howard graduated from Ligonier High and did general farming on his own. In 1921 Howard married Evelyn Franks, and they went into dairying and had a milk route in Ligonier for a number of years. He was elected to the Noble County Council and was in those days a promoter and director of R.E.A., and was for 20 years President of Noble County R.E.M.C. They increased the herd, and bought a DeLaval Milker. Then Carlysle was born in 1923 during the Farmers Depression. He was the only child. In Ligonier he got into the Vo. Ag. program, became interested in dairying and when he graduated in 1941 he took over the farm, really taking over in the fall when he was a senior in High School.

Howard had been in Jerseys but Carlysle switched to Holsteins, Commercial dairy herd then married Lulubelle Howell of Cromwell. (1943)

Claudia was born in 1945 and Tom in 1947. Soon thereafter they tore out the box stalls and increased the stanchions up to 36. By natural increase and purchase they got the milk cows up to 50.

This is when they built a 5000 capacity laying house and pushed it for 7 years. During these years 3 hired men were involved, but in 1965 they went to open housing, holding pen, and milk parlor and went up to from 90 to 100 milkers.

Claudia graduated from Ball State in 1967, and Tom went to Purdue for Agricultural Short Course. While there he got into the National Guard, requiring two weeks training each summer.

These requirements are now completed and Carlysle and Tom are now partners in the Farming Operation, and they are back to 1 hired man. In 1970 they closed out the dairy and went to feeding beef. They also irrigate 240 acres. They feed around 500 cattle on a rotary system. Through inheritance and purchase the land holdings have been built up to 900 acres.

Tom has married Cyndee Brockett from Ft. Wayne, and they live in the little white house built by Howard back in 1923 (just south of the homestead). They have no children. Claudia is married, lives in Chicago, and has 2 children.

The Heralds are all Presbyterians. Carlysle has been an elder in the church more than 20 years. The family is well established in the community and Carlysle and Lulubelle have built her "dream" home in a patch of woods off the road to the south and in a long lane into the trees.

Carlysle has been on the County Council 18 years and was one who helped hire the present county agent, Arthur Howard. Carlysle says, "I try to follow the Golden Rule 'Do to others as you would that they should do to you.'"

HERMAN HESS — Foraker

Herman and Vernon Hess bought the Jay Rohrer Garage in Foraker May 1931. They sold Studebaker (the Willy Overland cars) and did a general garage repair business. Herman married Charlotte Anglemyer January 1, 1935. They have 3 children (daughters).

They secured the franchise from the Case Implement Company in 1945 (Racine, Wisconsin). They also secured the franchise on the Harvestore Silo about 1955. Later in 1960, Vernon went full time in Harvestore and Herman and Charlotte stuck with Case and the implements.

They also handled Fox, Brady, and Bush Hog, also various kinds of wagons and implements. Ron Cleveland, June's husband, is a part owner.

Herman has been a member of the Union Township advisory

board for 30 years, project committee chairman of the Elkhart County Agricultural Society, a member of the volunteer Fire Department and his family is in Union Center Church of the Brethren.

They are 100% on cooperation with extension, 4-H, County Fairs, and have participated in many demonstrations and contests.

There is no limit in the extent to which Herman will go to assist a farmer in trouble with a tractor or implement. He is a master mechanic.

The Hess family stands high in the estimation of the people of the area, which is more than a local community as people travel for miles to bring their troubles to him.

HOLDEMAN & BROWN HORSE SALES — Elkhart County

Abner Holdeman worked with his father Abraham Holdeman near Olive Church about 7½ years and was married in 1885 to Emma Dodge and Abner rented the Joe Holdeman farm (140 acres) until he bought it, when Warren was 12 years old, that being at the turn of the century.

He first built a hog house and started in the registered Duroc hog business. He raised and sold Duroc gilts and boars. Later on he became interested in horses.

He would buy horses in the fall at the end of the season and feed them all winter and hold a sale in the spring, about March 1st, when horses were in demand for spring plowing. The first sales offered from 10-20 horses, later as many as 60 horses would be in a sale.

He bought a registered Percheron stallion imported from France and charged $15 for stud service to farmers in the area. At one time he had 4 Percheron and 2 Belgian registered stallions.

Soon after the sales were started, Abner took into partnership his cousin Ira Brown, Abner Brown's father. Many horses sold from $200-$250 and some as high as $400 and a closely matched team from $500 - $700 and more.

People came from East and West and the Wabash train from Chicago would stop at Abner's crossing right at the farmstead on the day of the sale.

The job of the boys and helpers would be to spend a few weeks to curry and clean the horses, and then at the sale to lead the horses in a trot to show action and then to run each horse for a short distance to test his wind.

Abner became an expert draft horse judge and people sought his advice on individual animals, as he had an uncanny ability to predict how a colt or young horse would develop.

Abner became leader in the Holdeman Church and the community. He was on the local Holdeman Mennonite Church board on Mennonite Missions.

In 1925, with the tractor coming in, and horses less in demand, Abner quit the horse business and farming and moved to Wakarusa where he died in 1939.

Warren took over the farm for 15 years and then went into teaching full time and taught 42 years; a leader in educational work and retired but still has a small herd of Hereford breeding cattle near Bremen.

Walter became a big farmer on the County Line and has ended his large dairy herd and feeds young Holstein cattle on his 160 acre farm. Florence lives in Wakarusa. All the others are gone.

THE HOOVERS AT FIVE POINTS

William Hoover was living (renting) with his wife's father, Christian Shaum, on a 20 acre farm, teaching school in Jimtown in 1889, and in 1890 Warren was born. In the Spring of 1891, he rented the John Musser farm (the Lee Loucks farm) and continued farming and teaching school.

In 1896 he rented the Martin A. Hoover estate farm (where Paul Wittmer now lives) of 158 acres which were mostly cleared at that time. A suitable barn and house were there. In 1898 William stopped teaching for twelve years. He had been crippled by a hatchet cut, so most of the farm work fell on his son Warren and the hired men and, later, other sons: Lewis (1895), Maynard (1900), Paul (1904) and George (1906).

In 1898 the estate was settled; William inherited the 40 acres on the Five-Points corner (now known as the Rev. Paul Hoover farm), Mrs. Amos Wittmer inherited the 100 acres and Enos M. Hoover inherited the 18 acres south of the 40. In 1889 the house, barn and chicken house were built on the 40 acres, followed later by a corn crib and buggy shed.

William was an agent for Swift and Company Fertilizer, and he sold U.S. cream separators. He had started with dairy cattle (grades) and by 1905 he was milking ten cows. In 1901 he had bought a corn binder. In 1903 he had a Kalamazoo wood stave silo constructed, (only the second one in Harrison Twp.) and in 1904 he built another one, 12 x 24. He bought a Davis Swing Churn and sold butter and eggs, peddling in town until 1905 when Freese and Company built a skimming station; then he sold cream, feeding the skim milk to the hogs. William had the job of operating the skimming station, with Warren's assistance. That era ended in 1908 when Goshen Condensery began picking up milk. The Freese stations continued buying cream, however, and for several years the Hoovers had cream routes with team and wagon, hauling to the Freese station at the Five-Points corner. During this time, William had been teaching again for six winters in Harrison Twp.

In 1909 Warren took a winter short course in Agriculture on a scholarship at Purdue University. From 1912 to 1916 he was hired by the State of Wisconsin for Advanced Registery Dairy Tests (long winters at work, coming home in the summers). In that time he acquired part interest in his father's cattle. For two years, 1917-18, he did some dairy test work out of Purdue, and the following year did supervisory work over other testers in Wisconsin.

In 1919 he was married to Nettie Martin and they made their Home with Peter Hartman, a bachelor, with Nettie doing the housework and Warren farming Pete's 80 acres on shares. For several years Warren was employed by J.M. Yoder, manager of the Goshen Milk Condensery, to do weighing and testing in the condensery. In May 1926, he rented the John Martin (Nettie's father) farm of 80 acres, on shares, carrying on with a small herd of registered Holsteins. Warren and Nettie at this point began the story of a beautiful family life. Four children already born on the Hartman farm were: Martha May, Ernest, Martin and Arthur. In the next thirteen years there came Esther, Florence, Joseph and Carol. These were the uphill years in their lives, but one could feel the hospitality of the home by walking into the house. These were the depression years and Warren says they made it, by the Grace of God and the help of their eight children, with the small herd of cattle (about eight milk cows).

The 80-acre farm still boasted considerable wooded area, and to this day the Hoover woods is one of the few native forests in Northern Indiana. From 1915 Nettie's father had operated a maple sugar camp with a small evaporator, which continued to be used many of the ensuing years until 1966 when a new sugar house with a larger evaporator was built.

Warren says the hardship of the depression years was softened somewhat by the income from several cash crops, especially strawberries (sometimes as much as two acres of them) and as many as seven acres of potatoes. Also some heifers and cows were placed in the consignment sale at Wanatah in 1938.

Up to this time there was no electricity, no running water, no modern improvements, no tractor and not much machinery; all farming was done with horses. In 1945, the family bought the 80 acres from the John Martin estate. Then they bought a tractor and other machinery, and built a 12 x 35 silo. The next year, Martin conceived the idea of remodeling the barn, with a cement floor and stanchions, for a modern dairy operation, to meet sanitation requirements and for greater efficiency. They used a gas engine to operate the Surge Milker the first year. Then electricity came in 1947, which was later than in neighboring areas because poles and lines had not been set up on that stretch of road.

During this time Ernest worked away from home by the month, for five years. He turned over all his earnings above personal expenses to the family at home to accelerate their standard of living. In 1948 he was married to Lizzie Martin and they rented the 199-acre Charles Schantz farm on shares for about eleven years. In 1958 he bought the James Dunmire farm of 90 acres. He was then milking about twenty Holsteins.

In 1963 Warren held a dispersal sale, farmed two years after that and then the farming was turned over to Ernest, who had purchased an additional 60 acres of land from George Smeltzer. With the cows Ernest bought at Warren's sale, his herd totalled about forty milk cows. Ernest now owns 150 acres, has two Harvestore silos and all the equipment he needs for successful dairy farming. He has nine children and three grandchildren.

Warren's second son, Martin, graduated from Purdue in 1951, was married in 1953, moved to California where he secured his doctorate, returned to teach at Goshen College for five years, and later at Juniata College, Huntington, PA. He now resides in Elkhart and is in the heating and air conditioning business. He has four children.

Arthur married in 1946 and helped operate the home farm until 1962 when he took his share of the cattle to Sheldon, WIS. His youngest daughter, Lora, now manages the farm while he operates the trucking business. He has eight children and four grandchildren. His oldest daughter, Helene, is the secretary for Ira C. Mast & Son, General Contractors, Elkhart.

Joe was married in 1956, graduated from Northwestern University School of Medicine, and is now a general practitioner and surgeon in Fort Wayne, IND. He has four children.

Martha May is the bookkeeper and secretary at Hope Rescue Mission, South Bend, IND. Esther and Florence taught at the Sidon Girls School, Sidon, Lebanon, for three years. Esther is now established in the math department of Penn High School, Mishawaka, IND. Florence has taken special courses in flower arrangement and has become somewhat of an expert in that field; at the same time, she maintains one of the most beautiful flower gardens in the area. Carol is a math teacher at Laville High School, North Plymouth, IND. Her interests are horses and antiques.

Warren's brother Paul rented the Peter Hartman farm in 1926, while living with his parents. He had bought a tractor the year before and bought some additional implements. Thereafter, he rented the home farm. Paul bought some of the items at his father's sale in 1927, and built up a dairy herd, milking thirteen cows. In 1929 he married Myrtle Good. In 1944 he bought the 58 acres from his father, at which time his cows numbered twenty five or thirty. He was ordained a minister in the Wisler Mennonite Church, and preached at the Yellow Creek and Blosser churches. Paul has become a man of great influence in his community.

Paul and Myrtle have six children, including (for our purposes here) Clarence, who was born in 1940, went to school at Harrison Center and graduated from Wakarusa High School. He worked for his parents for ten years, and in 1971 he bought one-half interest in the livestock. At that time they had one hundred head of cattle, and were milking forty-five to fifty cows, selling to Golden Guernsey (Earl Weaver, hauler). With rented land, they are now farming 350 acres.

David, another of Paul's sons, is farming 300 acres and is milking fifty guernsey cows. He lives on County Road 111 about one mile from the home farm.

Lewis and Maynard have passed away, and William Hoover's youngest son, George, is with Goshen Implement Company.

THE HUFFS — Guernseys

James Huff, born 1930 took over the farm at age 16 in 1946. He was married to Loretta Hochstettler at age 18 in 1948. They were milking around 30 cows. Max was born in 1954 and Rex in 1958. They have 2 sisters Carlene and Kristy. Max joined 4-H in 1963 and has shown animals at the Argos Fair every year since. He has won many firsts, Reserve Champions and Champions, 8 or 9 others in the county competing. They buy their own bulls and do not breed by artificial insemination. They have 65 to 70 cows, a splendid milking parlor with automatic self-washing pipe line, into a 500 gallon tank. Sheets and Benson south of Bremen also have Guernseys. The average test on their herd is 5.1% fat. They own 250 acres and rent an additional 350 acres. They feed corn silage and hay mostly. They feed Super-Sweet Feeds, trading with Tom Mattern, manager Nappanee Milling Co. They are members of the Salem United Methodist Church in Bremen. Both boys say they like farming.

DALE AND DORIS INBODY

John Inbody was born in the year 1898 to Milo and Sara Weldy Inbody near Waterford; he was one of a family of 12. As a boy, he attended the Waterford Grade school. As a young man, he married Laura Haberstich, right after World War I, in 1919. They moved on an eighty acre farm north of Goshen, and to get a start, he drove a school bus pulled by horses. They lived there 5 years. Three children were born there on that farm, a boy and 2 girls. Then they moved northeast of New Paris in 1925 to a larger farm owned by Mr. Dan Neff, where later Dale was born in 1925. A few years later when Dale was one year old, they moved onto the Ernest Martin farm, (Pine Manor) and farmed it until 1936, when he bought the 40 acres we know as the John Inbody farm on County Road 38, just East of Dale's farmstead for $100 per acre. He also started driving a school bus again, rented some small farms, and started to build up a herd of Guernsey cattle. Soon thereafter he rented the 200 acres where Dale now lives from Fred Koerner, and milked 18 cows.

In 1943 Dale graduated from Goshen High School and started to work for his dad by the month. They built the herd up to 30 cows and some hogs.

A few years later, John wanted to cut down on farming, so Dale bought 12 of the cows and rented the 200 acres from Koerner. That winter he increased his cows to 20, and from the milk checks he was able to buy a Co-Op tractor and plow, a New Holland Baler, and a John Deere combine. He was still living at home and helping with some of the farming. He also drove a milk route part time. A little custom work also helped out for capital. So it enabled him to start in the purebred Berkshire Hog business. He joined the Elkhart County all breed Swine Association and consigned some of the top Berkshires in the Annual Sale.

In 1950 a small tornado took the top half of the large bank barn and damaged other buildings on the farm, and he salvaged enough good material out of the barn and other buildings, and used it to build a 26 x 46 implement shed and shop and corn crib until a new barn could be built. Mrs. Koerner then built a 46' x 92' concrete block barn with 20 stanchions. By 1952, he had built the herd up to 30 milkers, increased the Berkshires, and had a complete line of farm implements.

However, in March, in 1954 he was drafted into the Army, and had dispersal and implement sale. For 2 years he was stationed at Fort Bragg, North Carolina in the heavy Field Artillery handling 280mm Atomatic Cannon. He was discharged in March 1956 as a sergeant, and came back to Mrs. Koerner's farm. He bought new machinery and 10 Guernsey heifers at the State Consignment sale as a foundation herd.

During those years the writer was Farm Veterans Instructor at Dunlap for Elkhart County and Dale enrolled in the night school, and besides the monthly income therefrom, he was sure to get a new rigorous bookkeeping system for the farm. In March 1957 he married Doris Burkey a farm girl from Nebraska, who had become a Registered Nurse. In June 1958, Thomas, the first boy was born. The same year Dale was named the "Outstanding Young Farmer" by the J.C.s.

In September 1959 the "Farming in Action" show was held on

his farm, he fenced in 7 acres for the 3 day event and was a real help and host to our Elkhart County Agricultural Society. 9 Implement dealers crews helped 400 visiting farmers see implements work side by side. About this time Dale learned Mrs. Koerner wanted to sell, so he up and bought it at a very good price. It is now worth twice as much as he paid.

The end came for John in 1960, and Dale finished his school bus term, and farmed the home place until his mother sold it years later.

By this time his herd had grown too large for the quarters so he built a 40' x 90' pole building, a 14' x 44' silo and a 4 stall picture Surge milking parlor, set in by Bill Cripe. Then he increased the herd to 50 milkers. At this time Dale Culp, who was their milk tester, had 5 registered Brown Swiss for sale and Dale bought them just to try them out. They liked them so well, for one reason they produced larger calves, that they gradually switched over to where they were milking 60 purebred Brown Swiss. They started showing them at the County Fair and in 1971 had the Brown Swiss Premier Breeder's Award and started to consign animals to the Indiana Brown Swiss State Sale. During these years he hired High School boys to help chore and farm and in 1963 when Carla was born, they adopted Randy, the young lad who had come to live with them the year before.

In 1968 their herd kept growing and they started to feed dairy steers. So he built a 20' x 60' silo and pole shed 24' x 40' for raising calves. The boys have been in the 4-H beef club since they were 10 years old, and have shown purebred Shorthorn cows, and have won their share of awards. Since they were feeding dairy steers, they started breeding the poorer Brown Swiss to Charlais Bulls for better steers. Dale went to the A.B.S. school for Artificial Insemination and learned to do it himself.

By 1971 they were farming 600 acres, but after graduating from the Fairfield High School, two years later, Randy wanted to get out in the world and is now working for Disney World at Orlando Florida.

Thereafter they decided to quit milking, leased out the cows to young dairy farmers, and they get the calves, so that they can keep on raising registered Brown Swiss cows under the prefix "Prairie Haven".

Dale and Doris are prominent in the St. Mark's Methodist church

77

of Goshen, in my day they would have been "Pillars".

Dale has been on the Elkhart County Fair Board for a number of years, for years on the Project Committee of the Elkhart County Agricultural Society, 20 years on the Elkhart Twp. Fire Department, Delegate to M.P.F., Vice-Chairman of Elkhart County A.S.C.S. Comm., Vice-Pres. of Elkhart County Co-op Board of Directors.

After the children were of school age, Doris has been on the staff of the Goshen General Hospital part time.

Dale says, "Farming has been good to us and it is a good place to raise a family, as the basics of all living and worship come from the land" - - - - - - - - - Nice goin' Boy.

ALBERT WILLIAM JESSUP — Butch

Butch was the son of Bill and Frances Jessup, born in 1943. After Harrison. Center he went to Goshen, joined 4-H and won the Grand Champion Steer Award, graduated in 1962, and the next year married Karen Henschen, of Wakarusa. Then they moved on Blair Rieth's farm on County Road 32, east of the old church a half mile, cash-rented it for a few years, and later bought it.

They rented more land from year to year and now have the total acres farmed up to 940.

Also Butch farrows 45 sows and gilts twice a year in a 24 x 104 farrowing building and a 20 x 80 concrete outside feeding floor, feeding out about 750 porkers per year.

Butch is a pusher, and takes an interest in most of the worthwhile Agricultural activities. I see the children are starting into 4-H beef calf club, and I would not be surprised to see Butch and Karen's children emulate their dad's brothers and sister for the Purple Ribbon.

Butch and Karen make a very happy, and enthusiastic couple and Butch says, "It's hard work, but a good life".

WILLIAM S. AND FRANCES RIETH JESSUP

William Blough was born on a farm in Harrison Township, in Elkart County, Indiana, in 1845, went to Harrison Center School, and when grown up, married Mary Hoover, daughter of David and Susannah Hoover, and they had six children, and, for our purpose, including Arvilla Blough, born 1884.

Later William traded his farm for a farm owned by Samuel and Mary Weaver, which lay on the south side of County Road 32, just a mile east of Five Points. The deed was dated March 18, 1893, and was recorded at the court house in Deed Book No. 87, on page 31. It called for 128 acres. Soon thereafter, in order to start spring work, the Blough's moved there with their family. So by 1993 the farm will become a Centennial Farm, if it stays in the family.

Arvilla was later married to an Albert Rieth, so let us look him up. He was the son of Nicholas Rieth who had hundreds of acres of land along the both sides of County Road 45 (the old Goshen Elkhart Road) stretching from the Sugar Grove bridge to the old Kunderd's railroad crossing. Albert had two brothers, and at his father's death Guy took the 100 acre farm at Kunderd's crossing, and Elmer the farm towards what is now Fairview Grange Hall. Albert invested his inheritance in higher education. After high school in Goshen, Albert was graduated from Purdue in Civil Engineering in 1907 and married Arvilla Blough the next year. After Albert worked as a civil engineer in Detroit, they moved to the Rio Grande valley, near Harlingen, Texas, and contracted to build irrigation canals in the rich Rio Grande valley. There in several years, two children were born, Herbert in 1910 and Mary in 1911. In 1913 they returned to Elkhart County and he became County Surveyor until 1915. The next year, 1916, he established the Rieth Construction Co. Mr. George Riley joined him later and after many years sold out his interest to Albert in 1940; however, the name Rieth-Riley was retained. Blair was born on 6th Street, in Goshen, in 1913; Lee in 1915; and Frances in 1917, on 5th Street (now Mrs. C.K. Bender's home). Bill was then born in 1918, Richard in 1921, and Rose in 1923.

After Arvilla's parents passed away, the mother in 1920 and the father in 1921, she and Albert bought the homestead from the estate in 1921. Then the Rieth family moved to the farm, children coming of school age, going to Bashor and Dell Schools, but Albert kept the house on 5th Street. All eight children graduated from high school and college, so between Farmer Blough and Engineer Rieth there must have been some family influence. Let us leave the family there on the farm, a happy family, and go with Albert to Rieth-Riley.

The first job the firm secured was that of rebuilding the road (CR 32) from 5 points to Goshen, a dirt road which was transformed into a gravel, ridge graded road, with graded berm, which the people of Harrison Township really liked. The bid was for $25,000. Albert had a knack of finding capable help and surrounded himself with the right people. In 1919 Rieth-Riley was awarded the first contract let by the State of Indiana, part of the Lincoln Highway (now U.S. 33) in the Goshen-Benton stretch, for the sum of $248,000. New machinery and better know-how soon made them No. 1 as road builders. In 1943 Albert Rieth died and his sons Blair, Lee, and William took over running the construction business.

In 1954 the outfit was awarded the contract for the first two sections of the Indiana Toll Road for approximately $4,000,000, so the firm was on its way.

One of Albert's daughters is now on the farm and we need to bring her future husband into the picture at this point. William S. Jessup, a son of Fred and Euba Jessup, was born in 1916, went to Goshen High School, graduated from Purdue in 1940, and married Frances the next year. He secured the job of heading up the F.H.A. office in Kosciusko County at Warsaw. There Nancy was born in 1942 and Albert William (Butch, as they dubbed him early), in 1943.

After the Warsaw job, in 1944, Bill and Frances moved into the small house on the farm and Bill farmed the place himself, set up a milk route in Goshen for two years, and after that, 1946, went into Rieth-Riley, and later became Superintendent of Equipment for the outfit. Then David came in 1947, and Jim, later in 1954.

Bill and Frances bought the homestead in 1954, and then things started to happen. They remodelled the house completely. In 1946 the big barn burned and they replaced it with a pole barn. Since then they have added 300 acres - the Charles Weldy place and the Robert Paul farm from the Nelson Paul estate- and have built a couple farm ponds.

All four children were in the 4-H Beef Calf Club and the 4-H Saddle Club at the Elkhart County Fair. All were awarded many blue ribbons, Butch getting Grand Champion with his Angus in 1962, Jim getting Grand Cahmpion with his Angus in 1965, and David had Reserve Champion with his Angus steer in 1964. Nancy had Grand Champion pony with her Shetland stallion in 1958, and Butch had the Grand Champion Quarter horse at that same time.

Now, Nancy, who graduated from Stephens, is in Tacoma, Washington, a secretary; Butch will find his story elsewhere in the book; David, who graduated from Purdue in Civil Engineering in 1969, married Kennlyn Kurtz, lives in St. Paul, works for the State Highway Department, and they have one daughter, Julia, 5 months old; and Jim will be a junior upper classman at Purdue in the Department of Civil Engineering.

I have enjoyed working out this story with Bill and Frances, checking at the courthouse, and with Blair. Surely, they are all fine people.

THE JUDSONS

William Judson (1809) bought the Judson farm 1½ miles south of Bristol west side of the road in 1853. He then came here with his 5 year old son John in 1853 and built the house soon thereafter. This is where Ed Judson now lives.

He had 8 children, among them for our purpose John Lemon Judson who was later married to Sarah Jane Kinyon who was the first school teacher in those parts in the year 1876. John and Sarah had two sons James; born 1874 and Charles born 1876.

James Judson married Nellie Sigerfoos on New Year's Day in 1899 in the Kinyon house and they both taught school for some years. Then James purchased the 140 acres across the road which had been taken from the government in 1845. In 1923 he inherited the 40 acres of the home farm of William Judson's estate.

By 1846 John Lemon Judson had planted about 3 or 4 acres of seedling orchards. Several other seedling orchards were planted later. Much grafting was done, not only for themselves, but for neighbors.

There was a long period of time in which carloads of barrels of apples were shipped to Buffalo, New York. No spraying of any consequence was done until the year 1915, when the San Jose Scale spread.

The boys both graduated from the Academy and Otterbein College at Westerville, Ohio. Both of them were school teachers for 12 years thereafter.

Even as soon as he was out of College, James became interested in buying, breaking, and selling western mustang horses from Montana. He would buy them by the carload. After a little breaking he would sell the horse for $100 to $150. This continued for 15 to 20 years. Then he went into the melon business and set up a roadside stand by the driveway. The writer knew him well and listened to his stories by the hours. He set up grading tables in the barn which are there and still used by the workers to this day.

In 1900 James Edward Judson (Ed) was born, schooled in Hogwallow, Bristol High School, graduated at University of Illinois with a B.S., at University of Wisconsin with a M.S. and Ph.D. He taught at Albion Michigan, Florida State, West Virginia Wesleyan, 31 years as a professor. All these years he came home to the old homestead at Bristol and grew wonderful pink meat melons in the summers.

He was married to Emily Adeline Mackin in 1924. They had 2 daughters, Mary Alice Forbes in Long Island and Helene Alene in Indianapolis.

He had a hand in the development of the Honey Rock melon, and also the seedless watermelon. He served as president of the West Virginia Academy of Science and is listed in Who's Who. He is still selling cantaloupe by the truckloads delivering them to his old loyal customers personally as far as South Bend and Niles, Michigan.

About 1893, Charles Judson started the C.E. Judson Fruit Farm, buying 140 acres on the west side of the road with a small piece of ground where the fruit barn was on the east side and planted the land to raspberries, strawberries, cherries and peaches. The peaches all died in the late 90's as they could not control the yellows.

He hired a number of the Bloss boys from Bristol to peddle fruit in dozens of towns in Northern Indiana; even as far as Edgerton, Ohio.

Charles married Golda Hite of Goshen, at the turn of the century, a city girl from Goshen, and for a time continued to live at home.

About 1916, Charles and Golda moved into the brick Kinvon house on the east side of the road which he had bought from his grandmother 10 years before.

This is where many readers have bought fruit and melons from the fruit stands in the Charles Judson Fruit Roadside Market.

He was elected to the Elkhart County Council and served for years as one of the influential members;

Charles had 3 children, Violet who died in the LaSalle Hotel fire in Chicago, Jane, who still lives in the old brick house, and Victor, who was born in 1904, went to high school in Bristol and the Illinois Agricultural College. He became known for growing Honey Rock cantaloupe and invented the strip method of labeling the melons.

Vic was married to Charlotte Lake (farm to the south) January 15, 1938 (he was 34 and she 24).

He had planted the West orchard in 1934 and was growing fruit and mostly cantaloupe on the Fisher farm which he had bought for that purpose. Before he was married, he being engaged to Charlotte, had planned a beautiful home on the hill across from the folks.

About 1943, Charles and Charlotte built the Judson Nursery on the Fisher farm. Later, about 1950, a plant was built on Indiana 15 across from their home, which was later expanded.

A contract was secured to furnish Sears Roebuck plants and perennials on a large scale. This went on for years. Later they began to supply Montgomery Ward and other large nurseries about the country.

In the meantime Mr. Charles Judson gave Vic and Charlotte 50 acres of land north of the plant (across from the old homestead) which they planted to raspberries, apples and peaches on top of the hill.

About 1949 Vic bought with several friends some ground on which they established the Victor Coach business which continued for several years. After the trailer business was sold, Vic attended a nursery meeting in Chicago at which time he suffered a heart attack and in 1956 he died. Charlotte continued the business until they were burned out in 1967. Krider Nursery has since bought what is left of the Judson Nursery.

THE ELWOOD KAUFFMANS

In 1940 after high school Elwood was taken by his father on the 160 farm three miles north of Millersburg and one mile east. They bought another 80 and in 1955 Elwood took over the farm and the father, Ora, built the mill and elevator on Indiana 13 and moved there.

Elwood had married Irene Kauffman in 1944 and Elwood, Jr. was born in 1953. Senior and Junior became partners in 1972.

Elwood and Irene have five children. Ora had died in 1971 and Senior and Junior are now partners in both the farming of 400 acres and in the mill and elevator business.

Lester Davis once told the writer in 1946 that Elwood, Sr. made the best grades of any boy who ever graduated from Millersburg High School. The Kauffman farm became a Centennial farm in 1972.

THE KAUFFMANS — John Deere

Clyde E. Kauffman lived one mile east of Foraker and secured the franchise to sell John Deere implements in 1936. Harvey went into the business with him, they stored the new implements in the old hog house, and Dad continued to farm the 80 acre place, general farming. They stayed mostly in the Elkhart County area.

Two bottom plow tractor with steel wheels sold for $605. The first John Deere tractor was sold to Allen Smoker. In a few years they set up a store in Goshen, back of the Shoots Building and ran both locations for 10 years. Noah bought out Dad's interest in 1944.

Then they built their present plant on U.S. 33 West, and that is the year that Dad died. He had been a great supporter and Director of the Elkhart County Fair. Within a year they sold the farm to Will Ramer, a neighbor.

Many people Clyde had sold other brands of machinery, switched over to John Deere and are now buying from the third generation of Kauffmans.

The firm was in on the ground floor when the Elkhart County Implement Dealers Association was formed and they started showing exhibits in the fair and participating in plowing contests and demonstrations.

In the next ten years they built several other buildings. Randy married Grace Weaver in January, 1971, and bought out Noah's interest in the firm. Noah went into semi-retirement and died the next year.

Harve has five children: Randy, Janice in the office, Sharon in Texas, Angela in a dress shop in Bloomington, and Craig, a carpenter in Maine.

They took over the New Holland line about 1949. Helen, Mrs. Kauffman, taught school about 20 years; five at Model School and after that at Fairfield. Now she enjoys her home in the woods on Clinton Street with many friends.

Harve says, "Through the years we have gotten our share of the business in one of the best counties in the United States". They still keep him busy.

OTIS KERCHER

William Kercher came from Ohio in 1850 and bought what is now known as the Ed Neterer Farm (formerly known as the Abe Holdeman farm) on Elkhart County Road 40, west of County Road 19 (120 acres at $30 per acre) and did general farming, a few horses, some cows, some hogs and chickens (1852).

A year later Abraham was born and at school age was sent to the old Kime School, east on the corner, now a residence, and in 1874 he was married to Anna Buzzard, daughter of John Buzzard on the Lehman Centennial farm, on County Road 38. They rented the Otis Weaver farm (now owned by Dr. Snider), and did general farming for a few years. Oliver was born there, 1875; Cora in 1876; Wheeler, the orchard man in 1879; and Venetta in 1881. Then they rented the Charles McDonough farm, 40 acres from his father, William Kercher, (40 acres) and carried on with general farming. There Lawrence was born in 1884. A year later, 1885, they bought what is now known as the Otis Kercher farm, 117 acres and set out to clear more of the land. (about 1/3 of the farm was woods).

Here John was born in 1886; Noble in 1888 (died in infancy); Oscar in 1890 (living in Ft. Worth, Texas); Otis in 1892 (now the present owner), and Merrill in 1895. Half of the ten children graduated from high school and College.

Otis entered the old rural one-room Kime school in 1898 and was transferred to Waterford in 1901, when Consolidation came. When the children would drive to Waterford in the horse and buggy they would pick up Merle Roher who later on married Nipper Neff.

After Waterford, Otis went to Goshen High and graduated in 1910; he was the Villain in the class play.

That fall he matriculated at the University of Illinois at Champaign-Urbana, Illinois in the Agricultural College. He had made $75 from his potato patch on the farm by peddling potatoes to Goshen housewives at 45¢ per bushel. This paid for his fees and his books and started him out in college. He then waited tables and soon had a job in the Presidents office, running the printing shop and later set up the "University Press". He started at 15¢ per hour which was later raised to 40¢. He graduated from the Ag. College in 1914.

That fall he was selected as one of the first Agricultural teachers in the country to set up a program at Homer, Louisiana at $83. per month ($1,000 per year) on a 12 month basis. This was when the Smith-Lever Law set up special funds for Agricultural Colleges, and Extension Departments as well as possibilities in the field of 4-H. He had all his students select special crop and animal projects and supervised them all year including the summer months. Otis was years ahead of the Vo. Ag. people which was not set up until the Smith-Hughes Law set up money for its organization. (1917) There he was married to Genevieve Williams. His program and work gained National Recognition and he was asked to move to Lexington, Kentucky, where he became State leader of the "Pig Club" and later was made State Leader for all 4-H clubs. This work he carried on for 4 years, emphasizing the breeding of Registered Swine.

In 1919 he became the first Farm advisor in Illinois at Pittsfield, for Pike County (called County Agricultural Agent in Indiana and Michigan). At this time his father died on the farm in Indiana, and Otis bought out the heirs and took over ownership of the home farm, with Fred Jessup farming it until he died and then Ray Leatherman took over and has been farming it for the last 10 years for Otis. He was transferred to Danville, Illinois in 1923 as the County Farm Agent or Advisor and served there for 12 years. Here two children came, Richard in 1925 and Martha in 1930. He was V. President of National Association Co. Agents 1925.

In 1935 Otis resigned at Danville and came back to his farm, was not here but several weeks, when the Regional Director of F.H.A. at Champaign, Illinois offered him the job as Supervisor of F.H.A. Farm Loan business for Northern Indiana. He took the job.

He had the final approval more than 600 Farm Purchase loans in the area, 40 of which were in Elkhart County. He was in this work for 17 years. It was during this time that the National Pres. of the A.F.B.F. in Chicago had him take off 3 weeks to go to North Carolina to organize the state Farm Bureau there in the state.

Richard volunteered for the Navy and on his return took the Ag. course at Purdue, and graduated in 1950. He is now the big operator-owner of the Goshen Floral and Landscape Company on Chicago Avenue, south of the Kroger store. He has 3 children and they are all

Presbyterians as his father and mother has been for over 50 years. Martha graduated from I.U. was married, has 3 children and they live in Phoenix, Arizona.

In 1953 he retired, farmed a few years, qualified the woods as a Tree Farm, and keeps one of the most beautiful farmsteads in the the area "Immaculate". Otis says "You can't fight inflation by increasing salaries and wages, the farmer needs more consideration".

THE KING TWINS

Carl King was reared on his fathers farm and bought 120 acres before he was married in 1924 to Bernice Artley of Middlebury.

Later he inherited 480 acres. They built up a dairy herd and paid special attention to good leafy hay and rich pasture, selling their milk to Goshen.

Both of the twin boys, William and Robert, were born in 1931 and graduated from Bristol High School in 1949.

Robert married Peggy Leister of Constantine in 1951 and the next year William married Anne Young from the same town. Then the twins took over the farming in 1952.

They built 2 silos 24' x 84' and increased their dairy herd. They set up a milking parlor and loose housing. They bought 150 acres of additional land, and in 1970 bought another 150 acres. They now rent 300 additional acres farming in all 1200 acres. They are milking 80 Holsteins and have 250 young calves and heifers, and 5 breeding bulls of their own.

Bill has two sons, Ronald and Scott and Bob also has two sons, Robert and Gerry.

They swear by the John Deere line of tractors and farm implements. The land is rolling to hilly and is light enabling the Kings to plow, and seed and plant early.

A happy bunch are the Kings. They are widely known and exceptionally well liked.

GLEN AND CARL KLINE — Northwest of Vistula

Glen was born in Missouri in 1901 came to Indiana, and married Nina Sommers in 1922. They lived with his folks 2 years, rented another place 2 years, and then bought the homestead of 250 acres, in 1926. They milked cows and had some hogs, and made a happy home for 5 children, including Carl who is going big guns with a farm across the road, another farm up north, and now offers to buy the homestead from Glenn, who has been laid up for years from a machinery accident. Glen has been my friend for 30 years. I will never forget him as long as I live. When I took on the promotion of Live Stock Exhibits for the fair in 1944, Glen was the first one to offer to exhibit hogs. Carl is now Registered Poland China Swine, and just landed the big one, Grand Champion Poland China Boar at the Michigan State Fair.

Carl has 4 children Becki, Jenni, Greg, and David; they are all in 4-H in the Elkhart County Fair, and David had the Reserve Champion Barrow there last week. Bruce farmed the homestead for years, but now plans to go into the ministry. FINE PEOPLE!

THE KRIDER NURSERIES

Vernon H. Krider graduated at LaGrange High School and after he graduated he started teaching at Adamsville, Michigan, and 8-Square, south west of Middlebury and started growing strawberries and small fruits, two miles west of Griner Church and one-half mile south. This is where Kenneth V. Krider was born in 1907.

When Kenneth was one year old they moved to the Carmien farm one mile north of Cornell School on what has been the Arthur Weldy Farm (100 acres). They set up a general line of Nursery Stock and the first mail order catalogue, in 1908 (about 16 pages), listing nursery stock of all kinds. The business increased and he built a nursery building and shipped orders by mail all over the U.S. He also established a landscaping service. His first truck was bought in 1927. Then in 1923 he bought the Teeters Farm (120 acres) on County Road 8 where a corporation was formed, including Kenny and Dr. B.F. Teeters, the Middlebury physician. After the death of B.F. Teeters, about 1927, M.S. Teeters, his son, served the company as president for 40 years.

Many of the buildings were built in 1923 and 1924, one building 200 x 160, and in 1925 all the nursery buildings were burned down and were later rebuilt.

In 1933 and 1934 the Corporation had a display garden at the Century of Progress (Chicago World's Fair). After the world's fair the company mailed as many as 250,000 catalogues, having secured a large mailing list at the Fair. They secured orders from all over the U.S. some orders being shipped to foreign countries.

In the meantime they bought several hundred acres including the old Mathers farm on County Road 14 across from Norval Poyser.

In 1928 Kenneth was married to Doris Nihart, daughter of Joseph and Jennie Nihart, and they settled down in the house directly north of his present home. He lived there for 25 years and then bought his present home.

Kenneth served 12 years on the Middlebury Town Board, eight years as president. Kenneth became secretary of the company and has continued as secretary of the company for 40 years. When M.S. Teeters was killed in 1969, Kenneth became president in his place. (The first Krider to become president of the company.)

Three sons, Roger, Ross and Rex, were born from 1929 to 1940 and were later taken itno the business. All attended high school and college. One daughter, Dian (Wilke) is a registered nurse at Elkhart General Hospital. Most of the Kriders are Methodists. During the thirties and forties, large flower and garden shows were held in which the Kriders were major supporters, along with the Middlebury Garden Club.

After Vic Judson died in 1956, Kenneth was appointed to finish out his term on the Elkhart County Council and then was elected for three consecutive terms, totaling 15 years. He served as vice-president for a number of years.

He has been a director of the First State Bank of Middlebury since his father's death, totaling 18 years.

He also served on the Middlebury School Board for ten years, several years as treasurer.

His sister, the bookkeeper says his motto has been all these years, "We still grow for those who want the best."

THE LAMBRIGHTS — Hatchery and All

Cleo Lambright was born in 1906 west of LaGrange. When he grew up, he was married to Orpha Hostetler from the Pashan School community. They did not settle down until 1930 when he bought the International Harvester agency in LaGrange, and to have a place to live they bought a small farm on County Road 25 north. There seven children were born, Eloise in 1931, a pair of twins, James and

Janet in 1934, another set of twins the next year, Richard and Robert, then after they sold the business and bought the Russell Walters farm, Vernon was born in 1942, and Wanda in 1946. The Walters farm was 275 acres, and they went to general farming, plowing with the Farmall 20 and cultivating with horses. They had about 20 cows, milked by hand at first, and then came the DeLaval milker. About this time he bought another 180 acres and fed as many as 2000 lambs in one year. Then he bought another 80 to the east of the old farm.

By 1945, he had sold all the cows, and went into the chicken business. He converted the old barn into a 3 story laying house (some 10,000 layers).

The Hatchery, was built and incorporated on the 180 acre farm in 1949. The next year they added the feed mill, and soon thereafter he bought the Ely farm near Plato (350 acres). During the Korean War, Dick and Bob spent 2 years in Greece helping teach new Agricultural methods to the people.

On their return in 1957 they built the big laying houses for some 120,000 layers, and the next year put up the 3 big Harvestores on the north side of the road for the cattle feeding project (Automatic Feeders).

Then in 1965 Cleo bought the 120 acre Garwood farm north of the hospital north of LaGrange and that was it.

He felt he wanted to get rid of some of the responsibility, so suggested the boys take over. Mr. Ivan Birky had a lot of know-how in the business so Ivan Bob and Dick bought the Corporation stock and took over, Bob in charge of sales, Ivan, Hatchery and Feed Mill, and Dick, Egg Processing and General Manager. Later the same year they built the Egg Processing plant. 2 years later they bought 100 acre Livingston farm and following that in 1970 bought all of Dads land but the farm at Plato on which Cleo wants to run some cattle. Since, the boys have increased the "layer capacity" by 75,000.

The Hatchery furnishes the pullets and hatches the eggs and processes the eggs from 750,000 layers. Of these layers 35% belong to Lambright's 7% are by contract, and 35% by independent producers. The Hatchery has an annual hatch of a million pullet chicks. The boys own 747 acres, rent another 128 acres, farming 875 acres. Besides they finish 350 beef cattle. They employ 85 people.

Cleo has always said "Honesty is the best policy" How True!!!

Eloise is married to Myron Summers, Supt. of Schools at Denver, Colorado and she is a graduate nurse at St. Luke's Hospital.

James is married to Virginia Pletcher, is a feed salesman in Goshen and has 100,000 layers of his own. Janet is married to Dale Kanagy, dentist in Elkhart, she is a graduate nurse. Vernon is a Vet in Decatur, and married to Beth Wolford. Wanda is married to Dale Mast, both are teaching in the Denver School System.

Note: After all this record what can one say but, "Good for them."

FRED LEHMAN — Soybean King

Fred was the son of Homer and Grace Lehman. His grandfather, Jacob Lehman was my dad.

Homer had almost a section of land, and according to Purdue, was the first farmer in Indiana to plant 22 inch Soybean rows.

Fred went to Madison to school and always had beef in 4-H as did his sisters. Fritz married Betty Menges of Bremen, and they have 3 children, Charles, Phillip, and Julie. Chuck was married last year to Susan Frick and they left the farm. Phil still is at it but Fritz is worried that they will all leave him. He says, "after Homer and I built up the spread, it is hard to see them not pitch in and keep it going, although Phillip still shows an interest".

All 3 children have been in 4-H, too. Homer died several years ago, and Fred has part of the section, and rents about 300 acres more. Neighbors say Fritz is the best farmer around Oak Grove.

They belong to Betty's church in Bremen, but Grace, Homer's widow, lives on the old homestead, and goes regularly to the Missionary church in Oak Grove.

This was a 5 page story, but Fritz has been hollerin', Uncle Elmer please don't brag me up too much". He is a very modest fellow, so it is real short, but I wish there were more farmers like Fritz, hard-working, and CLEAN AS A HOUNDS TOOTH. Bless them all!

HON. JOHN LESH — Goshen

John's father was a farmer in Wabash County on a little farm and when John was only 20 he was told he could not expect much financial help from his parents, so he had better strike right out on his own right then instead of working for his father until he reached his 21st birthday which was the custom at that time. John was born in 1846, so this verdict came right after the civil war in 1866.

John invested a few dollars in some standing trees, cut them down and sawed them into lumber, and lo, and behold he found he was reaping 7 times his investment. After 4 years in this activity, he found he had built up a capital of $15,000.

This is when he raised his sights, rented offices in Chicago, established a name, John Lesh & Co., an address and soon his company was worth several hundred thousand.

He had always liked the looks of Goshen, and the hankerin' became a fact, when about 1875 he closed John Lesh & Co. in Chicago after 9 years of operations, and moved to Goshen with his wife (Mary Ellen Clay), and two children, Joe, born 1868, and later Mayme. The Lesh house at that time was the big house, southeast corner of sixth and Washington, now the home of Rev. Robert Hartzler of Oaklawn Center.

In Goshen, John quickly became the Pres. of 3 outfits, Lesh, Sanders, and Egbert, Timber and Lumber, Lesh, Proutty and Abbot, realtors, and the Rock River Stock Farm, Racing and Stable horses. Everything John touched, turned to gold. He was a gifted man in timber. He could walk through a 20 acre piece of timber and without pencil and paper come out on the other road with an accurate estimate of the number of thousand board feet expected from the trees ready to harvest.

John's word became the rule; everybody sought his advice, and he was accumulating wealth.

It was at this time that Joe Noble built a factory across the tracks to manufacture hardwood school desks of oak, maple and ash. He became a competitor of John's and all at once they were each trying to outdo the other. John with a brick mansion east of the post office, and Joe, the next lot east with a higher turreted mansion (Dr. Mary Bartholomew, his granddaughter lived there for years).

Joe and Mayme were educated in the Goshen schools, Mayme married Jack Latta, and John made them, financially, and Joe married LaNeta Wanner farther south on sixth street, and Joe and LaNeta started to develop the stock farm, race and stable horses. This farm later became the location of the county fairgrounds.

By 1890 John had great popularity and influence and was elected Mayor of Goshen and from then on it was Hon. John Lesh.

The gobs of money John spread around Goshen was a great boon.

Brice Minnich, 418 South 6th, still living at 91, thinks we should say about John "He knew timber and lumber, especially hardwood; he was a real good organizer, promoter and money maker." (When the Goshen Grays beat the Chicago Cubs twice on the 4th of July, in 1899 Brice was the catcher). Forenoon score 4 - 0 Goshen. Afternoon score 18 - 3 Goshen.

My good friend Bill Bradford says his great uncle established many saw mills in the woods for the Lesh-Egbert outfit from southern Michigan to Missouri, but Northern Indiana was the center. My wife's uncle Mr. Ed Riggle was one of their best timber buyers.

John Lesh died in 1898 and the Abbott family (Frank's father) took over the brick mansion for many years. Frank was in Lita's class

LOCUST LANE DAIRY FARM

Marguerite's father came from Pennsylvania, married Elsie Kline, and built the first house in 1872. His daughter now lives in the middle of the woods on the same farm, on the shore of North Twin Lake, where she and her spouse enjoy a semi-retired life in the beautiful setting. Jim Kline who was her uncle, Agricultural Agent for more than 20 years, and Riley Case who succeeded him for another 20 years was a real friend.

Likewise, about 1842 John M. Kelly had a son Dan who had 430 acres (born 1861) and father and son both farmed all their lives north of Brighton. Ralph was born in 1898 and all his brothers and sisters graduated from Lima High School, and 4 of them taught school. Ralph A. Kelly and Marguerite Doll became friends in the Lima High School and were married in 1920.

Ralph had organized one of the first Boy Scout Troops in the county in 1919, later was a member the Pioneer Trails Council, Boy Scouts of America for several years, and was awarded the first Silver Beaver badge in LaGrange County.

Ralph and Marguerite were both pushers. They rented the Doll farm on shares and named it the Locust Lane when they established a dairy farm (183 acres). Then they did a smart thing; they made a contract with Howe Military Academy. This insured a ready market for their milk. They also started bottling milk in a 7' x 9' milkhouse. The first milkhouse was built in 1924. That year he helped organize the first 4-H Jersey calf club.

He served as Purdue Ag. Alumni Advisor from 1930 to 1945, then they bought the Beisel farm (200 acres) and later the 63 acres of the Craig farm.

By way of children, Eloise came in 1922, Richard in 1923, John in 1924, Ralph Allen in 1929, Jim in 1937 and Melissa in 1940.

In 1948 they started peddling milk door to door, also LaGrange and Sturgis, and reaching as far north as Mendon, Michigan.

Ralph was elected County Commissioner in 1948, and was Co-Chairman of the Volunteer School Study Committee for Consolidation.

In 1950 Ralph received the Purdue Meritorious Award and that same year they built Marguerite's life-long dream, "The Brick Castle in the Woods." It is on the Doll farm east shore of North Twin.

In 1963 they built the milk parlor and the big stabling barn, now quarters for 300 Jerseys. Ralph says, we found out long ago that Jerseys handle better for a big Commercial operation than any other breed. There are more than 200 adult cows, 30% of them registered and they milk an average of from 160 to 170. They stopped processing in 1968 and sell bulk at Constantine Co-op.

Eloise is now Mrs. Charles Geddes, edits a newspaper in Denver, and her hubby is a Professor in the University. Richard is in Sturgis, John is the Farm and Herd Manager, while Ralph Allen and Jim run the retail business, which is still quite substantial and Melissa is married to Robert Tobias, restauranteurs in Fairfield, California.

Locust Lane was incorporated in 1956, LOCUST LANE JERSEY FARM. They own 500 acres, rent 500 more so they farm 1,000 acres, 300 corn, 100 beans, 100 wheat, 25 oats, 200 alfalfa, and balance pasture. When Paul Reddick, the editor at LaGrange asked Ralph if he would recommend that a young man go into dairying He said, "That would depend upon whether he likes it or not." Over the 50 years we have had a regular income, which took care of a growing family, and while it has been very confining we have liked it. They are members of the Howe United Methodist, he was 8 years on the

94

conference World Service Commission and charter member of the Howe Lions Club, President 2 years.

JACOB HENRY AND OLIVER LOUCKS

Martin Loucks, born March 11, 1840, was later married to Hannah Kilmer and they settled on a quarter section, 1 mile south of Sailor's School. The farm is 3 miles north of Wakarusa. They had 4 children and for our purpose including Jacob Henry Loucks, born July 2, 1868, right after the Civil War. Jacob Henry attended Sailor's School 1 mile north of the farm. The snow drifts were sometimes 10 feet high. Then he was married to Margaret Warner Wenger and then they rented the home farm for 18 years (too long he often told Ollie his son). At that time he bought 80 acres in 1907. They had 8 children and for our purpose including Oliver, born 1895. Later Jacob Henry bought 7 purebred Holsteins and they were milking 18 to 20 cows in all.

Being a share holder in The Wakarusa Creamery, they bought a DeLaval separator and sold cream there.

They fed loose hay, and corn and oats ground together at Jacob K. Weldy's Mill in Wakarusa and bought soybean meal for protein. On the 5th of August 1916, Oliver was married to Anna Weldy, the daughter of Rev. Henry Weldy. Another house was secured and located to the south of the entrance lane, completely furnished and Jacob Henry and Oliver, father and son, became full partners. They went into the dairy business in earnest, building one of the largest dairy herds in the area at that time.

They started testing, keeping breed and production records, and soon established the first cow testing association in the county. It included Jacob Henry Loucks, Oliver Loucks and Tim Blosser on the Millersburg Brick Road 44, and Charles Weldy on County Road 27 north of U.S. 20. The first cow tester was a Mr. Campbell from Michigan.

At this time the Loucks family bought up many cattle in Indiana and Michigan in the fall months after pasture gave out, fed the heifers and cows over winter and then put on a big sale in the spring. They would have 50 to 65 in the sale. They had one cow which produced 100 lbs. of milk per day for a whole month. They showed cattle for many years in various fairs, at one time walking off with the Grand Champion Holstein in the Indiana State Holstein Show held at Kendallville, 1924.

In 1928 the partnership ended and Oliver and Anna bought the 80 acre Weldy farm, 1 mile west and 2½ miles south of Wakarusa. Ollie had 4 dispersals on this farm and finally in 1946, sold out completely.

Oliver had originated the Holstein Consignment Sale and after the third successful sale turned the chore over to Tim Blosser.

Oliver and Anna are living a happy retired life. He can entertain you on the mouth organ till your feet start to clog. They are still very active and busy, including Locke Township chairmen for C.R.O.P. for years.

LAMAR LOUCKS — Hilltop Hampshires

Lamar was born on the Loucks farm, 3 miles north of Wakarusa, on County Road 3, where Albert Weaver now lives.

He went to grade school at the Old Sailor's country school, a mile north of the farm, and when the school was closed, because of consolidation in 1925, he was transferred to Wakarusa.

His father, Oliver was a great Holstein man and a pioneer dairyman. With his father and Tim Blosser, he started the first cow testing association in the County (Holstein) and they gathered and bought up hundreds of up-graded Holsteins to sell at annual sales on their farm.

When Lamar grew up he married Vera, the daughter of Chester and Florence Gongwer Blosser, a graduate of Jimtown High. They then rented her folk's farm, and later inherited it and moved there in 1946, and named the spread (The Hilltop Farm).

They started with Guernseys first and later swung to the Holsteins. Lamar fell in love with the belted hogs and in the late 40's was showing boars and gilts as well as fat barrows at the Elkhart County Fair. He has supported the Hampshire Swine Breeder's sales, and the All-Breeders consignment sales all these years.

The writer influenced Wolfbergs of Wakarusa to put up a $50. Award Medal annually for the Grand Champion Barrow at the Elkhart County Fair, and Lamar won it year after year, then his son Loren, won it in 1956 and 1958.

Loren was born in 1945, and immediately as a young boy

caught his dad's enthusiasm for the black and white belted breed, so as soon as he was 9 years of age he joined the 4-H parade of Hampshires at the County Fair. He won both showmanship and high placings quite regularly and was a source of great joy and satisfaction to his father and also a right-hand young lad then at the chores. Only a young father on a farm loaded with work and responsibility can appreciate the tremendous lift he gets from a faithful, dependable young lad who is truly interested in achievement.

Loren is now married and lives in Goshen and has a father-son arrangement with his dad on the farm. He and his wife, Mary, have three children; Brian, Michelle, and Jeffrey.

Another son, Lynn was born in 1954. He was in 4-H Swine club 10 years and won Reserve Champion Hampshire Barrow in 1964 and Showmanship award in Hamps. He is now a Sophomore in North Manchester College.

Lamar has piled up many medals in Hampshire classes, including many champions at the County Fair. He was the President of the county Hampshire Breeders' Association for many years, and has consigned many, many boars and gilts in the consignment sales, both Hampshire and all-breed. He was a great pusher in financing and building the Swine barn and exhibition bldg. He is also a member of the Baugo Twp. Volunteer Firemen Corps. They are all Olive Mennonite members.

They have contributed much to Michiana Agriculture in influencing farm friends to change from lard to meat type hogs. Lamar says, "I don't know much to say, let somebody else say it".

JACK McDONALD

Jack McDonald married Florence Pletcher who was born on the Arthur Pletcher Centennial Farm, intersection of County Roads 35 and 36, on December 12, 1941. Sandra was born in 1943.

Jack was discharged from the army in World War II in 1945. James was born in 1946.

In 1948 they bought on County Road 34, and in 1950 they bought a 30 acre set-up across the road from the Pletcher farm, moved there after selling the little farm on the fairgrounds road.

Arthur Pletcher died a few years later, and then Florence inherited the homestead, and they moved on it, where they have lived ever since. Then they bought the Rev. Allen Yoder farm, where Dale had lived.

In 1950 Sandra secured a Black Angus Senior Yearling calf from Richard Barlow, and was the girl who entered the first calf in the Gold Medal Show at the Goshen Fairgrounds, which the writer helped organize, with the assistance of the manager and Superintendent of the Fair, and Purdue University which had tried for many years to set up a Gold Medal Show in Northeast Indiana.

The establishment of the Gold Medal at Goshen immediately had a heartening effect on the rebuilding of the Fair, and the McDonalds are to be credited. They became interested in the Fair, and later Jim had the Reserve Champion Steer at the 4-H Show.

After Jim graduated from Millersburg High School, Jack took him in as a partner, and they rented more land, mostly for corn.

They set up a breeding herd of Aberdeen Angus, 30 cows, but gradually became interested in feeders, and then they rented the Arthur Moore farms, formerly the Christ Schrock Peppermint farm. They now feed 550 mixed feeders, starting them at 450 to 500 pounds, and also feed 250 steers on their Centennial Farm.

They now farm over 1800 acres, they are a hard working happy lot of people. Florence is still teaching school at Millersburg.

THE MANWARING EGGS — Kosciusko County

This outfit was started by Arthur Manwaring in 1911. His son was Chester. Later Chester's three nephews, Charles, Miles and Richard came into the business. Richard is now in charge, Frank Jr. is Vice President and James is Secretary-Treasurer. Frank and James are sons of Charles.

The hatchery and the general offices are located on Indiana 25, 1 mile east of Mentone. The hatchery hatches 100,000 chicks per week, about 4,000,000 per year.

The Manwarings sell the chicks to the Midwest Poultry Service and they grow the pullets.

These pullets are then sold to either individual customers, or control houses, or corporation laying houses.

The eggs produced in these laying houses are then delivered to Gressel Produce, Mr. Phil Gressel produce manager and owner, Delphos, Ohio. Then the eggs are shipped to Buffalo, Pittsburg, Cleveland

and eastern markets.

One of the largest operations is in North Manchester where one farm has 5 houses, 60,000 birds in each house, total 300,000 birds. It is estimated there are around 100 flocks of layers in the area, each averaging 20,000 layers.

The Kosciusko County Poultry Association maintains a large monument in the shape of the egg to epitomize the importance of the egg business in the Mentone area.

It would take an entire book to cover the history of the Manwarings and the egg business, but suffice it to say, years of conscientious effort have produced a fantastic story, hard to believe.

How would you enjoy pushing a business with 2,000,000 Leghorn layers?

The Manwarings have had the know-how in breeding and management, and for that reason have contributed much to Michiana Agriculture.

Stop in sometime and meet these fine people. You might catch their enthusiasm. Since this writing Charles died, August 18, 1974.

MAPLE LEAF DUCK FARMS, INC. — Kosciusko County

Donald E. Wentzel, founder, was born in Monterey, Indiana in 1916. He became a feed salesman for Hale and Hunter Feed Company in Chicago, and selling duck feed to the duck raisers on Long Island, he caught onto the business, started the Wentzel feed business in Mentone in 1956, and contracted with a few local farmers to raise ducklings for him. He shipped them to Wayne Ohio, the Foster Duck Farm, to be processed.

Then, two years later, he bought 80 acres near the intersection of Kosciusko County Roads 900 north and 200 east and started a duckling farm of his own. Also he contracted with some neighbors to raise ducklings, and the first year they produced together 280,000 ducklings to process.

About this time the future-to-be son-in-law Terry Tucker was in the sixth grade in Mentone. He finished school there, enrolled in Purdue Agricultural College, and while still in college married Mr. Wentzel's daughter, Sandra.

He graduated from Purdue in 1963, they moved to Warsaw, and started right in with Mr. Wentzel on the Duckling farm.

In the next 5 years, they bought another 160 acres and started to develop a processing plant of their own, contracting with more farmers to furnish ducklings.

Mr. Wentzel passed on in 1968, and of course, Terry was the logical one to become head of the outfit and President of Maple Leaf.

Two of Sandra's brothers are part owners, but are not active in the enterprise, Terry being the manager and promoter.

Hatcheries in Ohio and Indiana supply Maple Leaf with day old ducklings, three times a week, which are then distributed to 20 farms within 25 miles of the plant, each growing from 5,000 to 75,000 ducklings per month.

Maple Leaf has a 160 acre experimental farm designed to improve growing techniques and conduct studies on feed and other supplies. Center of the experimental farm is a 10,000 square foot laboratory building designed to control environmental conditions, with 8 test pens, each containing 500 birds. The air circulation is controlled by thermostat.

The water sanitation control system is regarded as a model for the industry by Indiana State Authorities. During Peak production the plant uses 160,000 gallons of water per day, passing from lagoon to lagoon until it finally runs off into a swamp. Mr. Brick Meinert, Director of the laboratory, is certified by Indiana as a pollution controller. Maple Leaf Farms new processing operation is considered the most modern in the industry. The plant processes 6,000 ducklings daily in the winter and 18,000 in the summer. This year they processed 2,300,000 ducklings. Each bird gets 4 different inspections. When packaged the very tightly sacked bird is a picture to behold.

Bi-products are, down for pillows, and offal for mink farms. Terry has 3 children and 180 employees. He's a go-getter.

What a story right at our beckon!

Terry says, "The duckling business is moving West".

CONDA MARTIN — Marshall County

Charles H. Martin was killed at a barn raising on George Seymour's place, a large beam falling on him. Conda's brother took over the little 40 acre farm. They built a new barn first and the next year the house. Conda went to Drake School No. 11 in Bourbon Township. He also had two years in Bourbon High School as he was needed on the farm at age 16. He really took over later and built up the Guernsey herd 16 cows, milked by hand. In 1937 he married Freda Anderson of the Bourbon Community. He rented a 44 acre farm for cash rent, buying it after 2 years for $2900, and in 5 years had it paid for. In 1948 the Bates farm came up for sale (120 acres). He bought the farm using the bankers money. They switched to Holsteins, bought 40 acres of pasture land, then 70 acre farm south of Bourbon and by that time Richard was 12 years old and later became a partner. There were 5 boys, 4 surviving. All 4 of the boys had 8 to 10 years of 4-H at Bourbon. Two of these boys were state vice presidents of F.F.A. Each of them served as president of the local chapter in Bourbon.

Hogs being the mortgage lifter, they fed out a lot of hogs. Then they bought 200 acres west of Lake of the Woods, North Township, putting it to corn, soybeans, and wheat. They built a milking parlor, because the wife and son were milking 90 cows in 18 stanchions, when Conda broke his leg. The dairy herd has increased since by raising replacements.

With one boy staying on the farm in partnership, Conda bought a milk route. Hauling to Dean's at Rochester, Indiana, shipping 1½ to 2 tons of milk daily of his own milk plus 9 other dairy farmers. Recently purchased more acres (363) south west of Bourbon with the son a partner. This is nearly all farming ground with feeding facilities for the young cattle. Now land totals 793 acres.

Three of the boys hold Master's and Bachelor's degrees from Purdue University in Agriculture. One is affiliated with a large chemical and fertilizer company. One spent four years in Nigeria teaching agriculture and science and now at Purdue, one is employed at Washington, D.C. in the Census Bureau.

Mr. and Mrs. Martin are members of Mt. Pleasant Church of the Brethren, he serving as trustee for many years, and church board chairman. He is a member of Marshall County 4-H Fair Board, Marshall County Dairy Association, A.M.P. and delegate for 6 years and currently, also a member of Holstein-Friesian Association. He stated he owed his success to "udders", good common sense, plus hard work and his family.

MARTINS MILLS — New Paris

Jacob Martin came from Shipshewana to Goshen, corner of U.S. 33 and College Road and did blacksmith work for John Smokers sawmill 1 mile farther south.

Robert was born there in 1912 and when Smokers moved to New Paris in 1915, Jacob also moved.

In addition he made double trees and single trees and bolsters for wagons for the government in World War I near the present Smoker Lumber Co. on the Big 4 railroad north of Smokers.

Later he made the wagon parts for Montgomery Ward and Sears Roebuck.

By 1925, seeing trucks replacing wagons, he quit and was with New Paris Creamery until 1929.

About 1926, he bought the feed store from Elkhart Co. Co-Op Association where Kaser's plumbing now stands.

About 1928, he built a feed mill with John Bainter, Wesley Weybright, and installed one of the first hammer mills and mixers for custom milling in Elkhart County. It was in 1936 that Charles Neff first started working in the mill.

In 1938, Jacob bought the elevator in New Paris from William Menaught which had once been owned by the Goshen Milling (Frank E.C. Hawks). They built up a fine business and then the mill had a disastrous fire in 1944. This is when Robert enters the picture, and he and his father rebuilt the mill, with potential for formula mixing.

In 1946, they adapted the mill for the first pelleting machine in Northern Indiana. Since formula services have been provided, a feeder can now save money by hooking into a computer line to Atlanta, Georgia to find the right percentages of each feed ingredient in the ration based on todays prices to arrive at the most economical mix.

Joe Ladd was secured as sales and service man in 1946 and deserves a lot of credit for securing many new customers.

In the meantime, Charles Neff, who started from scratch about 1936, was brought into management.

The company now has a fleet of 12 trucks delivering feed within a radius of 100 miles and enjoys at this writing a volume of 7 million dollars in sales.

Robert attends nutritional feed conferences at Cornell to keep abreast and the broiler difficulties of 1967 are just a memory.

Bob has made a great success and enjoys the friendship of many people.

THE WARD MARTIN FAMILY — Milk Testers

Aaron Martin first farmed on the Isaac Basher farm on State Road 19 a few miles north of Nappanee (80 acres), then later moved to a farm north and west of South West and the 3 children went to school at South West grade school; Joe, 1900; Ward, 1904; and Fern, now Mrs. Devon Getz.

When Ward grew up, he took over his father's milk route, hauling milk for farmers in the area to Goshen beginning about 1909. (the condensery was built in 1908). Between Aaron, Ward and his son Joe, later, they piled up 27 years of milk hauling at $2.50 per day.

When Ward was 18 years old, he went to the Michigan Agricultural College at East Lansing, Michigan, and took a 12 weeks Short Course in Dairy Production. He started milk testing, was moved to the Owosso section to test, and there met and was married to Bernice Benton, a daughter of one of his customers, in 1930. Joe was born 1931. They moved later to the Pontiac area, Oakland County, living at Lake Orion, and built a House on Wheels, affording complete testing equipment as well as sleeping quarters. Jim was born there in 1933.

There they had the largest cow-testing association in Michigan, by quite a margin. They would stay on the road going from farm to farm sometimes for a day or two, sometimes for a whole week, until they would get fagged out and make it home for a little rest and relaxation.

About 1937 when the children were at school age, they "left off" with the "Wagon-on-wheels" and moved to Farmington, where Henry Ford's top man, Mr. Sorenson, had a large dairy Herd, and Ward became the herdsman. The 4 years there as herdsman were invaluable to them, as they moved to Elkhart County, bought 50 acres, across from the Yellow-Creek church, and built up a herd of registered Jerseys, about 50 animals, milking around 30. Ward even worked at Foster's in Elkhart to help get operating capitol.

Joe, who was in my Vo. Ag. classes at Wakarusa, seemed very much interested in testing and about then they set up quite a central milk-testing laboratory on their farm in a little building and set out testing for Elkhart County Milk Testing Associations.

By this time Bernice became invaluable in the business. Joe graduated from Wakarusa High in 1949. By this time Elkhart County had 4 milk-testing associations, and the Martins had 3 of them, testing regularly about 1,000 individual cows. Bernice had the area west of State Road 15, and after graduation, Joe had it east of 15. That was for the Holsteins.

Ward was also FIELD MAN for the Milk Producers Federation of Cleveland for 10 years from 1950 to 1960, and during those 10 years, Bernice worked 7 years in the testing laboratory of the Goshen Milk Division. Then Ward and Bernice went back into the business with the family, and they built it up to 7,000 cows in 127 herds, including Owner-Sampler and D.H.I.A. herds. Add up the number of each of the Martins serving as milk testers and you get 81. (Eighty one), counting Bernice's flare in Marshall County for the last 3 years. And now on their 10 acres for play across the road, and a beautiful home, it seems "quiet after the storm". The three boys are gone.

Joe is in Elkins, W.Va., Davis and Elkins college, a counselling Physiologist, and is twisting arrogant young lads around his finger, married to Shirley Pletcher, daughter of Miles Pletcher, and they have two children, Starley, age twenty-one at Chicago University, and Scott age nineteen.

Jim still sings like Caruso, is in Albany, Georgia, a Minister of Music, married to an Albany girl, a Southern Peach, and they have 4 children, Thalia, 17, Tammy, 15, Timothy 12, and Tory, 11.

Jerry, the pie eater, is married to Helen Parcell in Wakarusa, and works in Elkhart.

Ward says "Over the years my concern has been Mastitis, that we are too busy to look after little hazards that cause the trouble and do the little things, like real warm water for the udder at chore time to prevent it".

THE MARTINS SURELY DESERVE TO BE IN THIS BOOK, Farm Families who have built Michiana.

AGRICULTURAL WIZARD — A.T. Marvel

A.T. Marvel began teaching high school agriculture in Rolling Prairie where he met Ella Hillman who was to be his future wife and who had been teaching in LaPorte. A.T. was a Purdue graduate.

Tom went to Middlebury to take the agriculture department and in June of 1913 they were married in South Bend at the home of her brother Dr. Hillman. That year he set up a 4 year course in vocational agriculture. At this time he instigated the origin of The Future Farmers of America, working with Z.M. Smith, State Director of Agriculture at Indianapolis.

They lived in the 1st house south of Clarence Varns until the fall of 1915 when they moved to Dwight, Illinois where he taught agriculture for three years. In the fall of 1918 they moved to Pendleton to take the Vo. Ag. department for 6 years. During those years, 3 of their 4 sons were born, Tom, James, and Howard.

Then he returned to Middlebury for 9 years and through field trips, experiments and demonstrations became outstanding Vo. Ag. teacher in the country and gained national recognition as leader in Vocational Agriculture. Here Bill was born in 1925.

The 2 sons of Tobe Eash often say that they were so surprised that their father, a member of the Conservative Griner Church would do so much to sponsor field trips and tours for Mr. Marvel. A.T. sold the whole community on vocational agriculture. He went to Concord school to set up a Vo. Ag. course and in December he was drafted to become the Elkhart County Agricultural Agent for 2 years until J. Howard Brown replaced him. He went to Wolcottville and set up a course (2 years) and to Burnettsville and Idaville (for 5 years) ending up in New Carlisle 1943-1948 where he sowed the seed for what was to become a fantastic story of Evening Farmers Classes.

In 1948 he organized a class of veterans-on-farm students and did such an outstanding job that the veterans as they finished their entitlement insisted that he be relieved (by Tom Lake) in order to free him for working with all veterans in the area full time.

He taught evening farmer classes for 8 years reaching as high as 150 enrollment. He would take an ordinary farmer with little know-how and teach him new methods of fertilization and management and make him a success over night. The cars who followed the many tours would fill a pasture field from 5 to 7 acres. Purdue paid as much as $200 per year and many dealers helped sponsor the classes.

If you don't believe this story go to New Carlisle and talk to any farmer with two or more silos, especially Mr. Paul Cooreman on Tamarac Road 1½ miles north of U.S. 20 who will sing his praises until you come away convinced. A.T. raised Paul from 25 bu. of wheat per acre to 75 bushel the next year.

His success stories found their way into every Agricultural Journal of the land. New Carlisle renamed his street in his honor (Marvel Lane).

Their son Tom is still in Vo. Ag. (Anderson). Jim is a doctor in Evansville, Howard is a doctor, also, in Lafayette. Bill is in the legislative department of the Indiana State Farm Bureau.

A.T. passed away in the Home Hospital, Lafayette on November 29, 1968. Ella, rich in memories and surrounded by friends still lives on Marvel Lane.

HARLEY MAST

He was born in LaGrange County in 1925, and married Laura Miller in 1947. They moved to the Dewey Farm which belonged to her Father Elmer Miller, and bought half of the herd of cattle. (25). On this farm in the five years, 3 children were born, Duane, now with Monitor Coach at Wakarusa, Fern, a bookkeeper at the Mennonite Mission Board at Elkhart, and Nancy, a receptionist at Starcraft Agricultural Products at Goshen.

They bought the farm in 1960 and bought their first registered Guernseys at that time. The children were all in 4-H, in dairy and other projects.

They built their beautiful new brick country home in 1966.

Now they have a splendid herd with 70 animals, half of them in milk. Harley has been a booster for C.R.O.P. since 1955 and is appreciated as a neighbor and is ace high in our book.

He said some Dewey relative came around last summer to inquire, and he reported his understanding was, that a lumber company bought the farm from the Dewey estate, cut off all the timber, and then sold it to Mrs. Mast's father, Elmer Miller.

HERBERT MAUST — Milk Parlor King

The business was started in 1952, in a small office in the front of what used to be Mumaw's Mill, later bought by Hartman Bros., and for several years the inventory would be around $3,000.

Herb bought the inventory and business in 1954, and operated it under the Hartman Brothers name. The business was a general farm store, furnishing supplies for chickens, hogs, horses and cattle. At that time a farmer had a few animals of each kind, but as time went on the situation changed, the farmer specialized, and we had to make a decision as to which way to go. We decided to follow the path of the cow, and to become Dairy Specialists. Our goal then was to supply all the needs of the farmer around the cow.

We took on a line of milking machines, to be able to milk the cow, and took on milk coolers to be able to cool the milk, various feeding equipment was added to be able to feed the cow in many ways, with various set-ups and with different kinds of feed. There was also a need of cleansing the barnyards and barn, so barn cleansers were added to our line.

As the labor market became tighter, more labor-saving devices, and silo unloaders, bunk feeders, feed grinding and mixing equipment were used to save on labor. Then the dairy farmer became more technical, so a need was seen for an Engineering Department, and this was added. Our Engineer could plan a job of any size to fit the needs of each farmer. With total environment coming into view, the need for ventilation and air movement was seen, so we added a service of ventilating equipment to be able to engineer this job.

Each farmer is an individual, and has his own ideas and needs which we formulate into an efficient working operation. So as time passed, starting with a one-man operation of a small store, periodic steps were taken to enlarge in a steady and progressive way to the present operation of approximately 25 employees, and all the trucks and equipment that goes with it. Service has played a big part in our growth. We service what we sell, maintaining a service man on 24-hour call, and we have expanded our parts department 4 or 5 times. As equipment becomes more automatic and technical, the need for service and know-how will continue as a priority in future planning.

In 1967 the Hartman Brothers sold the Feed Mill to Ramon Pfieffer, and at that time the names were changed to the Wakarusa

Feed Center, and the Wakarusa Farm Center, but were still operated as separate businesses.

We can see, as we look back, over our business growth, that it has grown and prospered in relationship to the farmer's change and progress. We look to the future and hope to keep step with the farmer, and to be able to fulfill any needs he may have.

N.B: We asked to have Herb write this up himself so you will see it in the 1st person. Now for our comments; Herb graduated from the Wakarusa High School in 1946. He was in Lita's class and when I substituted, I had him. Both of us felt that some day he would come through BIG and he has done so, very conscientious, full of enterprise, and a great DESIRE TO SERVE. No one can measure his great contribution to Michiana Agriculture. I talked to Newman Brothers at Culver, and they thought he did a great job, and when I got the Pueschel story of 300 milkers north of Sturgis, Michigan, Ernest said there's nobody like him. MORE POWER TO YOU HERB!

THE MIDDLEBURY CO-OP CREAMERY

The outfit was incorporated as a co-operative in 1921 with 101 shares of stock at $100 per share, and the first Board of Directors was composed of Frank Walker, Pres., Sol Sherwin, Dr. M.A. Farver, Mose Yoder, Cyrus Steele, Dave Blough, and Sam Mauck, Brian's father.

There were 5 cream haulers, Luther Welbaum, Owen Yoder, and a Mr. Miller southeast of Middlebury. We do not know the names of the other two. They received the first cream on December 22nd, 1921. Glenn Dings was the buttermaker. They made 3,000 lbs. of butter the first week, and 162,000 lbs. the first year.

Ray Troop was manager from 1921 to 1922; Glenn Dings, 1922 to 1934; Melvin Plank from 1934 to 1952, and Brian Mauck from 1952 to now.

The Creamery distributes the butter in pound packages either whole or quartered by truck all over Michiana.

The Creamery has a tremendous contribution to Michiana Agriculture. Brian says, "A lot of people still prefer the old fashioned BUTTER".

REV. D.D. MILLER'S CLOVERLAND

Dr. Ernest Miller, past Pres. of Goshen College, drove me out to Cloverland Farm yesterday, south east of Middlebury 3 miles, where Little Emma Creek and Little Elkhart join, and relished the reminiscence of bygone days.

It seems that Daniel P. Miller, Ernests grandfather was born in Somerset, Pa., in 1837, came to Indiana, had 9 children, and for our purpose, including Daniel D. Miller, D.D. as everybody called him.

The 80 acre farm was across the Little Elkhart to the north and east, and D.D. spent his early years in Pashan country school, to the east on what is now U.S. 20. D.J. Johns was his teacher and had great influence on his life. He inspired D.D. to go to Normal School at LaGrange and Angola and become a teacher, against much resistance in the family and church.

He then taught in Missouri, and then at Emmatown, and there met Jeanette Hostetler, married her and they lived with her folks for a while, and felt the call of Evangelism, again found resistance, but finally won approval. He was made a Deacon at the age of 26, ordained a minister the next year (1891), and then he began his evangelistic work. One trip lasted 6 months, Missouri, Nebraska, Idaho, and California. He also worked in Canada.

During this period 11 children were born; Ora 1892; Ernest, 1893; Truman, 1895; Ida Mae, 1896; Clara, 1898; Wilbur, 1899, and that was the year they bought Cloverdale and moved there. Kathryn came in 1900 and Bertha in 1902, then the little barn was too small for the increase of cattle, hay, etc., and they built the big barn.

Alice first saw the light of day in 1903 and then mother complained that the house was not big enough and without conveniences called for a new one. So they built a beautiful large farmhouse which to this day makes a wonderful showing, running water and everything. That was a great year for the Millers. Instead of a crowded shanty, they had a mansion with all conveniences and the ensuing years were happy ones. Samuel was born in 1908 and Mabel in 1909. The cookie jar was seldom empty; Friday and Saturday would see a dozen pies of various kinds slide on the shelves for over Sunday, as there was sure to be company. D.D. was becoming very influential, and in 1906 was made a Mennonite Bishop. The Ordination service was in Forks, D.J. Johns, D.D's life-long friend, presiding.

From here on, anything new that was needed on the farm by way of equipment or machinery, they got it.

Everyone knows how the Mennonite and Amish women will be seen out in the garden and truck patch a good share of the day. So at Cloverdale the garden and truck patch made the winter months a "Cornucopia".

At one time D.D. started to register cattle, but the church thought it would be "yoking-up with the world", and they gave it up. D.D.'s mother died in 1906 of Tuberculosis. D.P. passed on to the spirit world in 1911.

It was about this time that the wood stave silo was built, one of the first in the area.

By 1921, many of the children had married or left and instead of being too small, the spacious farm home was now too large. They wanted to be closer to the church, anyhow, and Jeanette had her eye on "just the house" right across from the church, the Christ Stahly farm, so they bought it and moved there, renting their Cloverdale farm to Clara and her husband, Art Augsberger from Illinois. Art and Clara made Cloverdale bloom for 24 years. They were very prosperous and did much to help others in the family and the church.

In the big factional fights in the Mennonite church, D.D. was a peacemaker. He was a church leader in the church of great influence. All of his children graduated from high school, and 7 of the 11 from College, 5 of them from Goshen College, and the other 2 from North Manchester, because Goshen was closed.

Alice was married to Chauncey Oesch in 1925, a farmer and a teacher at Middlebury, then in 1945 Mr. Dan Oesch, Chauncey's brother bought Cloverdale and rented it to the Oesch family. They had 3 children, and for our purpose, including Myron who was born in 1929, right at the time of the Stock Crash.

Myron and his dad pushed the dairy herd, he was in 4-H and Vo. Ag. at Middlebury, went two years to Goshen College, and then married Murlene Garber from Metamora, Illinois, and lived with his parents 2 years, and had a Father-Son arrangement getting 1/3 of the profits. No house is big enough for 2 families, so Chauncey moved to Middlebury in 1953, and rented the spread to Myron, helping some on the farm, and working some in town.

Having had a stroke, Chauncey died in 1966, and Myron bought the 80 across the road to the west.

Two years later the barn burned to the ground, and Alice and Myron had to rebuild it from scratch, providing for loose housing, holding pen and milk parlor, with 2 large steel silos from New Paris, one for haylage and the other for high-moisture corn for dairy cattle.

Two years later (1970) Myron bought the 140 where the buildings stand, making 220 acres owned, and 100 rented, making a total of 320 acres farmed. Cloverdale now has 175 Holsteins, 80 to milk. Myron does his own cattle insemination, and the place never looked more prosperous.

Myron was on the A.S.C. committee 9 years.

Myron and Murlene have 5 children Marlys age 22 is a senior at Goshen College, doing practice teaching, and is just married to Randy Stutzman; Marcia, 21, married Larry Miller, (a student in Butler,) and they live in Indianapolis, she is a secretary with Herf-Jones; Michael, 20, is the right-hand man on the farm; Nancy, 19, will be in Hesston this Fall; and Debi, 16 is a Sophomore at Northridge and is a Varsity Cheerleader.

All of the children were in 4-H a number of years, and showed Holstein dairy calves at the Elkhart County Fair. Today they are all on-the-go.

Myron has been a real leader in the Forks church for years, and he says "The more we do and the more we give, the more we are blessed materially and spiritually."

Note: Orie married Elta Wolfe, became a shoe salesman for her father, later the manager, and then inherited it. Ernest finished Goshen in 1917, married Ruth Blosser, was in Alternate Service 2 years, Missionary, Dhamtari India 16 years, took his Doctorate in New York University, Personnel Director at Goshen College 1 year, then made President of the college in 1940 for 12 years, 2 more years in India, then Professor of Psychology at the college for 10 years, now at Greencroft. Truman died in 1952. Wilbur became Ass't Sup't Columbus schools, now retired.

SPECIAL NOTE: On October 8, 1974, the Elkhart County Agricultural Society named the Myron Oesch family "The Outstanding Farm Family of the Year".

EVERETT E. AND MAYME MILLER

Everett E. Miller, 1897, the son of Ira J. and Rebecca Jane (Rodi-baugh) Miller. The David Rodibaughs set up the Richard Barlor farm and were influential for early New Paris industry beginning at Baint-ertown. Power was obtained from the mill race for a grist mill, saw-mill, woolen mill and even a grocery store. His father, Ira J., farmed the land on which the old Baintertown schoolhouse still stands. His grandfather, John D., was the first white man to cross Turkey Creek west into Indian country, having made friends with the Indians by giving food, and a dug-out canoe, handhewn from a log, to them.

Mayme was born (1896) the daughter of John and Etta Smoker southeast of Goshen at Smoker's Corners. Etta was the daughter of Ben F. and Clarinda Stutsman. John, son of Jacob Smoker, was a manufacturer of wagon parts for the mail order houses. Other Smoker children were Eva, Ralph, Max, Mark and Chet. The family later moved to New Paris and Mayme and Everett were married in 1918.

After farming the Miller homestead a few years, Everett spent 40 years with the Smoker Lumber Company. Mayme turned her talents to music, and became a fine violinist-teaching, and directing the town orchestra and band.

Everett served as county commissioner for 12 years, and he gave it everything he had. In 1960, he retired, and now sells commercial ads for the Farmer's Exchange. He is a lifetime member of the Mis-sionary Board of the First Brethren Church. The Millers spend their winters in Florida. They have three children, LaVeta Immel of North Manchester, Rex, and Jeanette DeBoer, both of New Paris. The Mil-lers and son Rex still own and operate the homestead. "I could write a book about them", says Elmer Lehman.

JONAS MILLER & SON — Massey-Harris

Jonas was married young, but his wife died and he was married again after her death to Ethel Fervida. They lived on what is now the Forest Fervida Farm, south of Foraker. He farmed and auctioneered from age 19 for 55 years. In 1928 he took on the management of the Wakarusa Sale Barn.

In 1934 he moved into a home on North Elkhart Street in Waka-rusa, built by Frank Gotschalk and at that time secured a franchise with Massey-Harris Implement Co. of Racine, Wisconsin. One year he had a sale every day from January 2 to March 19. From 1942 on,

Ethel worked in the sale barn as secretary. They had a big Relief sale in January 1948.

In 1947, Kenneth joined Jonas in the implement business. The store on North Elkhart Street was incorporated J.A. Miller & Son in December 1962.

Jonas cried many sales at the Elkhart County Fair for 4-H as well as at the St. Joseph County Fair.

In 1948, they moved the old sale barn one mile east on Indiana 19. Jonas was made an honorary member of Wakarusa F.F.A. in 1952. In 1963 he was married to Mary Reed after Ethel's death. He lost his voice and died in 1966.

At that time Kenneth bought the balance of the stock and kept the store until he built the present plant in 1969. He had received the honorary F.F.A. in 1955.

In 1971 Kenn was taken into the business and when Robert graduated from high school he also became a member of the firm. The firm has always been supporters of cooperative demonstrations and contests with the implement dealers association of Elkhart County, and for several years Kenny was president of the association.

He has served on many boards and committees in the community.

Their exhibits at the Elkhart County Fairs for years have been outstanding. The firm now has a large trade in Indiana and Michigan.

L. ORVILLE MILLER STORY

Henry Shaum from Orrville, Ohio came to Indiana before the Civil War and settled on the northeast corner of Indiana State Road 19 and the Cable Line Road, just a piece north of the intersection on the east side of the road. Later he became a preacher of Shaum's Church, now Olive Mennonite, 5 miles north of Wakarusa.

In the meantime, Harrison Miller's grandfather bought across the road to the west what is known as the Bert Cook farm. His son Charles Miller bought the Roscoe Eby farm after he was discharged from the Civil War. In 1898, Charles' son, Harrison Miller, bought 140 acres to the south of the intersection on the east side of the road.

Later Orville bought 46 acres of the Shaum farm where his house now stands. Harrison, Orville and Ivan, soon became road contractors and later Orville and his wife became owners and operators of one of the finest restaurants in Goshen.

Orville then acquired 60 acres of the Jacob Paulus farm about 1934. In 1954, he bought the Harrison Miller farm from his father's estate, then totaling 226 acres of owned farm land. All this while, the Millers were developing the farms, built a large barn, a modern dairy house and named the happy abode "The Cherry Crest Farm". At that time they were milking about 20 cows (Jersey's) and sold the milk to Grady's of Elkhart. From then on they bought registered Jersey cattle, and started showing in dairy shows.

They built an addition to the barn and soon had from 75 to 100 cattle in the herd, 35 to 40 cows in milk.

About then the herdsman's daughter joined 4-H, picked out a good calf, and won Grand Champion in the State 4-H Fair at Indianapolis for 3 consecutive years.

The 4th year the Dairyman of the Year was up for grabs and was handed to our own L. Orville Miller.

About 1955 they had to disperse the herd because of the disastrous fire which destroyed the dairy buildings and 18 head of young cattle and calves, as they could not get out of the barn.

Orville made a great contribution to the county through public service. His first job was chairman of the Rationing Board. He says he will remember the rationing stamps to his dying day. He was one of the Directors and President of the Elkhart Co. Dairy Association. He served on the Planning Commission and Board of Zoning Appeal. Also he served 7 years on the school reorganization committee, Indiana State Dairy Association 2 years, Indiana State Fair Board 8 years, Park and Recreation Board 7 years, President of Elkhart Co. Fair Board 10 years.

In 1965, the Palm Sunday Tornado destroyed all the other buildings and the Millers have built a beautiful home on the same spot for their retirement years.

Orville has many memories of his years of service and hopes as one result, Elkhart County will be a better place to live.

WAYNE AND MARJORIE MILLIKEN

When Wayne was age 13 (1941) his folks bought the old Marker farm (120 acres) 1 mile west of the Dutchland Church (on Indiana 331) and ½ mile south.

They did general farming, milking 15 cows and a half dozen

sows and gilts.

Wayne went to school to Madison Twp. High School, St. Joseph County Indiana; graduated in 1945, bought some calves of his own as he was getting started on the farm; he was drafted into service (2 years) and after discharge was married to Marjorie Haas, born 1928, of Bremen in 1954.

Wayne entered Farm Veterans training and leased 120 acres on shares south of Bremen from Lee (Tubby) Nunemaker. Later Tubby bought another 120 acres making 280 acres.

Wayne built up a large herd of Holsteins; helped a great deal by Leonard Hibschman of Syracuse who sold to Wayne a number of well-bred heifers one of them producing over 1000 lb. of butterfat as a 3 year old. Wayne also went big in hogs.

Finding a splendid opportunity in Cass Co. Michigan, Wayne and Marj bought 180 acres southwest of Edwardsburg, Michigan. Later sold his dairy herd at a dispersal sale in which a daughter of the big producer brought $1500, a good price in those years.

Two children were born in Indiana, Janet in '56 and Jim in '58. The family moved to Edwardsburg in the winter of 60-61 making numerous trips, on 240 acre Roselawn Farm, making 420 acres to farm. They bought 5 cows at the C.B. Smith consignment sale and with the increase and other purchases built up another dairy herd and then Jill was born in 1963. At that time they bought the Earl Schwinkendorf farm (180 acres).

In 1967 they held another dispersal sale and later bought the Roselawn Farm and later the Runkle Farm, 120 acres. A few acres with buildings were sold off leaving 710 acres owned and now under cultivation excepting 30 acres. They have 24 sows farrowing twice a year, which means 500 market hogs per year.

The homestead where they now live on Conrad Road has the old brick walls, the last stop in the underground escape route for slaves which ended in Cassopolis.

In 1972 they had 325 acres of soybeans averaging 43 bushels per acre, 160 acres of corn, averaging 130 bushels per acre, and 80 acres of wheat at 60 bushels per acre.

They are all staunch members of the Grace Bible Church of Mishawaka and surely the Good Lord has blessed their labors. For pastime Marj and the youngsters each have a horse. Wayne just enjoys watching. What a story!

THE MISHLERS

Solomon Mishler, born in Holmes County Ohio in 1799, was married to Magdalene Keim, and moved to LaGrange County, Indiana in 1842. They had 9 children and for our purpose including Valentine. Then later they bought the Hazen farm where the Swoveland School stood, 160 acres for $1000. In 1964 he sold the farm for $2500 and bought what is now known as the Everett Mishler farm (160 acres) and moved his family there.

Valentine went to Swoveland School and when he grew up he married Nancy Miller of west of Foraker and took over the farm.

All eleven of their children were born in the little log house which still stands there in the middle of the farm. It was the custom at that time to build the house and buildings in the middle of the farm not on a line where a future road was to be surveyed, so as to be close to the field work. Milton was one of his boys. In 1880 Valentine built the present farm home and a big bank barn. They practiced general farming. Then Milton's father got an arm in the shredder, and he took over the farm and married Lucy Moyer in 1899. He bought the farm in 1907 and built on a large straw shed. He took a fancy to buying, raising and fitting horses and would trail them to Ligonier and ship to eastern markets.

Everett was Milton's son, born in 1918, born on the homestead, attended Swoveland school, took Vo. Ag. in New Paris and graduated in 1936. They were in Jerseys, sheep and grain, and Everett showed in the 4-H calf, lamb and corn club. As an achievement winner he was sent to the National 4-H camp on the banks of the Potomac, visiting all the governmental bodies and he says that is where he got the bug to go into politics later on.

Everett became a partner after his Vo. Ag. course at New Paris and married Kathryn Stahly in 1939, lived together for 2 years, and then Milton and his wife bought 80 acres to the east and moved there and it is now Nina's home (Milton having passed on October 1965).

Everett was elected to the State Legislature in 1964. After the Palm Sunday blow, Everett was put on the emergency disaster aid committee by Gov. Branigan. That is when the big bank barn burned. It was replaced by Freeman Burkholders outfit by a pole barn. They increased the beef from 100 to 150, much to the satisfaction of Milton who then leaned back and said "good" when he died 3 weeks later at the age of 91.

He had driven the tractor up to the age of 90.

Rex, Everetts son, was married to a Nappanee girl and became a partner with his father, and the project of feeding beef cattle has changed to growing and breeding quality Holstein springer heifers, 100 to 150 in the new facilities, 450 tillable acres, 43 acres of woods, with 450 sugar maple trees. Everett is also making a name as County Assessor.

They are all Union Center Church of the Brethren, Everett having been on National General Board 9 years. It would be hard to find a person more honest, conscientious or dedicated than our friend Everett. His word is his bond!

CHARLES MOSER AND SONS

Gotlieb Moser, born of German and Swiss parents in 1868 came to Kansas with his folks at age 16 from Switzerland. Later the family moved to Illinois and bought 120 acres. Mary Danzer also came to Illinois at age 9 with her parents and in Illinois was married to Mr. Moser in 1888. Eleven children blessed the union, and for our purpose, including Charles.

Later in 1809 the family moved to Millersburg, Indiana and bought the Juday farm, where the original Juday School stood. General farming was followed and Gotlieb died in 1931, early in the depression following the 1929 stock market crash. These were the hard years with poor farm prices.

Charles was married to Beulah Emmitt in 1928, and moved into the farmstead across from the main Emmitt farm, but share rented also the main farm. They were started with 3 horses, 4 cows, 1 brood sow, which they bought from the Emmitts on time at 6% interest. By the increase the cows got up to 15 by 1943 and within 2 more years the 30 sows were producing 400 to 500 hogs farrowing 2 litters per year.

By this time the Emmitts bought another 90 acres on the road a mile south of the Emmitt farm, which Charles immediately looked over, tore out all the stalls and put in 50 steers (loose housing). Several years later Charles switched from share renting to a cash rent basis.

In 1949 the oldest son Eugene was married to Helen Rogers of Millersburg and rented the Claude Loy farm west of Burr Oak

Church.

Three years later, Bob, facing the draft, enlisted in the Air Corps, later met and married Donna Hagendorfer while in the service and when his service time was up moved onto the Juday farm until it was sold, then moved onto his uncle Ben's farm on Indiana 13. Bob later bought the George Berger farm.

In 1952, Charles bought the 2 Emmitt farms and the next year built a beautiful 3 bedroom home on his south farm. He then put in several miles of 6 inch tile for drainage and put up a 3000 bushel corn crib. When Jack came back from the service he took over the farms on a 1/3 basis and later married Deana Fought in 1957 when he was 23 years of age. Charles had remodeled the old Emmitt home and bought the 90 acres a mile to the south.

Then in 1958 he sold the dairy herd, put up a Harvestore silo for high moisture corn and a finishing hog barn for confinement feeding (34' x 120') and rented everything to Jack on a 50-50 basis. Later he built a nursery barn 20' x 144' on Jack's side. In 1967 he bought the 120 acre Denny farm on Indiana State Road 5. This increased his holdings to 400 acres.

In the meantime Jack moved up to Buttermilk Corners on Indiana 5 and Charles now rents to other renters and has bought a lovely lake home on Dallas Lake 5 miles east of Topeka where he moved in 1972.

Now the amazing part of this story is that after spending the last 40 years with his 3 boys in which he hopes they have learned something about farm management, the show case reveals:

Eugene owns 550 acres; farms 200 rented acres; raises 2500 hogs per year.

Robert owns 450 acres; farms 500 acres (rented); raises 2000 hogs per year.

Jack owns 540 acres; raises 2000 hogs per year.

MOYERS ON THE BAUGO

William Moyer lived on County Road 24, one mile west of Jimtown from 1858 to 1896. He had 80 acres and did general farming. There were 6 children and for our purpose, including William H. Moyer, born in 1868. At school age William H. went to Jimtown grade school, grew up, and married Saloma Shaum in 1892. Then they moved to Elkhart off of Prairie Street, there Vernon was born the next year. In 1894 they moved to the Dave Moyer farm the next place west of the homestead, and Merle was born there in 1895.

Following this, William H.'s father wanting to give them a chance, moved off the farm and went to Elkhart, and let them take over the old homestead. There Ruby was born, Carl followed a few years later and Glen the baby in 1910.

William H. encouraged the children, and they all went to Jimtown High School. Their cash income was from dairy cattle, loose hay sold to outfits in South Bend having large numbers of horses, and through the years they hauled hundreds of loads of hay.

Merle married Vera Elder a Baugo Township girl who lived on West Indiana Ave., and had gone to Jimtown High School, they lived and worked in Elkhart a number of years, Max was born there in 1917 and Anna in 1920.

When Merle's father bought the George Cook farm on County Road 1, they rented it on a 50-50 share rent basis and moved there. On October 4th, 1920 the house burned to the ground, and while they were planning to rebuild, Vera took the children with her to her folks, and Merle and the cattle went to stay with his folks. Then William H. bought another 80 acres with buildings to the north, which had been a part of the original great grandfather's farm, the house was on the north side of the road and the barn on the south, Merle and Vera moved there with their two children in 1921. They started up again, buying livestock and machinery, and that is when Merle became a calf buyer. He would buy up three day old calves and as soon as he would have as many as a half dozen, he would call the buyer from South Bend to come and pick them up. Merle would pay, like $5.00 a piece and turn them over for $8.00, very slim pickin', but in those days, a dollar was a dollar! Income from the hay also helped. Merle remembers one load of hay to South Bend that brought $42.00 in 1928, just before the stock market crash.

Frances was born in 1925, and then misfortune struck. Max, the oldest son was killed loading hay with a hay loader. The banks were closed over the country, by Executive Order, and how to take care of the burial expenses was a monumental problem. Dewey Lienhart of the Wakarusa Funeral Home, said if they could produce the cash, he would give them a bargain on a coffin, but where to get the cash?

They finally found it; Harve Bechtel in the Exchange Bank of Wakarusa loaned them the money.

No sooner had they gotten the loan repaid, than the house by the cemetery, in which they were living also burned down. So they went across the road where the barn was (south side) and made a little summer house type of building for living quarters, while Orin Weldy from Wakarusa built a new house. Lemual Brown was the apprentice and he built the cupboards. Very nice. By August the new house was ready to occupy, and it surely felt good to move in.

In 1942 Merle became a car inspector for the New York Central Railroad, 2 P.M. to 10 P.M. shift. He would have all forenoon to work on the farm and then go to work in Elkhart after lunch. But people would call Mrs. Moyer and ask her if she wanted to buy a calf, and she became the calf buyer. She not only bought calves, but she became a cattle dealer, recalling a man from Tennessee who bought a bull and 12 cows on one trip. Our Farm Veterans Class would meet Tuesday and Thursday nights, and at the coffee break some veteran was always reporting that they had sold a calf to Vera. She carried on this calf business for dairymen for over 7 years, and for this service alone they get in my book.

Gene graduated from Jimtown High in 1953, and his first job was billing clerk in the New York Central Office, later he secured a position as bookkeeper in the First National Bank of Elkhart, and was married to Cherel Kuehm, a daughter of Paul and Charlotte Kuehm, of Jones Street, Elkhart. They bought a trailer home, landed it on his folks farm, and after a year Cherel's father bought the 80 acres Walter BeMiller farm and they rented it on shares, later buying it. Now it is completely remodelled and Gene and Cherel have it made. Martin was born in 1957 and 2 years later, Karen. Now they are age 17 and 15 and in Northwood High School.

Real fast Gene has achieved a place of importance in the Banking and Agribusiness of the County, and with his mathematical mind no doubt is headed for the top.

At this time he is Manager of the Nappanee Branch of the First National Bank of Elkhart, Treasurer of the Elkhart County Agricultural Society, and a member of the Elkhart County Fair Board.

Gene is proud of their Centennial Farm family history of 5 generations, and says "I feel Rural Elkhart County is our whole life,

Cherel and I love it, both children love it, and we think you can't beat it, with any other place in the world". Amen, and Amen!

SHERMAN MYERS

Joseph Myers owned a quarter section of land on Elkhart County Road 50, ½ mile west of County Road 3. (south side in lane), in the early 19th Century, and did general farming. Also, he became interested in breeding Clydesdale horses and bought a Clyde stallion for stud and also a jack for breeding mules. Originally, $5.00 was the charge for stud service. He was married to Sarah Robinson and from her and 2 former wives had 7 children, including for our purpose, William, Sherman's father, John, the wagon-maker in Wakarusa, and Rufus Myers the auto dealer, where Jerry Myers ran the Chevy business for many years. He handled E.M.F. and Auburn and was quite a dealer in the area.

William was born there on the farm in 1861 and Sherman says "Dad's first job was with Dr. Aaron Sensenich as his hostler in Wakarusa, and more than that, when he was not busy currying the horses or driving the doctor on calls, he was filling bottles with capsules and pills, cream of tartar, sulphur, soda, etc.

He was there for a number of years until he was married to a Clay girl, a relative of Will Clay the druggist who was a brother-in-law to the doctor. They had 3 daughters after which his wife died, and he remarried to a widow. Anna Wisler Clouse, who had a son and a daughter. From the new union were born Nina, in 1897, and Sherman in 1899.

When Nina and Sherman were school age, they attended Locke Center school ½ mile to the east, and Nina died afflicted with the scarlet fever while in school at age 12. Sherman received his diploma from George Ellis, the County Supt. in 1914.

Sherman remembers that they had lots of hogs on the farm and the profits helped the farm income. After summer farm work was done, Sherman began to follow farm sales during Fall, Winter, and Spring months, with the lunch wagon which he had bought from Joe Robinson, and he would set up the 'chow wagon' right beside his competitor, Irvin Stump of Wakarusa, a close friend of the writer's family. The hamburgers sold for 5¢ and a bowl of delicious soup for 10¢.

121

In 1920 Sherman married Wilma Buss, and they moved in with the folks on the farm. Sam Whisler had started Sherman's father in the peppermint business, selling him loads of mint roots at $8. to $10. per wagon load, and showed him how to bury the roots. Sherman offered to build the still with his own hands and money and soon they were champions in yields. One year a tub of mint hay produced 40 pounds of oil. In 1926 the oil went up to $26.00 per pound. The usual price was from $2.50 to $8.00 per pound. The mint oil buyers would usually, contract with the mint growers to buy their crops at a guaranteed price. During the Depression some of the buyers went bankrupt.

In 1928 William and Sherman had a joint sale and Sherman and Wilma moved to Nappanee and he got a job with Coppes Cupboards and built sink tops. Incidentally he built the first "Linoleum" sink top in the country. These were the happy days! He had answered an ad in the paper placed by Elkhart Truth Radio station WJAK for musicians for their program. He tried out, was put on and for some years he became known as Nappanee's singing Guitarist. Also he entertained at the Chicago World's Fair. He worked for Coppes for 18 years and had built a beautiful home at 608 West Walnut, and in 1946 he built a shop in the rear of Tan Tile, and established his own repair shop in the building and sold and repaired lawn mowers by the hundreds. Wilma died in 1964, and Sherman retired in 1970, and later was remarried to Nora Lehman Sawyer. Sherman says all my life my motto has been "Only the best is good enough" BLESS THEM! Nora is my baby sister, we buried her Saturday.

THE NAPPANEE MILLING CO.

The mill was built in 1886 by a group of people which soon got into financial difficulties at the turn of the century, and sparked by Daniel and Harold Zook, and a Mr. Coppes, the Coppes, Mutschler and Zook outfit took over the assets and the liabilities of the mill. According to Firm Troup, who was the railroad freight agent of the B. & O. up until 1906. Harold Zook and his father Daniel ran the mill for some years.

Mr. Troup took a job in 1906 with the conglomerate as a bookkeeper, and he remembers that the mill would ship wheat in and ship flour out by the carload, and under the "Milling in Transit" clause would receive a rebate of around $25.00 per carload on all carload shipments.

About that time, Harvey Miller started at the mill at the age of 17 as an office boy at $12.00 per week. He would take in the wheat the farmers would bring in to sell, like at $1.00 per bushel, and the farmer would take a sack of "Peerless" flour and receive a check for the balance due. Or he might choose to take a storage receipt for the value of the load of wheat, and then pick up sacks of flour as the family needed it, "against the account".

He would also pay a farmer for a load of corn. Sometimes a farmer would come to town with a load of corn and oats for grinding, and Harvey would charge him like 10¢ per cwt.

Harvey was drafted into the Army in World War II, in the year 1942, was in training 4 years and on his return, became a mill hand. In 1950 Harvey was made mill manager, and at that time they built an addition, and equipped the building to grind corn meal and shipped it all over the country. At that time the flour business was being dominated by the big National Milling Companies, and the mill had to make a decision, either to spend a fortune to re-steel the mill and in fact just about rebuild the whole plant, or to end the FLOUR ERA, and this they did.

Later Harvey was asked to come into the new NAPIANA plant farther east on the B. & O. in Nappanee, as purchasing Agent and he decided to accept the offer in 1962.

Later, in 1968, both the Nappanee Milling Co., and Napiana wholesale plant were sold to SUPERSWEET, a large feed outfit, with headquarters in Minneapolis, Minnesota, and with 17 huge branch plants in the midwest. Harvey was made plant manager at the wholesale mill, and Tom Mattern remains manager of the retail mill.

The Supersweet dealers of the county form a share in the sponsorship of the Annual Kick-off dinner held at Harry Eby's Pines each November.

ELMER NEFF FAMILY — LaGrange

Mahlon Neff was married to Mary Kauffman, and they rented 80 acres on 450 West and did general farming. They had 7 children, and for our purpose, including Elmer Neff, born 1921. The children had some sheep and calves of their own. Later he bought 40 acres to the south. He was also a carpenter and a contractor.

Elmer attended Green country school and afterward worked for his father until he was 21, then was drafted into World War II, and taking alternate service, spent 3½ years on a dairy farm at Sun Prairie, Wisconsin with 40 Holstein milkers. After discharge, rented a farm with his brother Vernon from Cleo Lambright, north of Plato, had a dairy herd there for a few years, then went back with his father and later married a neighbor girl, Martha Lou Atwater, and they settled down on the farm north of the father in 1952.

The next year Craig was born, and 2 years later Dianne came, and then they bought the present farm in 1955 on U.S. 20, and later added 60 acres to the east, and 91 acres to the north, and at that time they were raising 10,000 pullets for Lambright's. Ronda Sue came in 1963, and Martha Lou who has been a nurse's aid for 24 years at the LaGrange hospital had to drop out a few years. Also she has driven a school bus for 6 years for money to help with the expansion.

They went into beef cattle, at first, like 20 steers. Then they started putting up Harvestore silos, and increased the cattle.

Now they own 412 acres, rent another 100, and have 6 blue silos, 2 for haylage, 2 for shelled corn, and 2 for silage, and feed up to 1,000 beef per year. All 3 children were 4-Hers. In 1974 they incorporated with the 2 older children. They all say, "There's lots of people in the world, and we have to help feed them all. How True!

THE EMERSON NEFFS

Henry Neff, who was the son of Abraham and Lydia Neff, who had bought a farm on County Road 127 from Oliver Dalrymple, a homesteader, was born in 1863 (on what is now the Mahlon Martin farm, formerly known as the John O. Smith farm).

At age 18 he married Mary Lou Nettie Cripe (1881) and they bought 40 acres to the south, now known as the Emerson or Robert Neff farm.

By the turn of the century Henry was taking his boys with him and going to the stock yards in Chicago to buy beef cattle, ship them to New Paris, and then drive them on foot to the farm to feed.

They also bought a farm to the east, where Bill Weybright lived when he died (Elsie still lives there) Raleigh was born on that farm, and at school age went to the Gilbert school to the south, graduated from New Paris High in 1905, attended Manchester College a year, taught a year in a local school, and then married Amanda Deeter, a Milford girl, and moved in with his folks and farmed with them.

Raleigh was very religious, and much interested in the Free Ministry of the Church of the Brethren, was ordained, and served there 30 years.

Emerson the first child came in 1909 and Mary, 5 years later in 1914.

As the Henry Neffs fed steers, so Raleigh did likewise. So when Emerson got into the harness, he went for beef too, along with all the rest of the farming.

The farmer's depression of 1922 and 23 was not so bad, but after the stock crash of 1929, say about 1932, when hogs brought 2½¢ per pound and corn was 10¢ per bushel, it was pretty tough. Corn was so cheap they even burned it for firewood to fry the sow belly.

Emerson met a Millersburg girl in 1933, Miss Alice Roach, and the next year they were tied up. The Roach children were in Lita's old Juday school about 1912 on the corner of Ben Moser's farm.

They took over the old homestead, lived elsewhere a while and moved on the spread in 1937. Three children came during the early years, Eleanor, Shirley and Robert, and Nancy, Richard and Peggy were born after they moved on the old farm. Later in 1947 Emerson and Alice bought the old farm from his dad.

By this time Robert was at 4-H age, and was in several projects, chiefly Angus Beef. He meant business, right off, and took the Purdue Short Course, had a great experience in Belle Glade Florida, where he was in charge of a Migrant Children's camp for the Church of the Brethren's Volunteer Service.

On discharge, he took the Lincoln Welding training course, and now does most all of his repair work on machines. He has gained a reputation in the community as a welder.

In 1963 he was married to Rita Whiteneck from Virden, Illinois, whom he met at a Church of the Brethren Youth Retreat at Wabash.

Then a shift took place; Emerson and Alice bought a mobile home set it in a lovely spot in the trees to the south a couple hundred rods, and have made a lovely home of it, allowing the young couple to move into the old homestead, which in a few years will be dubbed a CENTENNIAL FARM.

Now Bob and Rita have Ruth Ellen, 6, and Randy Lee, 2, and they bought the 175 acres, and rent 210 acres more, farming 375 acres.

Raleigh passed away in 1969, Emerson is retired and Bob has become quite a person in the community; into everything, a C.R.O.P. worker for years, Jackson Twp. Crop Chairman for Uncle Elmer.

THE NEFFS FAIRLAWN

Abraham Neff came from near Roanoke, Virginia, and bought a quarter section of land, 1 mile north of the old Gilbert School on U.S. Road 6 and on both sides of the Road 127, being what is now the John Smith farm and what is being farmed at present by Mahlon Martin.

Then he married Lydia Whitehead and 5 children were born and for our purpose, including Henry Melvin Neff the 4th child, September 30, 1863, during the Civil War.

They kept on clearing the farm, burning even the beautiful large logs, as there was no other way. Of course some of the logs were used for the log cabin and timbers for the frame of the barn later on. Henry was married by 1881 to Mary Lou Nettie Cripe and they bought 40 acres of the farm to the south, now known as the Emerson Neff farm, built a house and barn and moved there. Not counting a child which died in infancy, three boys were born to carry on, one Raleigh who became an ordained minister in the Church of the Brethren and for our purpose Abe Neff, born September 14, 1895 and George G. Neff born August 23, 1903.

By the turn of the century, Henry was going to Chicago with his boy Abe to buy feeder cattle at the stockyards on Hastings Street. He would go with an open mind, decide when he saw the pens, buy a carload, ship them to New Paris and drive them on foot 4 miles to feed. Usually steers were the choice. This went on for ten years and then Henry kept watching Fairlawn Farm near Baintertown, a beautiful spread of 306 acres, owned by Jack Latta's mother Mrs. James Latta. A mammoth brick home with servants quarters, riding and stable horses in the huge barn, so on September 11, 1911, he bought the dream and moved there the following March. Raleigh was married and stayed on the old place. The beautiful home was accidentally burned following a belling and had to be rebuilt.

By the time George finished at North Manchester College they were buying more land doing a complete remodelling of the barn to accommodate more feeders. That was in 1927.

Henry died in 1938 and Abe and George ended up owning all of Fairlawn, 465 acres.

By the time Phil and Rene were ready for 4-H, Abe and George sponsored contributions for a beef calf weighing scales which was eventually donated to the fairground.

In 1963 they built a pole barn and feeding lot for beef and soon thereafter there was a corporation formed by the two brothers and their sons, 4 people, and Abe and George retired and built 2 beautiful homes on Indiana 15 at Fairlawn.

Abe was a director of the Farm Bureau Credit Union for 30 years and still is a member of the committee. He is also a director of Martins Feed Mills at New Paris.

George has been into everything and has made a big success of every assignment. He has been a member of, a committee member, a director or officer of 36 groups, since 1939. Suffice it to say he has sat in committees thousands of times for thousands of hours and has served faithfully, to mention especially, Director and Treasurer of Goshen General Hospital since 1962 and member of the Elkhart County Council since 1946 and President of the same since 1962. George and Mildred are Mr. and Mrs. Farm Bureau to many.

We could write a book on the Neff family alone.

HAROLD NETTROUR

Harold's father, Wilbur Nettrour, rented farms west of Bremen and Harold went to Bremen to school until they bought a farm on Riley Road ½ mile west of State 331, then he went to Madison Twp School. They went into Holsteins, selling milk to the Goshen Condensery.

Harold graduated in 1947 and was drafted into the army in 1951, discharged in 1953, and then married Fern Seese, who lived west further on Riley Road. Then they rented the Lulu Wine farm (150 acres) on Miami Road just north of the B & O, north of U.S. 6. They started in at once building a Holstein dairy herd. They had room for 20 stanchions and the number of animals climbed from that number to 35 and then 50.

Harold was in the Farm Veterans Program with Uncle Elmer for 3 years, and the main topic of conversation on the bi-weekly farm calls was the NEW FARM ACCOUNT BOOK, put out by Purdue. The house caught on fire 3 times, one time bad enough to require a trailer home for 6 months for temporary shelter. But when the barn burned it burned to the ground. Then they built a pole type barn (shed type) with a milking parlor, and enlarged the herd.

Cheryl was born in 1958, and after Harold finished our Farm School, Dean came in 1962, and Craig in 1963. Then in 1962 they bought the Wine farm and ten years later he bought another 80 acres, and put up a large silo with automatic feeder. Things have gone good with them.

Harold is not a joiner, but has cooperated with folks, especially the Bremen F.F.A., helping them with field trips and demonstrations, and in turn, the Chapter presented him with a plaque "Honorary Chapter" award. Now they own 230 acres and rent 135, and farm a total of 425, with a herd of 85, milking 40. All the children are in 4-H. Cheryl won grand champion in Handicraft. Harold says "Look on the bright side".

THE NEWMAN HOLSTEIN FARM

Charles W. Newman, whose father farmed before him and died of pneumonia during the Civil War, was born in 1854 near Tiffin and came to Francesville, Indiana and later to Lake Cicott.

They moved to Culver in 1898, and bought a quarter section of land on what is now Upas Road south of 20th Road. They had four boys, Claude, 1883, John, 1885, Dale, 1890 and Dick, 1893. His wife was Mary E. Rickenbaugh. They all took to farming.

Charles and his sons secured the contract to furnish milk to the Culver Military Academy. The academy sold them all 20 of their cows to put them into the dairy business. They were all grade cows. This was in 1905. Two years later they built a 35 stanchion barn and the milking was done by hand. Then they up and bought their first Registered Holstein cow. She came from Peter Hammes at Monterey, Indiana. The herd kept increasing and the Culver boys got lots of milk.

128

John was married to Lovina May Warmbrod in 1913 and soon thereafter took over the farm. The herd of dairy cows was divided at that time into three farm herds and the same sires were used for all three farms, and between themselves they kept on furnishing milk to the Academy; in fact this went on until 1957.

In 1920 John helped start the first cow-testing association in the county. Then in 1924 they did official testing in the herd, and began to show animals at the State Fair. That year one cow made over 800 pounds of butterfat in 365 days.

John was awarded the Master Farmer designation in 1926 by the Prairie Farmer Farm Paper and also he helped organize the Marshall County Farm Bureau and was president of the group for 10 years in the early part of the program.

Charles G. and Jesse, John's sons, joined the 4-H dairy club in 1928 and showed senior calves. Charles W. Newman, Sr. had bought ten calves for the club in Wisconsin and the boys drew for their calves from the "hat."

In 1932 John showed 4 paternal sisters at the Indiana State Fair, and won 1st prize "Open Class", "Get of Sire" as well as a first prize for "Dairyherd." About this time John became president of the State Holstein Association as well as the State Dairy Association.

In 1940 the Newmans started breeding their herds artificially. Charles G. doing the inseminating and requests from neighboring herds soon put them in the business; it being the first artificial breeding service in Indiana. At the peak they bred 8,000 cows in one year, and shipped semen all over the United States. Two of the most famous bulls used were Posch Ormsby Fobes Eden, the sire of Minnow Creek Eden Delight, and Maytag Ormsby Fobes Dictator, the sire of many famous offspring including "WIMPY", who was the All-American Holstein cow for 3 years straight.

The Newmans have truly contributed much to Michiana Agriculture, and for that matter, statewise, and nationally, too. Charles W. died in 1946, and then John Newman & Sons continued operations until John died in 1969. Now his sons are carrying on as the Newman Holstein Farm, farming over 700 acres, with a herd of registered Holsteins (200) and milking 90 cows. "Wimpy" is gone but will never be forgotten. Bless her memory! Ralph, J. Allen and Jesse say, "The good cow pays the bills".

JOHN NUNEMAKER

John Nunemaker married Doris Wenger, daughter of Charles Wenger, August 28, 1948 and settled down on Carl's farm (the father) on County Road 40. They farmed there 25 years, general farming, milking about 30 Holsteins and as many as 2000 layers.

In the meantime, they bought 3 places (200 acres). The boys kept on farming and including the 150 (Carl's old farm) they farm 200 acres of John's and rent 80 more totaling 430 acres farmed.

About 1960 John set up a large fertilizer plant catacornered across from the old Bowser country school on County Roads 40 and 15.

John bought a compensator liquid feed from Allied Chemical these many years and now mix their own liquid feed and fertilizers, also W.R. Grace, and Royster bulk fertilizer.

John and Doris have 5 children: Dale 1950, Sandra 1953, Robert 1955, Bryan 1959, Connie 1961. Dale lives on the old Snider brothers farm with the round barn (80 acres) on County Road 40. All have gone or will go to Bethany Christian High School at Waterford. They are all members of the Holdeman Mennonite Church west of Wakarusa.

They are co-sponsors of the annual C.R.O.P. kickoff dinner at Harry Eby's. John has really been a friend of C.R.O.P.

At the plant, besides John, there are 4 full time employees and part time workers.

People ask John why he has his fathers name on his mail box and he answers it has been good to be in a community where our people have been established and favorably known for so many years.

W.W. OESCH AND ELVA

Bill graduated from Goshen College in 1910 and married a school teacher from Nappanee, Elva Garber, and they bought 101 acres on Indiana State Road 15 and named it "The Spring Valley Farm." They specialized in truck farming and set up a wayside market roadside stand laden with fruit and vegetables. They rented a stand in the South Bend Farmer's Market and hauled the produce in a covered truck. This continued 31 years until 1948.

He served on the A.A.A. County Committee as a member for 20 years and was chairman for 14 years. He was followed by Clint

Zollinger, Ezra Lovejoy, from Vistula, and James Dunmire, of Jimtown, were on his committee. He also served 40 years on the Federal Land Bank Board, locally, with M.M. Bassett 1917 to 1957. Elva served as Social and Education leader for the Farm Bureau for many years.

Alice was born in 1911, Hubert in 1915, Harold in 1918, and Rosemary in 1921.

He started to work with the Farmer's Exchange in 1946 and a few years later became associate editor. He knew most of the farmers in the county and his many contacts were a great help in his work.

He visited many farms where exceptional stories and pictures could be secured and would be on the job with every group where exhibits or demonstrations would be taking place.

He served the Farmer's Exchange for 24 years until 1970, continued to go to Florida in the winter and then in 1972 sold his home on Indiana State Road 15, and now Bill and Elva have a nice apartment at Greencroft Retirement Home. They eat breakfast and supper in the apartment and take noon dinners in the dining room with about 25 other residents, luncheon charge $1.50.

Alice's oldest son, Dr. Allen Kelly at the Oklahoma State University, Stillwater, was voted the professor of the year in 1973, and Hubert's son, Gary is studying drama in England, sent there by Ohio State University. There are now 12 teachers in the family, children and grandchildren. What a story!

ROY W. PARKER AND SONS

Roy was born 3 miles south east of North Webster on an 80 acre farm in 1892. Then there was no hybrid seed corn, but open pollinated corn, chiefly Reed's yellow dent and Boone county white, yellow corn for yellow corn meal and white for white corn meal. At the turn of the century he was selecting best ears from the fields and giving them or selling them to his neighbors for seed, after drying them under roof using a stove and wire hangers. Roy had 6 children but for our purpose, the boys were born there James in 1923 and Dale in 1925.

Roy read about Hybrid seed and wrote to Purdue for information and started in the 1930's with 2 fields of Hybrid corn. Then he bought 140 acres 1½ miles south east of Cromwell and moved his family there in March, 1936, and pushed Hybrids. Then the next year, 1937, he bought an onion storage building in Kimmell and equipped it as a processing plant and drier.

In those days Chet Troyer of LaFontaine and Roy W. Parker were the only 2 dealers producing hybrid seed corn in Indiana. Ben Leonard of the Leonard Hardware Store in Wakarusa was one of their first dealers. At first the price per bushel was $7.00. Very quickly the news spread that hybrid seed corn was raising the yield tremendously, and some farmers wanted to try it. They would drive to Kimmell for miles and talk for hours before buying some seed. James finished Cromwell High in 1941 and was married in 1942. Dale finished in 1943 and in the summer went into the U.S. Service for 2 years. The drier by the viaduct was then built, using fuel oil. When he returned in 1947 he was married and they enlarged the drier. In the meantime they were buying other farms, now totaling over 1000 acres, about 400 acres being used for hybrids.

Single Cross produces only from 5 to 20 bushels per acre, and because of other factors the prices range from $16.00 to $30 per bushel for flats. James has 3 children, 2 of them married; Dale has 2 children, both married. They incorporated in 1964, other Parkers have stock but Roy, James, and Dale push the business.

James is a Director in the Cromwell Bank, and Dale is wrapped up in Hybrids, has his own plane hanger in Kendallville and flies all over the country to push hybrids. Dale's wife keeps the records. Roy died January 13, 1974.

ELLSWORTH PETERSEN — Farmer, Statesman

Henry Petersen was born in 1887 and married Ruth Rowe in 1912, and rented a place on State Road 5, north of Ligonier.

Later he bought the Elmer C. Yoder farm, 1 mile south of Burr Oak, but died before he got to move there. But his family then moved there, and it was not long until Ellsworth took over, and according to Mr. Tom Hite a friend and neighbor to the north of Ellsworth's present spread, the young lad really took over real well.

Ellsworth was born in 1914, Graduated from Ligonier High School in 1933. He was "father" to the family for many years.

In 1939 he married Kathryn Yoder, daughter of Erman and Gladys Yoder of Topeka, lived with his mother on the farm a year, and then bought the old Hostetler farm, straight north of the Perry School.

They went into Dairying and feeder cattle during those years.

Four children were born, Gary in 1940, Karen in 1941, Linda in 1945, and Barbara in 1947. Additional land was bought, the 80 acre Roy Slabaugh farm, and the 150 acre Ollie Larimer farm.

Ellsworth was interested in Public Service early in life and became Trustee for two terms, served on the Noble County Council for 6 years and gave it everything. On the death of Kathryn's father in Topeka, they acquired the insurance business, and work it out of their farm home. Kathryn's desk is always loaded.

Gary took Vo. Ag. in Ligonier High, and all of the four went through many years of 4-H. Karen had Grand Champion Steer one year, Gary had Reserve, one year, and the others won many blue ribbons.

In 1959 Ellsworth was elected to the Indiana State Legislature, and began serving in 1960, and outside of a 2 year stretch, has served continuously since that time.

He is busy on the House Committees, and so they lessened up on the cattle business and Gary has taken over, a father-son arrangement.

Ellsworth is now on the State Budget Committee and that takes more of his time.

Now, Gary is married to Nancy Carper of Ligonier, they live east of the spread, and have 2 children, Carla, age 9, and Bradley age 6; Karen is married to Tom Hull, from town, they live there, and have the "Emergency Radio Service", and have 3 children, Brian, age 11, John, age 9, and Mark, age 6; Linda is married to Rick DeBolt from town, and he is a payer for Rieth-Riley, and they have one youngster, Stan, age 9; and Barbara is a teacher in Lebanon, Indiana, and her son is about ready for school.

Pete says "God has been good to us. My service to Community, area, and State makes me feel I can do something in turn for others".

BILL PHILLIPS AND SON — Irrigation Sales

William Phillips was the son of John and Dora Phillips and came with his parents to Elkhart County from Illinois, having seen the first light of day in 1904, first in York township, then they landed on the Knapp farm. (Dale Thwaits lives there now). V.V. Clark (Virgil)

133

was the administrator of the estate, who rented them the farm on shares, 50-50. They did grain farming, with some cattle and other livestock.

Then in 1930, right in the depression he married Miss Frances Brant of Jefferson township. The going was tough the first years and Frances remembers that in 1934 the sand was so dry, Bill sat down one day and cried as the corn burned up. No doubt Bill got his first inspiration for irrigation from these trying days. Charles, now the President of the outfit, was born there in 1936.

They became members of the Vistula Grange and became very active through the years. The Grange has from the very beginning been a farm organization centered around Farm Family and Religious Life and that fellowship was what Bill and Frances needed right then.

In 1942 they bought the Bickel farm on Road 8 northwest of Bristol (140 acres) and moved there, switched from Jerseys to Holsteins, and after that (1946) they set up an irrigation system for potatoes and tomatoes on this farm, and were so impressed with the results, they became agents for irrigation supplies for a Detroit firm.

At first irrigation was used mostly on special crops, but in the middle fifties the crop farmers took hold, and since that time, the interest has increased by leaps and bounds.

At school age, Charles went to Bristol to school, and at age 10 got into 4-H with Pete Rink the county Beef Calf Club Leader. He completed 11 years, with 54 project years, and graduated from Bristol High in 1954.

The next year he took over the farm (140 acres) as Bill was giving his full time by now to the irrigation business, setting up operations across the road on the river on Howard Ferm's broiler set-up.

Then in 1963 Charles became a partner with his father as The Phillips & Son Irrigation Sales. The Operation is on County Road 8, 2¼ miles west of Bristol, right on the north bank of the St. Joe river. By the early seventies, irrigation sales went sky high, and the pressure was heavy for Bill. He passed on last year having given his life in service for others. Now Charles works until late at night trying to complete projects and get them in operation in order to try to save the crop. His calls take him as far as Indianapolis. The projects this year involve 2300 acres of crops. A sister of Charles, Barbara is the office secretary, and Frances is still back of it all. Another sister Norma and her husband Dale Yoder have 30 acres of potatoes under irrigation.

Charles is doing a tremendous thing in irrigation and it is impossible to measure his splendid CONTRIBUTION TO MICHIANA AGRICULTURE. Charles attributes most of his success to the ground work so well laid by his parents, Bill and Frances. Bless them!!!

PAUL PHILLIPS AND RACHEL

John Phillips, son of Peter Phillips, came to Elkhart County in 1836, cleared some land and had 7 children, including for our purpose, Peter, born in 1840. Peter was on the school advisory Board, Township Trustee, and a Road Supervisor. His son Frank was born in 1868, grew up and bought the farm on Road 34, two miles east of the present fairground, 80 acres. He had his schooling at Brown country school a mile to the east. Paul was born there in 1908, and went to the same school, attended Goshen College Academy 1 year, Millersburg High, 1 year, and then graduated from Goshen High School in 1925.

About that time his father bought another 60 acres, across from Leonard Yoder, now Crazy Corners, and Paul worked with his father and alternately went to North Manchester, graduating in 1931. The times were so hard, that at times they had to burn corn in the house furnace to keep warm in the winter.

He was married to Rachel Hartsough of Millersburg, and the first year they settled down on the 60 acres. Hartsoughs gave them 12 layers, and they had eggs the next morning for breakfast. Facing the summer harvest he bought a John Deere Combine against the advice of everybody, in 1937 and then in 1939 Janet was born. That same year they bought the Michael farm of 120 acres, where Fernlee Runchey now lives, on County Road 19 south of Road 36. They borrowed the entire purchase price from F.S.A. (Which is now F.H.A.) at $100. per acre and Roy Rensberger said "you poor young fellow". The only good thing about it was that the interest was only 3%. Hard times or not, Paul and Rachel started to tithe, put their first heifer in the Heifer Project, and have never missed a year since. Three children born there on that farm, were, Eugene 1942; John, 1943; and Joseph in 1945. In early 1946 (Feb), Paul organized a Committee to sponsor the big Relief sale at the sale barn, thousands of people attended, and from the proceeds, exported 3 carloads of oatmeal, bought from Quaker Oats, all this for Refugees from the war. Later that same year they bought the 140 acre Bill Chiddester farm on County Road 38 east of Rock Run church, moved there and later sold the Michael farm. For six years he was a director of the Bethany Theological Seminary in Chicago. For a while they went into O.I.C. hogs, bred some of the gilts from a 14 litter of pigs and would feed out from 100 to 200 porkers a year. For several years he was President of Mens Work in the Northern District for the Church of the Brethren, sending many shipments abroad.

Betty was born in 1950, and Barbara in 1952, and then they got out of hogs, and switched to Hay and Grain, storing as many as 13,000 bales of baled hay in the barn and some outside under tarps.

About this time they developed quite a business in small grain Certified Seed, Oats, Barley, Wheat, and Soybeans.

In 1950 the C.R.O.P. program was launched, and Paul was right in the front ranks from the beginning. He was County Chairman for one year, and then became a canvasser in Clinton township, canvassing as many as 9 square miles in one fall. He has been Clinton township chairman several times. Now they are one of the Sponsors for the big "Kick-Off dinner in the Fall at Harry Eby's.

They have also been signers for 2 foreign Refugee families.

Frank died in 1950 and Paul's mother in 1953, then Paul bought the old home farm, and has farmed it ever since.

In 1959, Rachel happened to be near a grain drier, when it blew up and was badly injured. The damages insurance is what has paid for the beautiful new brick home which replaced the old house, in very bad repair. It took 5 years to settle the claim.

Now to bring you up to date; Janet is married to Marlin Chupp, delivers mobile homes for Jay-Co; Eugene married Janet Wiles of Wabash, and is in the ready-mix business; John is a practicing Physician in Missouri; Joseph married Anita English, in I.U. Medical School; Betty is married to Keith Metzger, who teaches at North Manchester, and Barbara is still home.

All these children went through high school, 5 attended college, three graduating.

Rachel is supervisor at Rosalind Long's Credit Bureau, where she has been now for years. Paul and Rachel have had about every job in the Rock Run Church of the Brethren, and most of the family are or have been members there.

Paul and Rachel say "The Good Lord has always been good to them, so they have always been tithers". Long Live Paul and Rachel!

PIKE LUMBER CO., INC. — Fulton County

Howard Utter was born 1909 in Possom Hollow School District 5 miles northwest of Akron, son of Oliver Utter. He attended Possom Hollow one room school and attended Akron High School. When he was 14 years old his father died and when he was a Junior in Akron High School he went to Canada to work in the lumber camps, Ontario and Quebec. There he learned to love the forest and logging. He returned to Akron in 1933 during the depression and found a job with the D.A. Pike Lumber Co., Mr. Pike and his daughter, Helen, who was an expert in the woods, being working partners together.

Howard and Helen were married in 1934. They had ideas of their own and branched out in a separate division. Early they recognized the necessity of providing raw materials for their saw mills if they were to assure permanency in the business they loved. Immediately they launched into a tree farming business, conservatively harvesting old growth timber and planting seedlings. This they did on their own woodlands and also encouraged other woodland owners to do the same.

In 1950 Mr. and Mrs. Pike were killed in an automobile accident and Helen donated the land for the beautiful park in the east end of town in the name of D.A. and Eva Pike with a suitable marker in 1955.

The big emphasis in Pike's tree farming program took place when Dean Baker became head of Pike's Timber Department as a Vice President in 1967 and with the capable assistance of Channing Utter, their son, as plant manager and vice-president. Up until 1950, Pike furnished 80% of farm lumber in the area. At that time carpenters went to pine, fir, and hemlock, because it was easier to handle, and later pole barns came in because of economy. But Pike Lumber Co. works primarily with hardwood timber sold to and used by customers they have had for 50 years. Always, northern Indiana has been the world center for the world's most valuable hardwood veneers. Howard and Helen have 3 children Kay, Channing, and Lynne. Howard is not a joiner but his life is in the forest and the mill. He says, "People are our most important resource, meaning co-workers." He is a frontiersman in today's battle to replenish our timber, our only remaining natural resource.

ELTON POWELL — Clydesdales

Elton Powell bought the 97 acres at the Penn Central RR on U.S. 131 west and south of White Pigeon and having bred horses since 1956, he started anew with Clydesdales and breeds, trains, and sells horses.

This year he exhibited 9 animals at the Centreville Fair. He says a good Clydesdale sells for $800 to $1000 or $2000 for a matched team.

He built his own head harness for a 4-horse hitch.

Elton was raised on the farm west of Constantine and has been with horses all his life. He is in on the money every year with seconds firsts and grand champions at the Centreville Michigan Fair. Elton says he remembers missing only 2 Centreville Fairs all his life, one year with a hurt foot and one summer when he was in the Army.

The Clydesdales are beautiful horses with white feathered legs. Elton has his own stallion. The tandem team of 4 horses hitched onto a decorated wagon is one of the judging classes at Centreville. Elton does much of his harness sewing by hand with the awl. He is still employed by the Power Company to get additional funds to develop a larger operation.

He has great dreams and has a host of horseman friends who hope to see his dreams come true.

Funny thing, horsemen more than any other kind of farmers, do not generate jealousy in their competition, probably because ingrained in their heart and soul, is the feeling, let the best horse win, and further, since the sire and dam place their stamp on the progeny, a grand champion is not so much what his master made him, but what his sire and dam made him.

NORVAL POYSER

Dr. Harley Poyser was a veterinarian in Middlebury. His wife, Norvals mother, died and he felt he should give him to his sister to rear, Mrs. Curtis Blood, 1918. A year later Mr. Blood bought the 80 acre Mather farm on County Road 14, one-half mile west of County Road 8 (when Norval was 1 year old).

Curtis did general farming and taught Norval early to work and do chores. Norval went to Middlebury to school and graduated from High School. He was in Vocational Agriculture, hogs as a project, and was state secretary of F.F.A. which his Vo. Ag. instructor, A.T. Marvel had originated through Z.M. Smith, State Director of Agriculture.

In 1939, Curtis and Norval bought the 40 acres to the west. At that time they had 15 sows and were marketing several hundred hogs per year. He had bought his first registered gilt when he was 10 years old from a breeder south of Rochester at a sale, Levi Moore.

In 1944 Curtis died and in his will left the estate to Norval.

He was then married to Jean Dings, a Middlebury girl. They continued in breeding Chester Whites and after Bill Weybright died they were the only Chester White breeders in the county. They had been selling some registered gilts to some Vo. Ag. and 4-H members through the years.

In 1954 they bought the Vernon Krider 120 acres to the west. Later 40 more acres were acquired south of the home place.

Their religion is Lutheran and their machinery is International. His hobby is woodworking and he has made or refinished nearly all their furniture. When they were in Guernseys, he was on the board of the Middlebury Cooperative Creamery and president for 10 years, a director of the Elkhart County Farm Bureau Co-Op. He was a supervisor of Soil and Water Conservation and has been a director of the Middlebury State Bank for 20 years.

Norval opposes the existing philosophy of trying to GO BIG, but instead agrees with A.T. Marvel that you should take better care of what you have.

RUSSELL PRICE — Seedsman

In 1952 the Syler & Syler Elevator burned to the ground and a seed house building was constructed for the use of two of the former employees John Robinson and Charles Gerkey who incorporated to start a new business.

In 1954 Russell Price came into the firm somewhat as a plant manager, looking after the cleaning of the various kinds of seed and grain. After 6 months Russell bought some stock in the corporation.

The business increased gradually and in 1957 the name was changed to Robinson and Price as Mr. Gerkey left the business.

One of the reasons the firm is so widely known is that they carry a complete line of corn, small grain and grass seed from crowned vetch to Reeds canary grass.

By 1968 John's health left something to be desired and he sold his stock to Russell and retired. He passed away in 1970. Now Russell and his wife (Katherine Meese Price) own the business.

Russell says his best slogan of success has been to tell the exact truth on every occasion, then it saves the trouble of trying to remember what you said yesterday. Russell and Katherine are devoted members of St. John's Lutheran Church in Nappanee.

Russell is not a joiner, they have no children and he and Katherine devote their whole lives to the seed business or anything connected with Agriculture. He has the know-how and the dedication to the seed business, one reason it is about the number one seed outfit in Central U.S.

ERNEST PUESCHEL

Ernest was brought up on a farm in Allegan County near Hopkins (80 acres) featuring general farming and a dairy of about 20 grade cattle. He was born November 23, 1910.

He went to District No. 4 school 2 miles north of Hopkins. He moved to Sturgis, Michigan in 1936 and worked for the Kirch Co. 8 years and married Margaret Schroeder of Sturgis.

In 1944 he bought the Fred Yunker farm west of Sturgis on the river road. He kept on working at the plant 2 more years and started buying heifer calves and when he quit and went to farming he had 20 cows and bred heifers and they gave him his start in the dairy business. He bought the Frank Waite farm on the County Road 139 north of Rd. 140, in 1953, where he added land and now owns 1500 acres. Herb Maust of the Farm Center in Wakarusa built the huge milking parlor. They set up 324 free stalls. The milk tank is a picture to see. He now has 6 silos filled about half with corn and half with grass.

Marilyn came in 1938 (later married to Larry Kelly), David in 1940, John in 1946, Linda (now in Detroit) and Karen later in 1961.

The boys showed Holsteins in Centreville Fair and now married David, John, and Marilyn and her husband, together with Dad make

4-way partnership.

They usually have 500 acres of corn, 500 acres of soybeans, and 200 acres of wheat.

David now does some artificial insemination, buying the semen from Michigan Breeders Association, but ¾ of the cows are bred by their 4 purebred bulls. The cows are grade. They milk 300 cows, sell milk to Babcock Dairy of Toledo, about 20,000 pounds every other day. Babcock outfits pick it up.

What do they do for recreation? Each of the 4 families gets every 4th Sunday off and goes to the Lutheran Church in Sturgis and takes dinner out. They can also fish on their own shore on the 40 acre lake to the east.

What Vet work they need comes from the LaGrange Vet Clinic.

Ernest was on the school board and the citizens committee of the Sturgis School. He says "There are still a lot of good opportunities on the farm, if you are willing to roll up your sleeves and go to work and forget about the 40 hour week." What a story!!!

QUAKER HAVEN

In 1874, two hundred and forty acres of land on the east side of Dewart Lake were owned by three LeCount brothers, James, Zachery and George. One hundred and sixty acres were later acquired by inheritance from Zachery and purchased from George by Miram, son of Zachery. In 1926, Miram, a Presbyterian minister, gave the Dewart Lake frontage for the establishment of Quaker Haven park. Later, the son of Miram, R. Dale LeCount, sold the remaining acreage of the two farms to the Quaker Haven Foundation, reserving some three hundred fifty feet of Dewart Lake water front for his summer home. Dewart Lake is name after the mother's family of Dale LeCount.

The son, Dale, graduated from LaGrange High School in 1916; Hanover College, 1920, and from McCormick Theological Seminary, Chicago in 1923. Now retired after fifty years in the ministry. In 1932, First Presbyterian Church of College Hill, Cincinnati, gave him Sabbatical leave of six months for study at New College, Edinburgh, Scotland; June 1933, married to Dorothy Margaret O'Brien, professor of organ and piano at Western College for Women, Oxford, Ohio; summer of 1934, studied at American School of Oriental Research, Jerusalem; 1943 accepted call to Sixth Avenue Presbyterian church,

Birmingham, Alabama; retired in June, 1962; accepted invitation to be Assistant to the President of Blue Cross-Blue Shield of Alabama; retired again in 1968.

Two children; Sylvia, two sons, Brian and Alan, lives with her husband Don Harder in Memphis, Tennessee. She graduated from University of Alabama in 1958. The son, R. Dale LeCount, Jr., graduated from Princeton University in 1962; later earned his doctorate from Columbia University; presently Dean of Students at Muhlinburg College, Allentown, Pennsylvania. Married to former Miss Margaret Nutt in 1966; they have three children.

JAMES REED — Woodland Farm

Abraham Reed bought the George Reed farm in 1885 (120 acres) and later bought several other farms. He had 4 boys, including George Reed, born 1888 who at school age, attended Stryckers school to the east. From the beginning George took to hogs. When he grew up he married Alice Shoemaker from Etna Green in 1923, and they went into the Registered Hampshire Swine business, furnishing many purebred boars and gilts to F.F.A. and 4-H boys and girls in Elkhart and surrounding counties.

Jim was born in 1931, Marilyn in 1933, Frank in 1935, and George Jr. in 1937. All 4 took the full swing at 4-H and all of them graduated from Nappanee High. Jim was in Corn Club as well as Tractor Maintenance and later became a T.M. leader for the county. Marilyn was in clothing and Frank and George Jr. were often winners in the barrow, gilt, and litter clubs.

George Sr. had been showing belted hogs at the Elkhart County Fair for many years, and when the writer was Swine Supt. of open class hogs at Goshen, George was one of my best supporters.

Jim remembers they bought their first International Tractor in 1943. They usually had a dozen sows and fed out close to 150 hogs. Many of the pigs were selected as gilts and boars and would never become porkers.

Jim was married in 1953, served in the army at Augsberg, Germany, and when discharged, enrolled in the Farm Veterans program at Concord school where we worked with him for 3 years after he had qualified by renting the Dr. Amick farm on New Road east of Woodland 1 mile. Going into hogs from Yen and training, he also started to build a herd of Holsteins for the monthly milk checks. The place consisted of 160 acres and he rented it from 1956 until 1969, when they bought it.

They farrowed 20 sows and gilts and sold about 300 porkers, also 35 to 40 Holsteins, milking around 15 to 20.

In 1958 the barn burned and Dr. Amick rebuilt, with 2nd floor hay storage, also milking parlor and bulk tank.

4 children came, David in 1954, Jerry in 1955, Patty in 1956, and Roger in 1959, and then Jean said, "Thats it". All of them are in 4-H, David has graduated, Jerry is up for a cap and gown this June, and the other two are still at it.

Counting the 5 years in Elkhart County, Jim has been a Leader in Tractor Maintenance for 13 years, and still going.

Now they have 350 Holsteins, milking about 100, and Jim does most of his own inseminating. He has several good cows by Newman's famous Dictator bull. Also they feed about 80 Holstein steers. Besides they rent 540 acres so they are farming 700 acres this year. David is 20 and has his own 80 acres.

This is a close-knit family and they are a happy, hard-working lot, and judging by the huge skillet of liver, they eat well. They are all members of the St. John's United Church of Christ at the north edge of Woodland on the Wyatt-Mishawaka road.

Jim says, "My only worry every night is whether there will be any of the kids around at milking time in the evening"

(Of course if there isn't, there is always Jean)

BILL RILEY — Oliver

In 1946 Albert Riley and his son William cut down the trees in the Merril Fields woods, on the old Middlebury Road (County Road 22) on the Norton Lake, and set up a garage to repair tractors and trucks.

In 1952 Bill bought his Dad's share and in October 1954 he secured the Oliver franchise (J.D. Oliver Chilled Plow Works) now known as the White Farm Equipment Company of Charles City, Iowa, a subsidiary of White Motor Corporation of Cleveland, Ohio (Having bought Oliver in 1960).

Bill held his own in competition and made inroads into the farm machinery business. In 1956 one of his customers Robert Clahorn, tenant on Richard Barlor farm south of Goshen, with Bill's assistance, entered and won the Elkhart County Plowing Contest, and won the second in the nation, using an Oliver 88 Diesel and a model 4240 and a three 16 inch bottom plow.

Bill co-operated with the Extension Department and Farm Veterans class in many demonstrations including the Ag. Society Progress show on the Dale Inbody farm in 1958 at which over 400 farmers were in attendance.

In 1959 the plant burned to the ground January 22nd and the farm veterans class invited the outfit to bring shipments to the old Ford garage which the veterans were leasing for assembly furnishing practice for the 44 veterans in the class. The class also fabricated steel tables for Bill for his new plant to be constructed. By March 20, 1959 a new building was up and ready to go. In 1964 Bill added an office area and parts room and in 1970 built on another shop for truck repair. He now has about 7,000 sq. ft. area.

His son Tim has now been taken in as a partner. Bill says they like to stay with every purchaser with a follow up, to insure complete satisfaction.

ELLIS AND BETTY RINK

When John Rink lived north of Millersburg on the Musselman farm, his brother George lived across the road and up the lane on the Lebold farm. Their children included William F. who was later married to Elizabeth Groff, a daughter of Jacob Groff, Sr. Eventually, George gave William 80 acres, and then Betsy bought the 65 acres to the east from her dad. (Now the centennial farm).

Bill and Betsy developed a custom butchering business, and would get up before dawn to hitch up and drive for miles to arrive at the farm by daylight to start in. Their son was Boston Rink, Buck as we called him, and he took over after being married to Ethel Corbin.

Ellis was born in 1917, and when grown married Betty Barnes of Schoolcraft, Michigan, farmed the home place 2 years, and then bought the 60 acre farm south of Mark Pfeaster, Jr., and moved there, where their children were born, Charles in 1944 and Ellen in 1948. Then they started to expand, buying the 80 acre Margaret Cripe farm, where they now live. Then they built a 16 x 56 foot cement silo, and went into the beef cattle feeding business. Later they bought the 55 acre Ed Rogers farm on County Road 40 across from Shirley Rink, and later added the Ralph Bates farm of 80 acres, and finally the 33 acre Luther Vance farm across from Orlando Whirledge.

Charles had 2 years at Michigan State, enlisted in the air force, served 4 years, and during that time married Carolyn Hershberger of Goshen, and they now live on the farm where he was born. They have 2 girls, Sheri, age 8, and Shannon age 4. Now Ellis and Charles have built 2 Harvestore Silos on the homestead, and feed from 350 to 400 beef a year, also have a combination farrowing and finishing hog outfit, with 30 sows and gilts finishing 350 to 400 porkers per year. Charles is planning to take over the whole 408 acres. Ellen was just married to Robert Fieck and live on the Bates Farm. She graduated from Western Michigan in 1971. Ellis says after tearing out miles of fence rows, and picking millions of stones, he would hate to tackle it again.

THE MILLERSBURG RINKS

John Rink was born in 1844 in Clinton Township, one of seven living sons of George Jacob Rink, an immigrant from Germany. He was reared on a farm one half mile north of Millersburg. When his son William was married he started farming a mile north of town and a mile east on what is now known as the Shirley Rink farm.

Another of John's sons Jacob Frank Rink, bought the Dewey farm, a mile north and a mile west of town (77 acres, Dewey retaining 3 acres). Dewey wanted to reserve the strip because it had a large Poplar tree which later yielded 7,000 feet of lumber, sold to Goshen Veneer. Later Frank bought the rest of the quarter section, 83 acres. Later Frank bought another 80 acres to the north, where Richard (Pete) Rink now owns. (from Hezekiah Bowman), then later another 40 to the east.

Frank was married to Zoa Ott, and they lived there until 1922, when they moved to Millersburg. They had 10 children here, three died at an early age, Russell and Harley worked on Power lines, and Chauncey farmed. Of the 2 girls, Elva married John Prough, and Edith, a registered Nurse, married John Luke (U.S. 20 by Elcona Golf). The remaining two sons Fred and Shirley carried on with farming; Fred on his dad's farm, and Shirley on his grandfather's farm. Later Shirley bought the spread where Paul now owns by the

145

viaduct.

To show how things went, Frank bought 15 feeder calves at 3¢ per pound and were sold for the same price, the profit coming in the gain in weight. Some job for a little profit! The calves were tied in individual stalls, watered by hand, and fed individually.

He also fed hogs, which were hauled to market by wagon, but the next lot of steers were fed in the lot and when finished they were driven to the Millersburg stock yards on foot, many neighbors helping in the drive at intersections, and every housewife in town, out to guard their own yards and gardens. The cattle were then shipped quite often to Buffalo.

In winters Frank went into the wood business. He hauled logs to the Veneer Co. in Goshen, sometimes two loads in a day. He also did quite a stove wood business, hauling to the railroad to load a freight car for shipment, and also doing quite a business in town as well as in Goshen and surrounding towns.

When Fred and Shirley married, Fred took over Frank's operations and Shirley took on the grandfather's farm east of town (a mile north and a mile east. Fred married Florence Rockenbaugh and Shirley married Hazel Musselman.

Fred and Shirley had quite a round at custom threshing. They bought a gas engine and a threshing separator but the engine was too small so they bought an oil pull Rumley in 1924. They had 3 different separators, one a Keck Gunderson, and made the rounds. No one who lived in those days will ever forget those big threshing dinners, nor the stories, nor the dirty tricks. But the Rumley gave way to the new combines, and in 1946, the separator was pulled to Goshen and sold for $75 as junk. They had also done clover hulling and custom silo-filling when the corn was cut in the field with a sled and hauled to the cutter-blower by the silo.

Fred remembers the butchering ring, Fred has 5 children; Mrs. Frank (Virginia) Turley a school teacher living in New Jersey, Mrs. Dale (Alice Ruth) Schrock with Goshen News, Richard (Pete), 4-H beef calf club leader for many many years on the farm north of the homestead, Fred Jr. known as Junior Rink, on the old homestead, and John, with Lazar Center in Las Alamos.

Shirley had a boy and two girls, Paul, on the big spread west of the homestead, Eva, (Mrs. John Jr. Emmert big cattle feeder near

Hex school) and Bernice (Mrs. Paul Worthman, on State 13 south edge of Millersburg , Dairy then beef.

The 5th Generation of Rinks are well established and well known, and have been active members of the Millersburg United Church of Christ from the beginning.

CALVIN C. ROGERS

About 1845, Jacob D. Rohrer of Clinton Twp. Elkhart Co. heard of a soldier of the Mexican War who had a land grant for 160 acres of land southwest quarter section bordering State Road 13 and County Road 38. He went to Cincinnati, Ohio and bought the 160 acre grant for $1600.00.

John Hoovens, his brother-in-law, bought the west half. He was the father of Amasa Hoovens who later became a businessman in Goshen.

Orlando Whirledge now runs the east 80 acres of this 160 acres and Lawrence Rockenbaugh owns the west part.

When the railroad came, Mr. Rohrer, Jacob W. Groff Sr., John Pence, and David Knisley, cut and sold 500 cords of 4 foot wood to the railroad for $2 per cord to be used to be burned in the engine.

Jacob Rohrer built the buildings on the Whirledge farm and Hoovens built the buildings on what became later the Cal Rogers farm.

William Harvey Rogers, Cal's father, was born August 3, 1852. He had 3 brothers and when their father died, his widow bound out the 4 boys, Cal's father to Levi Pearman who lived on what is now the Lewis Swinehart farm. When he reached 21 he was given a suit of clothes and $8 in cash. Then he went to work for the afore mentioned, Mr. Rohrer, for $5 per month and keep. Later he married Mr. Rohrer's daughter, Sophia Rohrer, February 15, 1882 by the pastor of the Rock Run Church.

They farmed several farms and then worked as a section hand on the New York Central Railroad, and moved to Millersburg. Two children were born on the farms and the rest of the 7 in town. Cal was born there in 1893.

In 1904 they rented a farm 2 miles north of town, they rented the Dewey farm where Harley Mast lived another 4 years and then in 1911 they bought the 80 acre Phillips farm. So it became the Harvey

Rogers farm and James Groff now owns it.

In 1918 when Cal was 25 years old and he returned from the Army, he married Carrie Stiver and they bought 60 acres of the Rohrer farm. They built up a dairy herd and a few sows. Cal became chairman of the advisory board of the school for 24 years. He represents the Agricultural Society on the Fair Board, and has been a leader for years in World War organizations. He served on the Goshen Hospital Board for 9 (nine) years. Cal says, "What is worth doing at all is worth doing right."

THE ROOD TILE MILL

Wilson H. Rood (Wick as he was called) was married to Cora Bemenderfer, and settled on the farm on the northwest corner of the intersection of County Roads 13 and 32 at 5 Points, 5 miles west of Goshen.

Later he acquired land to the north and then his holdings stretched for the whole mile to County Road 30 (Bashor Road).

He soon found out that the clay in the bottom land west of the farm buildings were of the proper consistency to bake into tile for tiling land.

He built himself an oven; set up forms and was soon in the tile business. The tile kiln was right near the road going west out of 5 Points. Tile would be corded up at times but buyers came so fast as a rule and the tile would be picked up as soon as they were ready to load.

The county being so hilly, water would stand in low fields and could not be plowed until it was too late to plant.

It has been said that ¾ of the tile under the land in Elkhart County came from the Rood Tile Kiln, even though the Bremen yard was not too far away. Dave Martin was his right hand man. The tile were of a good quality quite uniform and well baked, even so, many have had to be replaced in ensuing years.

With modern methods coming and lumber companies offering a smoother product at about the same price the dream ended, the marker on the old fire station recording the beginning and end, 1884 to 1916.

Wilson became County Assessor from 1918 to 1930 and moved on 6th St. in Goshen. Winnie and her husbnad, Mr. Jamieson, lived

148

on the farm a few years and left later. Wilson died in 1956, Winnie in 1959. Ralph is still in California. "Rosebud" the Jersey cow is gone too.

THE SCHALLIOLS OF KLONDIKE

David Schalliol was born in Germany in 1824 and was married to Frauline Margaret Hauptreis and came to America in 1853. He first moved to Holmes County, Ohio, where Augustus was born in 1857.

Later David and Margaret moved to Madison Township, St. Joseph County, Indiana, and acquired the 80 acres on New Road, one-quarter mile east of Beech Road on the south side of the road. David had three sons and for our purposes, including Augustus.

They cleared the farm gradually, burning all the logs but enough to build the buildings, and lived there until his death in 1892.

Before Augustus took over he had been teaching singing school at age 17, and taught public school for some years in the Township. When he married Dorothea Bollenbacher on April 30, 1882, they lived at Oak Grove for several years, and then settled on a farm on Patterson Road one-half mile west of Dogwood Road.

About 1898, he moved with his family of nine children to the corner of Beech and Madison Roads where they erected a three-story building for general store and a dwelling upstairs, and gave the establishment the name, Klondike. At the same location he operated along with the general store, a creamery for Schlosser Bros., of Bremen.

In 1902 he built a new home and installed the rural Klondike Telephone Exchange. Some time later he acquired the Wakarusa Telephone Exchange, which Victor, his son, operated for several years. One winter in a sleet storm poles blew down and lines snapped and Klondike was out all winter.

Augustus had ten children, Walter, Victor, Thaddeus, Grover, Ida, Nora, Amelia, Minnie, Elsie and Mabel, who died in infancy. He and his family were active members of the Zion Evangelical Church. At one time the whole family was organized into a band, which played for many events in the community.

When Augustus died in 1938, Grover bought the Klondike complex. Over the years the family heritage of industry, integrity and dedication will attest to the fact David and Augustus left their mark. Vic went big in Black Angus for a while. In 1965, on Palm Sunday, Vic's buildings were all destroyed.

Vic's son, Carl, went big in dairying, milking around the clock, milking as many as 120 Holsteins and later switched to grain farming. (300 acres).

Tod's son, Roger, also went big in livestock and farming operations. All of August's children are now gone but two girls. Grover died in the summer of 1973. The family will long be remembered.

DEAN SCHIEBER

Dean graduated from the Wakarusa High School in 1950 and bought one purebred Hampshire gilt from Orin Weldy and one from Harvey Weaver. He was living at home with his father, Lawrence Schieber, on County Road 3, two and one half miles south of Wakarusa, where he was running the farm because of his father's heart attack. In 1951 he started to show at the Elkhart County Fair and won a first place with his spring boar. In 1954 he rented more land and increased the Hampshires.

He was drafted in 1956, went into the army and his brothers farmed until he came home in 1958.

When he was home on leave in 1956, earlier, he was married to Lainada BeMiller, daughter of Morris BeMiller. At that time he secured a part time position with Excel in Elkhart, which he has held ever since. They bought the Ed Kehr farm and built a beautiful home on County Road 42.

After discharge from the service about 1960, Dean and Nate started showing at the Indiana State Fair.

Collin, the oldest son, was born that year. Later Darin was born, 1962, and Dirk, 1964.

In 1963 at the Indiana State Fair, they had the Reserve Senior Champion Sow. In the meantime Dean had pulled down many firsts and champion.

In 1966 they had the Senior Champion at the State Fair, and the same year won the Champion Carcass at the Northeastern Indiana Barrow Show at Columbia City.

In 1971, Collin had the Reserve Grand Champion Barrow at the Elkhart County Fair and the next year, the Reserve Champion Hampshire 4-H gilt at the State Fair. The following year Darin got a ribbon for the same thing.

The Schieber spread does not load up fat hogs for market, it produces registered gilts and boars - Hampshires.

ROMAYNE SHERMAN — Auctioneer

Oliver Sherman, born in 1883, was married to Sadie Yoder of Prairie St. Road, Elkhart in 1905. They farmed several farms in Harrison Township and Concord Township, and then moved northwest of Bristol, on Road 21 south of Coddins dairy farm, and there Romayne was born in 1913. They later moved back to the Jonesville school district, and Romayne attended Jonesville and also Pleasant Plains schools. He graduated from the Elkhart High School in 1930 and then met Miss Ruth Bleile at a literary society at Nappanee and later married her.

Then they rented the James Wogomon farm on Oaklnad Ave road, and another 40 acres of his father's. After that they took over Ruth's father's farm southeast of Nappanee, across from Stanley Burger, and did general farming with mules, with 12 milk cows and a few sows. There Gene was born in 1934. (He later died at age 14). While farming there, Romayne did some sales with Harley Loncor. Later they moved to Bremen and farmed the Bellman farm of 80 acres, but the auctioneer bug had bitten him, and within 2 years, he quit the farm, had a sale, and went into Auctioneering full time, moving east of Goshen on Indiana Road 4, near Ora Thomas with whom he soon teamed up to buy livestock, and then bought the Goshen Communtiy Auction from O.O. Kauffman in 1938, and relocated the auction east of town on State Road 4. At this time Robert was born, 1938, and then they built a big new sale barn, the first one in the county to sell livestock by weight.

People brought in and consigned livestock for 50 miles around, dairy cattle, feeder pigs, young cattle, hogs, and butcher cattle. A horse sale was held in connection every other week, horses coming from as far as Iowa, and going to Southern and Eastern buyers. Later a daily hog market was established, with Ora's brother, Alvin J. Thomas as the chief buyer. At that time Alvin lived right across the road from the sale barn.

In 1940 Romayne and Ruth bought their first big farm (114

acres) the Truex farm on County Road 19 south of Road 38.

The third son, Dana, was born in 1944.

Also in 1943 they bought the 190 acre farm, on County Rd. 40.

Gene died of Rheumatic fever in 1948. Later the same year, a beautiful brick home with 20 acres, was for sale right west from Alvin's home, and Romayne and Ruth purchased it from Walter Eldridge.

Then, in 1950, Romayne and Ora, and Lloyd (Ora's next brother) bought the Topeka Livestock Auction from Grover Castner. Today, the Topeka Livestock Auction is the largest one in the State of Indiana.

Romayne's demand as an auctioneer rose very rapidly, twice in that period he scheduled sales for 60 days straight (except Sunday). He even travelled to Bangor, Maine to auction horses 3 times, and he has cried Registered cattle sales in 9 different states. He has been crying the Indiana Draft Horse sale in Indianapolis for 12 years.

In 1966 the Goshen Community Auction was sold to Gerald Lambright and future interest was centered around Topeka Livestock Auction.

Then in 1972 Romayne and Ruth sold their home across from the sale barn in Goshen, and built a condominium with 4 other couples on College Road right east a piece from what used to be the College farm, how the Dan Slabaugh farm.

Robert graduated from Colorado University at Boulder in Civil Engineering and married Charlene Mast in 1958 (A Goshen girl), and he works for the state; they have 2 sons, Roger, age 15, and Rodney, 11; Dana graduated at I.U. in Accounting, married Ruth Eshleman from Harrisonburg, Virginia, in 1965, and he is now the controller for Goshen College and they have 2 sons, Chad, age 6, and Brett, age 4.

Romayne's motto is "No auction is too large or too small".

SHIPSHEWANA YARD GOODS STORE — Ora & Grace Yoder

Ora M. Yoder was born to Masellas and Mary Ann Gardner Yoder in 1906, on a farm near Shipshewana, went to Shore Country School and graduated from the high school in 1925. He worked for his dad two years and then graduated from Goshen College in 1931. He worked for the Keller Store in Goshen for a year and then went to North Manchester to take Normal work in order to be able to get a teacher's license. He married Grace Smeltzer in 1933. He taught at Shipshewana and Farver a year at each place, then accepted the challenge to take over the Business Department in the Shipshewana High School. Here he taught for 16 years, working for Kellers store on Saturday. Little did he imagine how the experience in that store would help him so much in years to come.

It was during these years, the 4 children were born, Janet, Marion, Leon and Elaine.

Ora joined the Shore Mennonite church when real young and has been in the harness from then on, Sunday School, Sun. Eve. Moderator, Cemetery Committee, and Building Committee.

In the larger area of the church, he was Treasurer on the Indiana Michigan Mission Board for 7 years, handling funds for the Mission Board Church Conference, Elkhart General Board, Bethany, Goshen College, General Conference, and M.C.C. Then at the end of the month, the monies would be sent on to the proper agencies. Besides the Board operated over 20 mission stations in Mich, Indiana, Ky, and Florida, which included the job of getting workers. When the Mennonite church decided to build Bethany Christian High School, Ora served on the school board 15 years.

In the early '50's with others he helped organize the Disaster Service, was Sec'y, V.P., Pres and now chairman Region II, 9 (states).

In 1942 he had bought his dad's 80 acre farm, and later bought another 40 nearby. A farm pond, and wooded areas are the things that enable him to relax from the busy-store pace. Popcorn is the main crop.

Ora had learned to like store work, so they bought a store in Topeka in 1944, and called it the Yoder Department Store. They started on a shoe string with less than $5,000 capital. The business prospered and in a few years they bought another store in Shipshewana, except that this store had groceries along with the drygoods, and shoes. This store also grew rapidly, and then in 1959 they purchased another store in Shipshewana. Then they decided to make the one all groceries and the other one a Department store, specializing in yard goods. A few years later they sold the grocery store in Topeka. Again they outgrew the quarters and decided to build the Shopping Center. The ones interested were; Miller & Sons, Wana Hdw., Dr. Brubaker, a dentist, and Dr. Martin, M.D.

During one of their travels, they got the idea from a shopping center in Halifax, Nova Scotia.

Their Specialty over the years has been the yard goods Dept., as they were in an area doing a lot of sewing, and for the last 30 years, have kept pace with the new ideas, and types of fabric, until at the present time they carry over 7,000 bolts of yard goods materials. Many people travel over 100 miles to select from their large supply.

Men's and Womens clothing and footwear suitable for any farm boy or girl is appreciated, yankee or Amish, take your choice.

Recently, Ora has been serving as Pres. of the Menn. Aid Assoc. of Mich. and Ind., and is on the Exec. Comm. of the Re-insuring agent, Menn. Indemnity, Inc. He helped organize Shipshewana Merchants, The Perrin Lake camp, and Riley Case says "Ora was the motivator, and with his big Yard-Goods service to Amish and Mennonites, must be in the Book."

Ora says "We get a lot of relaxation out of our Farm Pond, we need it". Janet is manager of self help in M.C.C. Marion is Pediatrician at Hyde Park Goshen, Leon died 1965, Elaine died 1974.

THE SIMPSONS

The Simpson farm was homesteaded by George Simpson in his brother-in-law's name. The farm was one mile east and one-half mile south of Millersburg. It consisted of 80 acres of level land covered with heavy timber. He built a log cabin and a log barn. Over a period of time he cleared part of the land, burning most of the logs and brush and cutting wood into four-foot lengths which he corded along the New York Central Railroad. At that time the name was "The Lake Shore and Michigan Southern." The railroad bought the wood and used it to fire the engine.

He went back to Union County for his wife; they had 16 children and among them for our purpose, Aldo's father, Edward H. Simpson born February 7, 1862. The children attended the school near Brown's Cemetery, one mile south and a little west of Millersburg. Later on the Hilbish School was built right across the road from the homestead.

Edward was married June 20, 1891, and Aldo was born in 1892. George died 1893 and Alfred Juday bought the farm from the Simpson heirs. Then Aldo's father was married and rented the farm on shares. Aldo was the only child.

General farming was followed. The judge, as a boy, graduated from the Hilbish School across the road in 1908.

Edward bought the farm from the Juday heirs in 1911. Aldo went two years to Millersburg High School and finished in Goshen High School in 1912. He attended Valparaiso Law School and graduated in 1914.

Working at home on the farm with his father and helping neighbors, he started practice of law in South Bend for two years and then established an office in Goshen at which time he was married to Mae Chiddister, June 20, 1917, and later went in with Lon W. Vail, a lawyer of considerable reputation. They established a partnership January 1, 1920.

For four years Aldo became Deputy Prosecuting Attorney. He was also Goshen City Attorney for four years. He was Republican County Chairman also for four years and a Director of Salem Bank for 24 years. He was appointed Circuit Court Judge by Governor Harry Leslie on December 5, 1932.

The Simpsons have two sons, James A., at present City Judge and a practicing lawyer, and Richard A. presently owner of Simpson Nursing Home and Elkhart Township Assessor. Richard died January 1974.

His parents died in 1936 and 1937 and Judge became the owner by inheritance as the only child and then bought 93 more acres. He has since share rented the entire acreage to the east tenant who has now been there 19 years, operating as a dairy farm.

The Simpsons reside at 414 South Sixth in Goshen and enjoy a host of friends and supporters.

DAN AND LEROY SLABACH

Dan J. Slabach Sr. was born July 30, 1906 on the old Mose Weaver place 2½ miles east of Griner Mennonite Church south of Middlebury, Indiana. On an 80 acre farm, farming with horses. When he was 3 years old his folks moved to Midland, Michigan and that is where he received his schooling.

In 1930 he returned to Indiana, and married Amelia Graber, and rented 160 acres, Clark and Koerner farms, on County Road 142 (320 acres), milking 16 Guernseys and grain farming.

In 1940 the house burned and they lost most of the furnishings. Then they bought the Goshen College Farm in the same year and moved there (120 acres). They rented about 400 additional acres. They established Dan's Dairy, Milking 45 to 50 cows and peddled the milk in Goshen. This continued 7 years.

The children were coming on, 6 girls and 3 boys, including Leroy born in 1935. Leroy stayed at home and farmed choosing that instead of higher education. He always wanted a field of popcorn or something else to do for himself.

Dan became interested in Christian Rural Overseas Program (C.R.O.P.) about 1956, became quite a leading canvasser, and later when C.R.O.P. started the farm leases, was outstanding with his machinery.

Leroy was married in 1956 and farmed with his father for 3 years. The next 3 years they lived in Milford and farmed there.

Now he has bought a farm just north of the Herbert Fervida spread, has constructed a new ultra-modern dairy setup and is building up to a 100 cow dairy. A place to see!!!

Dan quit farming in 1971 and works with Willies Construction, home builders (300 new homes in Elkhart in 1972) in Elkhart, and enjoys it.

He and Millie go to Florida for 5-6 months in the winter and have a home of their own on Bahia Vista at the corner of Conrad, just west of Pine Croft. Pine Croft is the winter and all year home of thousands of Amish and Mennonite families, where you can get a good meal every day except Sunday for just a little over a dollar.

Dan says "I plan to work as long as I am able. Too many sit down when they retire and don't last long!"

JOHN O. SMITH

This family traces their family history back for 100 years on both sides of the family. John H. Smith was born on the homestead in 1845, married Elizabeth Young in 1866, and was a farmer and carpenter. His son Oliver R. married Nellie Cook of Jimtown, and they had 6 children including for our purpose, John O. Smith. John O. graduated from Concord in 1935, peddled bread as a young man, joined the army and became a first Lieutenant in the Field Artillery, sold pies for a while after his release, and then went in with his father farming in 1947, and shortly thereafter married Frances Whisler. He joined Uncle Elmer's Farm Veterans class and that helped them get started. He bought a small place south of the homestead and stayed there until after the folks died and then moved into the homestead. They had some hogs at first, but decided to push dairy cattle, bought a milking machine, enlarged the milk house, installed a bulk tank, and later remodelled the barn.

Around 1950 he built 2 large chicken houses and put in 2600 layers and sold eggs. Ron and Ross did not like chickens so they converted them to calf pens. Built their herd of cattle up to 31, gradually switched to Registered Holstein and Ayrshires, started showing at fairs and won 9 Grand Champion and Reserve Champion ribbons, mostly with Ayrshires.

John also became agent for DeKalb Hybrids in 1948 and the $800. per year helped a lot. Then John bought the farm and let the folks live their time out on the homestead. Oliver died in 1961 and Nellie in 1970. Then they remodelled the old house and moved there in 1971.

Frances, too has a great family history, the daughter of Jonas Whisler, the Whisler Meat Packing House baron, and a great Grange booster all his life, so Frances and John came by it honestly. Both of them have had practically every job in the book. Frances is a Ball State Graduate and has taught most of her lifetime. Ron graduated from Purdue, and is now a Vet with Doc Weldy. Ross and Heide still keep things on the move.

The Smiths believe in working keeping all bills paid, whether it is an individual or the government. If you can't afford something-go without! They believe that you only get out of anything what you put into it!

SOIL AND WATER CONSERVATION DISTRICT

Records indicate that the original townships involved were, Washington, Jefferson, and parts of Osolo and York, excluding the town of Bristol. It was first called the Elkhart County Soil Conservation District. Later in 1960, the name was officially changed to S & WCD to include water. The District was not certified as a government subdivision until February, 1941. The first supervisors were J. Bernard Myers, Chairman, Harry S. Eby, Vice-Chairman, Glen C. Bowman, Secretary-Treasurer, Howard Stark, and Fred Bourn, members. The first meeting of the group was in the Bristol Town Hall, June 3, 1941. Oscar Ackerson, area conservationist was present, as was J. Howard Brown, County Agricultural Agent.

The first meetings of the Supervisors were to develop a program that would meet with the approval of the National Office for a mutual memorandum of understanding, so that an office could be established for a center for operations. First SCS personnel for the office were then, Oscar Ackerson, area conservationist, Mr. Henry Dugan, District conservationist, and Mr. Wm. Vanderbosch. When Oscar first came, he was Area Conservationist. He was later made State Agronomist, and continued working out of the Goshen office under the direction of the State office, and later developed quite a program of Minimum Tillage for the entire State of Indiana.

1941 to 1949 were the years of "Do what you can", Cal Dunifon replaced Vanderbosch and later Fred Geiger replaced Dunifon in 1967. Fred, then retired in 1974.

Mr. Don Smith from Terre Haute, graduated from Purdue in 1939, was Farm Security Administrative Supervisor at Albion from 1943 to 1949, and then was moved to Goshen as District Conservationist, and the program was on it's way, as we know it today.

One of the major contributions of the S & WCD to Elkhart County has been getting the county soil survey completed for all Elkhart County land owners to use the valuable resource information. Another major contribution was to get irrigation started on the "Goshen Prairie" and Don Smith was largely responsible for this.

In June, 1967 the District received county funds to hire a District Secretary on a part time basis. The first secretary was Eileen Whirledge. In June 1968 Alice Graff became the office secretary, and from April 1972 it has been Jackie Berkey. In January, 1974 she became a full time secretary for the district.

In July of 1971, Don Smith retired and Leroy Holtsclaw has become the District Conservationist. Now in June 1974 Fred Geiger, Soil Conservation Technician has just retired after years of very fatihful service. He will go back to his "Farming in Retirement at Ligonier". The Area Conservationist is now Joe Branco.

It is hard to assess the service of this great outfit in Elkhart County, but we are sure the S & WCD belongs in this book, as it has contributed much to Michiana Agriculture. Bless them all!!!

The SCS is located on the second floor of the Spohn Building on Clinton Street in Goshen.

Supervisors as this book goes to press are: John Rouch; Chairman, Lamar Huneryager; Vice-Chairman, Everett Lienhart; Secretary of the Board, Jackie Berkey, Office Secretary and Treasurer for the Board, Kenneth Lechlitner, and Robert Moser.

THE SOMMERS FAMILY

Noah Sommers was born in Miami County southeast of Peru in 1901 of humble parents. Later they moved to Howard County and Noah attended school there.

When Noah grew up he married Esther Ruth Strebin and they rented a farm and followed general farming for 5 years after which they bought the Amos Kendall farm (60 acres) and continued with general farming.

He also rented another quarter section (160 acres) which he operated for 30 years. They had 7 children, and for our purpose including Wayne, 1922, and Darlton, 1931, during the depression.

Wayne grew up and married Susie Keim, 1942 and they bought 90 acres in LaGrange County near Howe, because land was cheaper than in Miami County. However the toll road came through and cut their farm up and looking around for a farm bought the old Irvin Snider farm (160 acres) on County Road 50 at the corner of County Road 17 in 1954.

Later, 1965, they bought 96 acres to the north. They have 5 children, Arlee, Darrel, Lorraine, Fern and Dallas.

Darrel is the one interested in the Holsteins. They milk 40 cows and have from 75-80 animals, sell milk to Burgers. Also farrow 11 sows several times a year.

Wayne has been Supt. of the Waterford Mennonite Sunday School and active on the Boards. The family received The Outstanding Farm Family of the Year from the Agricultural Society in 1971. They are now putting in a new milk parlor.

Darlton was born 1931, went to school in Miami and Howard counties, grew up and married Martha Bontrager in 1950. They have 5 children. The third son Stephen is slated to follow farming. They milk 45 Holsteins, farrow 22 sows spring and fall and feed out 350 hogs. Darlton won the Outstanding Young Farmer in 1959. They sell milk to Deans in Rochester. They own 80 and rent 260 acres, farming 340 acres. Noah and Ruth have put the spunk in this family.

IRVIN STAHLY

Irvin Stahly born 1885 was the son of Peter Stahly. Peter's father, Henry Stahly, was one of the 5 boys, with their sister brought over to America from Germany by their mother.

When Peter grew up he bought the farm opposite Northwood School where Gerald lives and called it "Pinelawn Farm". Peter and Irvin later raised Red Polled cattle and became interested in Belgian horses, bred and produced the line, selling surplus animals. They showed Belgians for years at the Nappanee Onion Carnival.

Irvin was one of the first farmers to use a Fordson tractor. At one time he was much interested in Cheviot sheep. He was married to Olive Snyder and had 2 children, Gerald and Erdean, who is now the wife of Lowell Moyer of Wakarusa.

He was elected and re-elected for 3 terms as trustee of Locke Township (12 years) and also settled many estates and became a real friend of the people.

One of the hardest jobs he ever had was serving on the tire rationing board. He also handled insurance for the Farmers Mutual Aid of Elkhart County. His friendly counsel and advice to friends in the area have earned for him the name of "Mr. Locke Township".

The Stahly's have always been members of the First Mennonite Church of Nappanee and Gerald and Irene have both undergirded the programs there for many years. John was in 4-H and the writer had the joy of bidding off one of his 4-H pigs in the 4-H auction sale.

Irene served a number of years with the writer on the personnel committee of the County Church group.

She also teaches in the Nappanee Schools.

Gerald says he is going to get back into hogs and what he says he will do, he usually does.

This family has served the community well through the years and a host of friends will testify to that. Bless them all!!!

BURNS STARK & SONS -- Sugar Grove

Howard Stark married Lydia Burns, 1885 and bought the Helman farm on County Road 17, one and one half miles south of the 6 Span bridge, three miles north of Sugar Grove Church. Blue Grass Grange was so named because it was built on the Stark farm called the Blue Grass Dairy.

When Howard homesteaded in South Dakota, he froze his leg and was crippled so he sent his oldest son Burns Stark to Purdue, because he could not follow the plow himself.

When Burns came back from the short course he built a large herd of Holsteins, paying Mr. Bert Stutsman $100 for a three day old calf. He married Carrie Lynn in 1911. He built the herd up to 80, milking 50 cows. Lewis, his brother, drove the milk route in Elkhart while Burns did the farming (244 acres) with several hired men.

He bought the first milking machine in the area. He started his first alfalfa field at this time. Later Lewis was drafted, which put a crimp in the Blue Grass Dairy. At the stock market crash he secured a Federal Land Bank Loan and bought out his family's interest in the estate after his father died.

Later he sold the land to Ralph Dull and started over again on the Sigerfoos farm (80 acres) what is now Elcona Golf Club, and went into Jerseys.

He added land his neighbors wanted to sell until he had 400 acres and 75 head of cattle, milking 50 cows. He also built up a flock of sheep, as many as 100 ewes. He planted 40 acres of spearmint and peppermint and between the sheep and the mint income he was able to pay off all his indebtedness. In 1946 he sold all the land but instead of retiring he bought 160 acres (the Lamar Martin farm) on Road 30 and bought 65 acres of the Russell Stutzman farm. He had five boys and three girls and then sold out in 1954 and gave each of the eight children a helping hand and moved to Elkhart.

Since, he bought several small farms and raised popcorn. Mrs. Stark died in 1965. Of the five sons, Russel farms 300 acres and milks 20 to 30; Burns Stark, Jr. farms 500 acres and milks about 60 cows; Lewis has a dairy farm at Sugar Grove Church; Howard died, and his widow teaches at Northridge; and the other brother Robert farmed a while and then went to excavating.

Burns Stark, Sr. will long be remembered as a man of great

vision. At this writing he is 88 years of age and still dreams of farming. Now, July, 1974 Burns is ailing fast in Turtle Creek Nursing home in Elkhart.

ALVIN AND HELEN STEELE

Cyrus Steele moved to Indiana in 1896 and went on a 60 acre farm in Clinton Township. They had 2 children, John in 1904, and Alvin in 1907. They both went to the Middlebury school.

Then they bought the Mathers farm one mile east of Middlebury (80 acres) in 1914. A.T. Marvel was the Vo. Ag. teacher and Alvin was on the Poultry Judging Team at the Purdue 4-H round-up and made the highest grade ever in 1925. He won a 250 egg incubator for the distinction. Then in 1926 the folks moved to town and his dad carpentered and was Secretary of the Livestock Shipping Association and also preached without salary in the Middlebury Church of the Brethren. Alvin graduated from the high school there in 1928, and also worked at the Middlebury Co-operative Creamery and then was married to Helen Powell, daughter of Harry and Iva Mae Powell, in 1930. The Powell home was ½ mile northwest of town on County Road 8 on the left side of the road; here they built a new laying house 30 x 110 (1100 hen capacity), shipped eggs to New York, cleaning every egg by hand.

About that time Alvin got to doing custom work for farmers, first buying a baler with several other farmers, like around 8 to 10¢ per bale. In the fall and winter after baling he would work at the creamery. He was with the creamery there for 13 years with Glen Dings, Melvin Plank, and later Brian Mauck. He was in custom work for over 30 years; also was in liming 3 years for farmers, and the Nitrogen fertilizer supply service for 16 years. Helen also helped with the Nitrogen business, hauling the nitrogen tanks for supply.

Then in 1944 they bought the folks farm and moved back there. Donna was born in 1933, Darrel in 1934, David in 1940, and Delores in 1943. All the children were in Uncle Elmer's 4-H as he was the 4-H leader there in Middlebury for 7 years, as it was impossible to get a local leader there in town at the time. Many blue ribbons were won by the Steele children, Darrel had a Reserve Champion Hampshire one year, and the girls both showed at the State Fair.

Now, Donna is in Toledo, a secretary, with 3 daughters, Roxanne, 20, a junior at Toledo Univ., Angela 17, a senior in High school, and Beth, 14, in Junior high; Darrell, is married to Jeanette Swihart, Cookie's daughter, they live in Bellebrook, Ohio, and he is with Super Value Foods, they have 5 children, Gregg, a soph. at Ball State, (on the Dean's list), Scott, 16, a junior in high school, Brad 15, Laura, 11, and Grant, 10.

David is married to Linda Schamerloh of Ft. Wayne, a registered nurse, they live there and he is purchasing agent and draftsman for a Home Builder, they have 2 children Sanya, 7, and David Jr., 1; Delores is married to Dan Dotlich, in Heavy Crane Service, Indianapolis, with 3 children, Michael, 6, Marla, 5, and Trent, 2.

The Steeles have been prominent in church and communtiy. Alvin was a Supervisor for SWCD for 9 years, also A.S.C. Committee for many years, Director of the creamery for years, and for 9 years a member of the school board. Also he was on the F.H.A. committee for 3 years. Helen taught S.S. at Ch. of the Breth. for many years. By the way here is a modest woman who has served well in the community, in the Home Ec. club, Garden Club and 13 years in the Middlebury School Cafeteria. The students will never forget her.

After many health problems in recent years Alvin and Helen say, "We are still grateful".

DWIGHT STOLTZFUS

Dwight was born in 1920 near Hudson, Ohio, in Portage County, on a dairy farm. His father, Elmer Stoltzfus was also a Mennonite minister.

Phyllis was born in 1917, the daughter of Arthur Hartzler, who was the brother of B. Frank Hartzler, the man who taught music at Goshen College, Bluffton, and Hesston Kansas, still living in Phoenix, Arizona. The Hartzlers lived east of West Liberty, Ohio, near the caverns. Arthur for some time ran the flour mill at West Liberty.

Dwight and Phyllis attended Goshen College, Phyllis for 2 years, and then taught for 3 years south of West Liberty, and Dwight graduated in 1941. They were married the next year, in 1942, Rev. S.E. Allgyer assisting in the ceremony. Then they moved onto a farm in Portage County, Ohio, part salary, and privilege of having their own dairy, then in 2 years they bought 100 acres for $10,000 and went to dairying, selling milk to Cleveland. They had 12 Holsteins, about 4 cans of milk per day. The 6 children were born from 1944 to 1953.

In 1960 they bought the Colonel Jackson farm just west of the Jackson cemetery in Elkhart County, moving the cattle here by truck and milking them that night.

Later Dwight bought the farm across the road (130 acres) and the increase had pushed the milkers up to 80.

Soon after they moved here they got interested in irrigation, and Dwight served on the SWCD Committee for a number of years.

The family was named the "Outstanding Farm Family of the Year" in 1966 by the Elkhart County Agricultural Society at the annual meeting of the Society.

Dwight has served on Mennonite Mutual Aid for many years, and the family has been very active in the Waterford Mennonite Church.

All the children graduated from the Bethany High School, Fred, in 1962, Rosemary, '66, Tim, '67, Lowell, '68, Shirley, '71, and Helen in 1974.

Fred also graduated from Goshen College and is now in Germany, studying music. Rosemary also graduated with a Phys. Ed. major and is teaching in a Pennsylvania high school.

In 1972 Tim and Lowell became partners, bought the home place, (143 acres) 142 acres to the west and another 192 on U.S. 6, just east of Indiana 313. Total acreage 477.

They are still single and live at home with the family, and have built the dairy herd to around 200 animals, milking up to 100. This is a commercial dairy herd.

Dwight is now Director of Field Services for Mennonite Mutual Aid, and is also Vice President. They are great supporters of C.R.O.P. and Dwight has helped on the canvasses. He still owns the 130 across the road.

Here is a closely knit family. Families like this are the "SALT OF THE EARTH". every one of them "clean as a hounds tooth." Dwight says "One thing I aim to do is to share my time and money to help others".

THE STOOKEY HOLSTEINS — Milford

5 generations in our day have lived on the Stookey spread; John born at the time of the civil war, Millard his son in 1882, and Emra, born in 1913, and then his children, and grandchildren, and there you have 5 generations on what is now a 1,000 acre operation.

John started in Jerseys and Millard followed until about 1920, when Emra was starting to school, then they switched to Black and White.

The first blow came in 1930, when the big barn burned to the ground and had to be rebuilt; Emra was a junior in Leesburg High School.

He graduated in 1932, and 2 years later was married to Mary Anglin, the daughter of Roy and Allie Stackhouse Anglin, rented the 364 acres on shares and pushed the 34 stanchion dairy barn. The 3 children, George, John, and Jack, came during the next 12 years, and each of them was the full 10 years in 4-H and each of them took the Vo. Ag. course in high school, George, in Milford under Marion Stackhouse, and John and Jack in Leesburg.

In 1944 they bought the 120 acre Plummer farm on 700 north, and later in 1958 they bought the 200 acres farther east, where Jack lives, and the Loose Housing and Milking parlor with it.

On the 2 farms they keep 150 to 175 animals, milk about 80 cows, and instead of pushing volume, they push quality.

Early, in his career, Emra, became known as a very careful selective breeder, has shared many fine animals with other breeders.

George was married to Nola Meek in 1955, and they have 4 children, Lynda, Lisa, Laura, and Kenneth. George is now a Dr. of Preventive Dentistry, teaching in Indianapolis, at the I.U. center.

John married Geraldine Wildman in 1961, and has 3 children; Jeffrey, Gina, and John II. They are on the farm near Leesburg. Jack was married to Beverly Lueck and they have a son, Jackson.

John and Jack are both associated with Emra in the Dairy Farm set-up.

Here is a family of farm people who stick together on every thing, and results show that it pays off. They are people of culture and refinement, and you can feel the warmth of hospitality when you step inside - and a very nice home.

Mary says make the quote for Emra and me "Do the best you

can, with what you've got, where you are". They are humble people and I know they have lived up to that slogan.

Emra holds office in the State and Nat'l Farm Bureau, the last 2 years has been the V. Pres. of D.H.I.A. was a charter member of the Leesburg Meth. church, and last year showed in 9 different Local, State, and National Fairs, in Kentucky had 3 firsts, and Reserve Champion Bull. He has had Premier Breeder award 7 years at Warsaw. This year they shipped 2 heifers to Japan and several bulls to France. Last year their wheat went 60 bushels per acres. My! My! How's That? Nice people to know, stop by sometime, they'll treat you nice.

THE STROUP FARMERS OF MILLERSBURG

Two Stroup brothers, Samuel and John came to the Millersburg community from the Dayton, Ohio area in the western emigration of the eighteen hundreds. Samuel married Ann Parker and settled on a quarter section of land 1 mile north of Millersburg, now owned by Monroe Nisley, and John who married Eliza Stiver, bought 80 acres across from Junior Fred Rink, and a little north, where they farmed and raised a family of eight children, and 2 of them became farmers.

Of the eight children of Samuel Stroup, 2 were farmers, one, J. Cameron moved on the 80 now owned by Ezra Gingerich, and the other, Edwin, Herberts father on what is now known as the Stroup farmstead across the road from Rinks.

As a boy Edwin walked to school, Pleasant Hill, often called the Dewey School, which was 1 mile west of the Nisley farm.

When grown he was married to Libbie Culp. (1888) and he purchased the 80 acres on County Road 37 from his uncle John's estate. Here he did general farming. But in 1894, Libbie his first wife died and for 5 years he rented out the farm, then in 1899 he married Saloma Stiver, and the next year Herbert was born (1900).

He also fought the GREAT BATTLE of the country school at Dewey, and on consolidation the school was closed and he went to Millersburg.

Later Edwin bought another 40. After finishing high school in Millersburg, Herbert graduated from Heidelburg College in Ohio, and taught in Edgerton, Ohio for 3 years.

In 1925 Herb married Grace Musselman, and they went in partnership with his dad, milked by hand, fed pigs by hand, horses and a small tractor, and later bought a 40 acre tract for themselves.

Kathleen, Evelyn and Martha came along and Carlton, a son.

Carlton was in my Vo. Ag. class in Millersburg in 1946 and '47 and I cannot resist now to tell the story. I had just made some wild statement about the rewards of a heavy "Plow down" in the Crops class, and concluded with the "If anybody questions the merit of fertilizer, you can tell them for me that Uncle Elmer says they are crazy". Within the 5 minute break I was "Uncle Elmer" in the hall, by noon I was Uncle Elmer all over the school, by Friday night basketball game I was "Uncle Elmer" in the township of Clinton, by Fair Time the next summer I was "Uncle Elmer" in Elkhart County, and now they know me by that name throughout Michiana. The moral of the lesson is "Be careful what you say in class".

Well, Stroupy made it through school, up and married Sue Blood daughter of Mike Blood of Bonneyville Mill fame, set up housekeeping on a small farm his Dad had bought, went pretty big on layers until in 1963 "Stroupy" took over the farm and moved there, and Herb retired and moved to the chicken farm but dropped the layers after 4 years.

Now Stroupy owns 160, rents another 50 to 100, feeds out 120 steers a year and is the Beef Cattle Calf Club leader of Elkhart Co.

Carlton and Sue have 3 children, Marty, works for a trailer home outfit, Sandra is headed for Taylor Univ., and Tommy is getting to be quite a tractor boy on the farm.

Herb has been a Farm Bureau booster for 40 years, is now V.P. of the County Group, worked in various capacities for ASC for 20 years, AAA and all with Clint Zollinger, CROP worker since 1950 and has been helping placing voting machines in election years.

LOYAL STUCKMAN'S BERKSHIRES

In 1899, Lewis Stuckman bought and took over his father's farm where Loyal now lives. He raised potatoes and onions on the marsh. When peppermint came in, when Loyal was a boy, they set out ten acres of mint. The old mint still is right where it was 50 years ago.

They went into registered Poland China hogs keeping a number of sows. In 1919, Loyal graduated from Nappanee High School and taught four years.

In 1923, Lewis suffered a broken leg at the St. Joseph County

Fair in a horse race. Then Loyal stopped teaching and took over the farm.

He married Dorothy Slabaugh in 1926. About 1940, Loyal became interested in Berkshire Hogs.

Loyal bought more land and three children came, Mary Lou, Noel and Kent. They went to New Paris to school. Mary Lou was in Mrs. Lehman's Latin Class, an "A" student.

Loyal was instrumental in organizing the all-breed swine sales, and from the beginning an officer. He consigned many boars and gilts to these sales.

Loyal had worked with Purdue on muckland research. In 1943 he showed the first place spring boar at the National Berkshire Show and Sale and in 1944 he won Reserve Champion in the National held at Purdue.

In 1946 he had Champion and Reserve Carcass in the light weight carcass class and Champion Carcass in the middleweight class and the heavyweight class.

When Noel and Mary Lou got in 4-H, they showed at the 4-H show at Goshen as well as Ayrshires. They also showed at the State Fair.

In 1960 Loyal had the Grand Champion Spring Berkshire boar at the Indiana State Fair.

The Stuckmans have also done much to swing the trend of lard type hogs to meat type. They have made a real contribution to 20th Century agriculture in Michiana.

SUNRISE ORCHARDS, INC. — Max Kercher, President

Wheeler Kercher bought 40 acres on County Road 38 in 1922, at the age of 45, and planted fruit trees, apples, peaches, and sweet cherries; then he continued to work at Studebakers and Stivers furniture store until the trees came into bearing. Max graduated from Purdue, in Agriculture in 1928, and while still in school, was married to Rosemary Harper of Goshen, daughter of George and Myrtle Harper.

The oncoming Depression made it a poor time to get started with a fruit orchard, so Max became Supervisor of the Indiana State Institutional farms, with the oversight of 18,000 acres in all. Bill was born in 1928, and Dave in 1932.

In the meantime Max continued a father-son arrangement with

his father Wheeler and used the money from his salary to help buy farms from time to time. The Ernie Martin farm west of the river, 82 acres, the Spohn farm of 60 acres, and the 33 acre Mast Farm, finally totalling 224 acres. At Lawrence Kercher's death, Bill later bought the 80 acre farm from the estate.

In the early years the fruit was sold under a large tent, and after World War II, the large fruit market building was built on Indiana 15 at Kercher Road. Shortly thereafter, Bill graduated from Purdue in 1950, and is now manager of the outfit. Max is still President. 80 acres are devoted to melons and sweet corn. They supply grocers for a 50 mile radius, and ship apples all over the South.

Bill has Tom a senior in Goshen, and Janet an eighth grader. Dave is an Engineer in Schenectady with 5 children. All the Kerchers are Episcopalians. Before Wheeler died in 1962 he used to say "When I was young I never ate a good apple, we always ate the culls".

EARL SWIHART MAKES IT AGAINST HEAVY ODDS

Clarence Swihart, Earl's father was the minister of the West Goshen Church of the Brethren, and also worked at the Jefferson Barber Shop.

Having been reared on a farm in Jefferson township, he felt they should be on a farm to bring up their children, so bought a small farm right at the west edge of Goshen; they had been living right on the Lincoln Highway at the corner of Chicago, now Judd's parking lot.

They built a new house and a barn in 1911, but after 6 years of Goshen School, Clarence was called to Solomon's Creek church, and they moved out on County Road 146 to be near the church. But in 1921 Clarence suffered a cerebral hemorrhage and died in 2 weeks, so his mother sold out and moved to town.

Earl started in at Goshen High, but had to quit to help support the family, working at the Bag Factory for 25¢ per hour, and later at the Sash and Door. At that time the North Dakota Harvest wages looked big to young people, and Earl went. The 3rd year he went back he married the rancher's daughter, Rosamond Kout in 1928. The next year Alice came, and then they came back to Indiana and moved onto a farm west of Jefferson school, and raised truck and melons, bought the Bemendorfer school house, drove a school bus, and worked on the Messick farm a few years. Lois was born in the school house. At that time corn was so cheap, 15¢ per bushel, that they burned it for firewood. Hogs were selling for 2½¢ per pound.

Three years later the twins were born, Ruth and Roy, and a month after, Earl was hired by Mrs. Amasa Hoovens on County Road 36. (which later on was to become their homestead).

Mrs. Hoovens had 4 dairy farms and this was farm No. 2. The general farm manager was Mike Carpenter a brother to Adrian Carpenter, Roy's father. At the time Mike was living on the main farm, just a step to the south of the corner on County Road 33. For 5 years they pushed the herd of Guernseys for milk for the Hoovens dairy, and during this time Don was born, 1938, the first child to be born on what was to become their future farmstead.

Earl had sold the school house and had $500 saved up for when his chance would come, now in 1940 he began to smell success. His close friend Clint Zollinger was on the local Committee, and the local committee approved an $8,000 loan for Earl to buy the farm, plus several thousand operating, to buy some stock and implements, but when the papers got to Indianapolis, the big shots said Earl could never in the world make it and turned it down flat.

Clint was exasperated, as he felt the F.H.A. was set up to help farm hands like Earl, who were deserving and honest and ambitious, but with little or no capital. So they fought over it for a year, and in 1941, closed the loans, and lo and behold, Rosamond and the kids pitched in, did without, saving every dollar, and in 1947, when I had the Vo. Ag. Department in Millersburg, visited the family for 4-H and took supper with them, and that is when they announced the good news to me - that the loan was all paid off. What a Joy! Earl and his family had fooled them and paid it off in 5 years instead of 40 years.

Later Earl served a 3 year term on the F.H.A. Committee. Well, Earl and the children pushed the Guernseys up to 30 milkers, with only 26 stanchions. They bought the Hoovens farm No. 3 in 1949, went Bulk, Grade A milk and sold to Hoovens, and continued with Goshen Farms Dairy, when the Yoders took it over, and later switched to Cook's in Elkhart.

Alice was sent to the State Fair one year in 4-H dairy with her splendid Junior Yearling calf. Ray was with me in the pig club, and some of the children were later in the Corn club.

Even Earl had a special citation from Wolfe Grain for 148 bushel yield of corn per acre. Later one year Don had 156 bushels.

They built a silo, went to grass silage, and even rented Frank Phillips 80 acres on Road 34 a number of years. Gradually in the Fifties he was switching to Holsteins to supply changing demands. He was on the Board of Directors of the Farm Bureau Credit Union for 16 years and is still on the Committee.

They retired in 1966, sold the 100 acre Hoovens farm No. 3, and have put most of the rest of the land in C.A.P. program under ASC. Lukemia crawled up on Rosamond and took her in March 1974.

Earl says "We celebrated our 45th last September and have had a lot of very good years together".

Alice is married to Antonio Alvarez in Puerto Rico and they are in Poultry and Eggs, have 7 children.

Ray is married to Ellen Russell a teacher in Topeka, live in Fairfield and have 5 children.

Lois is married to Paul Chalfant, head of the Psychology Dept., in Texas Tech. 2 children and 3 step children.

Roy is married to Caroline Brock, a Ph. D. in Education in DePauw, they have 2 children.

Ruth is married to C.G. Roig, and they have the El Cid restaurant. Don is married to Joan Beathan, he works for Travel Equipment and has 3 children living with his ex-wife in Mississippi, and 4 step-children with them at home on Road 36 east a mile from Earl.

IRVIN, MAUDE AND WILLIS EBY — Swallowland

Noah Eby owned 80 acres on County Road 3 north of Wakarusa, and Irvin was born in 1892 in a log cabin where the garden is now laid out.

He went to school at Sailor's. There were 3 other boys, Willis, Ellis and Victor. Willis was a brain and taught school for 20 years in 8 of the nine schools of Olive Township. He is now a partner with Irvin with the 100 Guernseys, milking about 40 to 50. They sell milk to Burgers New Paris Creamery. Willis never found the right woman, but Irvin married Maude BeMiller, and she is still a pretty woman. The license was dated 1913.

They have 3 children, Ruth Louise, in the Waky Clinic, Wendell B. in Traverse City, Distribution Sup't of Consumers Power, and

Laurabelle, a Home Ec. teacher in western Michigan at Kalamazoo, Michigan.

Irvin was one of the first committee members of SWCD and helped Bill Oesch and Clint Zollinger sign up farmers for AAA in the Corn-Hog program. The whole family has been conservation-minded from the beginning. One of the big demonstrations of SWCD was carried out on their farm, and Uncle Elmer was there. Later Irvin was the County Grain-Bin Supervisor.

Cliff Swallows started nesting in their barn eaves about 1925, and Willis has shot as many as 1000 sparrows in one year as they would rob their nests. Willis is a member of National Audubon Society, and large groups come to observe and study the swallows. Louise, Mrs. Jim Cook loves the old farm, and comes often.

Maude says to make Irvin's quote "Why worry about tomorrow, when you can think about today, and enjoy it". What a wonderful philosophy and in line with the doctrine of the Jimtown Methodists.

DON THWAITS

Don was born in 1931 on a farm on County Road 27, the son of Robert and Edna Thwaits, graduated from New Paris High School in 1951, and then married Beverly Jean Miller, and rented the Charles Mishler farm west of New Paris for 2 years (160 acres). Debbie was born there in 1952. Then they rented the Charles Crow farm, for two years, where the Smith Wambridge Baton Twirling Camp now stands (140 acres). Then for ten years they did the Smoker Lumber Co. farm of 190 acres, where Bob Martins Demonstration farm is now operated by Richard Snider.

They went into Holsteins, like 50, milking 30, and Douglas was a new baby there in 1956. Also Dennis came in 1957. While there they bought their first farm, 40 acres, without buildings, and later bought the John Hibschman farm of 40 acres and moved there. David came there in 1965. By then Debbie was in the Angus Beef Club as all the other children followed suite. Then they started to expand, rented her father's place, bought the Moore farm of 100 acres across the road, and later the Bunger farm to the east, on County Road 50, after that the Dale Thwaits farm on County Road 25, also his Brother Bob's farm on the Huntington road, and last Herbert Blue's farm on Road 50 where they now live.

Now they own 643 acres, rent another 600, and farm a total of 1243 acres, have 45 Black Angus Breeding cows, and feed out 80 to 100 steers each year, also have a 25 stall farrowing house on the Hibschman farm and feed out over 300 porkers per year and sell some weaning pigs. Misfortune struck in 1972, when Dennis was killed in a tractor accident.

Now Don is a member of the Fairfield School board, on the ASC for years, active in Fairview Grange, Lions Club, Solomon's Creek Church, and Pres. of Fairfield Community Men's Club.

Don says "Be good to your neighbors".

TROYER'S POULTRY

Elroy was born on his father's farm on Indiana State Road 4, about 4 miles east of the Troyer Poultry plant. (120 acres), 1924, and they did general farming. They went into Peppermint like about 40 acres, and also had Registered Poland-China hogs.

At school age he went to the Clinton Community school which was built in 1924 during consolidation, and then he went to Millersburg High and was under Russell Luke in Vo. Ag. At that time Roy's dad bought the Mangus farm north of Leonard Yoder (102 acres), and did general farming with some turkeys.

In 1946 he married Alberta Cross, and then he became herdsman for Ike Roth on his farm a mile north of Goshen, milking 40 Holsteins. After several years he bought a 73 acre farm near Vandalia, Michigan and raised turkeys and chickens, and started the business of distributing dressed poultry, turkeys and chickens, first in southwestern Michigan and now from Muncie, Indiana to Grand Rapids, Michigan.

From 1949 to 1953, he would fill up the van-type refrigerator-truck at the Pringle & Roth Processing plant on State Road 4 east of the Goshen Livestock Auction. That is when they bought a lovely farm on Maple Street, next farm north of Ora Thomas. (Road 35)

Then Pringle and Roth bought the closed Farm Bureau processing plant south of New Paris, and ran it as "THE LAND OF GOSHEN" chicken. Roy stuck with them and would load up at that plant, and left the plant east of the sale barn idle for 5 years.

Then in 1958, "Land of Goshen" quit because of the problem of supply of birds, and then Roy bought the original plant on Road 4

173

and incorporated Troyer Poultry, Inc. Broiler Production had its problems, and Roy found it necessary to seek birds out of state, from Ohio to Mississippi.

Now they are delivering dressed poultry, turkeys, chickens, ducks, stewing hens, and Cornish game hens, as well as a full line of beef and pork.

Six children came from 1948 to 1959, Steve, Kermit, Sue Ann, twins, Levon and Levonda, and Joline. They make a happy family.

When Roy first began distributing chicken he counted up 600 pounds of chicken the first day. Now they are doing 450,000 pounds per week. Some growth!

The tremendous impact of a firm like this with its great contribution to Michigana Agriculture, cannot be measured.

Roy's brother Ora is the general Manager, and 3 of the boys have places in the plant.

Roy has been one of the Sponsors of the CROP kickoff dinner at Harry Eby's for many years.

Roy says "We attribute our success to our good employees". What a nice thing to say!

THE UMMELS

Joseph Ummel moved from Ohio after the Civil War and settled on what is now called the John Moyer farm west of Goshen six miles on the south side of County Road 30.

His son, John Ummel, Sr., later moved to a farm which is now known as the Ummel homestead (160 acres) on Prairie Street (County Road 9) six miles south of the original Post Office in Elkhart. It was all muck marsh until they put in a drain ditch.

There were ten children all born on this homestead, including for our purpose John Ummel, Jr. and James Ummel. There were also several well known missionaries, Joseph and Paul.

John Ummel, Sr. was known as the Potato King of this area. He had bought one of the original Mogul one-cylinder farm tractors which pulled three plow bottoms. The Ummel farm was one of the best equipped farms in the area as far as implements were concerned. About 20 acres were planted to peach trees but potatoes was the main crop.

After the farmers depression in 1922, the Ummels got started

174

in registered Holsteins.

John, Jr. and James bought the homestead when John, Sr. sold out in about 1935. Later James took over the 80 acres on the west side of the road.

Both John, Jr. and James developed herds of Holsteins on test and started to show cattle at the State Holstein Show held for a while on West Lincoln Ave. in downtown Goshen and then later on at the Elkhart County Fairgrounds.

Jim had the Grand Champion aged cow for a number of years (Old Reba). Both brothers always did well in the shows. They sold milk to Wambaugh's and Grady's in Elkhart.

In 1955 Jim sold out his dairy herd and began specializing in potato production. In the meantime he had won the Indiana State Championship in yield production, around 800 bushels per acre.

Herb Ummel, famous as a milk tester, is a nephew to the two brothers. James has been on the Missionary Campground Board for many years and is now helping the Missionary Church which has acquired and promoted the Cedar Road Missionary Church's Passion Play in Osceola, rendered annually at Easter Time.

John Ummel, Jr. has been a member of the Elkhart County Council for many years and has fought for good government on every controversial issue. He modernized the barn and built a 65 foot silo. He had been a delegate to the National Holstein Convention for a great many years. His great influence in the dairy field in Northern Indiana needs to be recorded. He now has sold the farm and has built a beautiful home south of the buildings by the little bridge.

All the Ummels have been members of the Bethel Mennonite Church to the south of the farm for many years. The name, Ummel, is tops in the County.

CLARENCE VARNS

Wise and Varns Hardware stood on the southeast corner of the square in Middlebury. In 1909 Clarence Hoover bought the Will Wise interest, when Mr. Wise died, and then it became Varns & Hoover. At that time the double store room was moved across the street on the other corner, and has been there ever since.

Clarence Varns was born in 1896 and went to the Middlebury School at the turn of the century, and attended Goshen College, and then volunteered with the Air Service in World War I.

On his return in the Spring of 1919, he went right into the hardware, and was married in September that year to Wilma Swartz, one of the popular Belles of the day.

They have done a large business for many years. Many of their customers are farm people. They also handle farm supplies, garden equipment and some machinery.

He has been a Director of the Middlebury State Bank for 25 years, was a trustee of Taylor University for 20 years, on the Elkhart County Zoning Board for 14 years, and a very influential citizen of the communtiy and the county. He is also a member of the 24 member board of the Elkhart County Agricultural Society.

One of his hobbies is his 200 acre farm just at the south edge of Middlebury, which he bought in 1938. This farm has been visited by people for miles around as an ultra-modern Dairy Farm, sometimes by farm tour groups.

Some of his tenants have milked as many as 50 Holsteins.

Another hobby is spending their winters in the south, where for years he has participated in the Boca Raton Bible Conference near that city.

In 1970 they sold the business to their daughter and her husband, Mr. and Mrs. Gerald Warstler. Clarence died in October 1974.

The Varns family is known far and wide and has a host of friends.

WCMR AGRICULTURAL NEWS AND MARKETS

The agricultural programming of Elkhart's WCMR Radio is an important source of information to many farmers in this Michiana area. Since 1959, WCMR has been keeping the farmer well informed with agricultural news, interviews and market reports.

Many dairymen as well as other early rising farmers are on hand from 5:55 AM to 6:30 AM each morning, winter and summer, listening to "Farm Fair". Hog producers tune in to the opening livestock markets at 10:40 A.M. A five minute agri-business report examines an important subject to agriculture daily at 12:15 PM. A detailed livestock report of local auctions and grain prices of the local elevators as well as Midwest livestock and the Chicago Board of Trade grain prices are the target of the farmer wanting to catch WCMR's market at 12:20 PM. each weekday. Twice daily county extension reports come from Goshen, Warsaw, and Cassopolis.

Local interviews with farmers and agri-businessmen are alternated with reports from Purdue, the USDA, Indiana Farm Bureau, and many other sources to keep WCMR's farm listeners up-to-date on the news of agriculture on "Farm Fair" and the noon program "1270 Acres."

The younger generation is featured each Saturday at 12:15 PM. on Today's Youth-Tomorrow's Leaders. WCMR is active in promoting 4-H and FFA activities with these programs and in many other ways.

Currently serving as WCMR's Agricultural Director is Larry Schuman.

WALKER — The Dondee Farms, Inc.

Don's father, Mr. Carl Walker (1887) came from Jay County, Indiana, and he found his helpmate, Laura Ford, in Berrien Springs, Mich. After the depression they moved onto the Billy Edwards farm ½ mile east of the Jefferson school and did general farming there. Don was born there October 29th, 1934. Soon thereafter, they moved north of Syracuse on Road Indiana 313 and Don attended Hex school and later New Paris High School where his project was "Calf Club" in F.F.A. Also the writer remembers a bear fenced in by the roadside for the amusement of the children of the neighborhood. This farm had been known as the Pierman farm.

Don graduated from New Paris High in 1952, got a job by the month on a farm near Milford, and the next year married Delores Hollar, a popular young gal in New Paris. Later he joined the army during the Korean War, doing duty in Japan, as a parachutist with the airborn Division.

He learned of the Farm Veterans-on-the-farm training on his return with an honorable discharge and after renting a 151 acre farm south of Union Michigan qualified to enroll in the class. His landlord was a teacher in Mishawaka, a good man to co-operate with a tenant as well as the Farm Veterans Instructor, who was, of course, yours truly.

Don was energetic and ambitious, pushed grain hard, but kept doggedly at the job of building up a herd of Holsteins to as many as 80, milking on the average through those years about 50. The writer remembers when their son Kent was 12 years old, he was handling the

177

whole herd, feeding, milking, breeding, record keeping with mothers help. This let Don free to do the field work.

By 1964 Don was starting in to buy land, and kept buying one piece after another until now he owns over 800 acres with around 700 acres of it under irrigation. Under this category, Don and Delores are entitled to BE IN THE BOOK, as he has demonstrated to Michiana that irrigation really pays off.

Don entered into a contract with Pioneer Corn Co. to grow Single Cross seed corn (Hybrid) 300 acres of the spread is for Pioneer seed corn.

In 1972 they decided to hold a dispersal sale of the wonderful herd of Holsteins, and people came from far and near to buy. Roger Hahn was the auctioneer and did a good job. The high cow brought $2200.00 and was bought by Matthew Schumacher of White Pigeon.

Then they decided to incorporate as a family farm, all 5 named in the papers, including Donna's husband Mike Allan. Mike and Donna the daughter were just married and live on one of the farms.

The outfit is too busy to "join", but are very devout members of the Kessington Community Church on Chicago Trail and Don has had high performance with N.F.O.

THE WARNERS OF GOSHEN

William Warner came from Germany and settled near Wakarusa in 1850. They had 7 children including for our purpose, Eli born 1869 and married to Addie Plank in 1892. They moved to Goshen and he became connected with Sanders Egbert as a mill man. They had 4 sons including Demain, born 1895.

Eli started farming on the Mehl farm, County Road 35, ½ mile north of Indiana State Road 4, on the west side of the road. Later he moved to the Chris Schrock farm where he died in 1906. At this time Addie moved with her 4 boys onto the farm home of her parents Mr. and Mrs. John C. Plank (the present Warner farm). That same summer Mr. Plank passed away.

Demain had attended the Schrock School as well as Rensberger. He took over the Plank farm in 1910, at 14 years of age on a share crop basis. There was some orchard there and they planted some additional trees. Their income at first was from some milk cows, some hogs, and some fruit.

Genevieve was born in 1921 and later was to become the wife of Dr. Kenneth Lehman of Goshen, later Topeka.

These were the lean years what with poor farm prices and increasing family. Phil was born 1931.

Demain had bought the farm (93 acres). They built a chicken house for 300 laying hens, the eggs being sold to the Farm Bureau Hatchery. They planted nearly an acre to strawberries and black and red raspberries, which helped with the income.

In 1937 Demain planted about 4 acres of apples, pears, peaches and sweet cherries.

About 1944 he rented the Eldridge farm across the road which Phil now owns, and Phil was becoming more interested and in 1945 started attending Purdue.

In the meantime, Demain had become interested in community affairs, serving as member and president of the township board 8 years, member and chairman of Triple A for 3 years, chairman of Goshen Farmers Institute for 2 years and chairman of the Extension committee 3 years. He also became interested in the Farmers Co-Operative movement and served as a director of the County Co-op 22 years, 18 of these years as president. The county set up began in 1927 and ten years later it was Demain who negotiated the purchase of the Frank E.C. Hawks grist mill from the granddaughter of Frank Hawks, Mrs. Dan Spohn. Also being in the fruit orchard business, he became Sec'y-Treas. of the Elkhart County Horticultural Society and served 21 years. He was elected a director of the Indiana Farm Bureau Co-Operative Association, served for 24 years, 6 of those years as president. He was director on the National Board of Co-Operatives for 3 years. The accolaids he received from many at his retirement witnessed to his service and influence. Serving on different boards of the First Brethren Church of Goshen, he was a member of the official board for 43 years.

Phil graduated from Goshen High School in 1949 and from Purdue in 1953, then enlisted in the Army where he was a 1st Lieutenant. He was married to Gladys Lung in 1953. In 1955 on his return from U.S. service, Phil took over all the farming on both farms, bought his farm, with Demain retaining title to his.

Since that time they have built up a dairy herd and at this time Phil set up a Landrace bacon type hog breeding program with Harvey

Hull of LaPorte. After 3 years he bought Harvey out and continued for several more years. He remembers selling one sow with a 3rd litter due for $1200.00. They have acquired other land and in 1972 he was farming 550 acres (grain farming).

He was elected to the State House of Representatives in 1972 and has already become an influence in the House. They have 3 children, Stephen, Jennifer, and Nancy, and are active in the Goshen First United Methodist Church.

Phil is on the Finance Committee and a member of the Administrative Board, and Gladys serves on the Pastor-Parish Relations Committee, and the Womens Christian Society Committee.

Demain's brother has just retired as president of Carnegie Tech where he has had great influence in rebuilding a great University.

WAYNE FEED MILL — Wakarusa

The Wakarusa Mill and Elevator Co. was started in 1896. After operation for 2 years it went into the hands of the receivers, Harman Bringolf, trustee in receivership. He operated it for 2 years and then it was bought at Public Auction on March 15, 1900 by Jacob K. Weldy, grandfather of Clesson Weldy, our postmaster at Wakarusa. They manufactured "Fancy" flour. Joseph Schryer, a methodist, was the flour miller. Buying of wheat and milling of flour was the main business. Feed grinding was also an operation.

In 1917, N.L. Layer and sons Harry and Bert, bought the operation and named it the Wakarusa Milling Co. During World War I (1917 and 1918) they operated around the clock, manufacturing flour for the U.S. Government.

Following the war years, the business changed somewhat, retail coal business was on the increase, commercial feeds started coming into prominence necessitating additional grinding and mixing facilities, and additional warehouse space. Shryer retired sometime after 1925.

In the early 1930's, the flour business was taken over by the large flour mills, and in 1931 the flour mill machinery was removed.

On March 1, 1932, a one cylinder diesel engine replaced the steam engine in the boiler room, George Brenneman (present manager) starting with the layers, to install the diesel.

For the first two years George initiated a novel service called the

"Pick up and delivery feed" service. Because of the bank holiday, the mill found it necessary to go on a cash basis with no charge accounts, and ingenious George, with a big heart, would take scads of 12 dozen egg cases on his delivery to offer to receive eggs for the grinding expense and then sell them for 9¢ per dozen to the Wakarusa Produce Co. (South Elkhart Street). The broiler business was coming on with improved dairy herds and beef cattle and hog business and George became the promotion man for the outfit even getting into and solving poultry troubles for the customers.

In 1933, Layer Brothers purchased the Pierceton Elevator, and in 1934 The Claypool Elevator. At this juncture a new name came for the 3 outfits, mainly "Layer Bros. Elevators", and George spread his specialized services to all the communities. The Layer Boys, Harry and Bert, met the challenge of the expanded business, and spent a great deal of money to improve all locations.

Due to expanded business, record keeping became of major importance and George was working into this part of the work, so when Bert took ill, George found the job was up to him (about 1939). Bert died December 11, 1942. Harry is living in Redlands, California.

In 1942, Layer Bros. sold out to Allied Mills Inc. (Wayne Feeds) who now operate the Wakarusa location.

George was made District Supervisor for the concern for 5 years after which he was made the manager of the Wayne Feed Supply at Wakarusa (1948). Since that time they have completely electrified the plant, put in 50,000 bu. capacity grain storage, a seed cleaning plant, bulk fertilizer storage building and many other changes.

George was born November 12, 1911. He went to Wakarusa Schools and a member of Bible Baptist Church. He married Arabella Haines from Nappanee in July 12, 1932. He and Mrs. Brenneman reside at 222 Wabash Ave. They have one daughter, Marcia Ann, who is a teacher in the Fairfield High School.

George says two years before retirement "Working for the public is not always easy, but it has its compensations".

MENNO W. WEAVER FAMILY

When Menno W. Weaver in 1910 purchased the former Longenecker farm of eighty acres in Locke Township two and one-half miles southwest of Wakarusa, he already had a record of years of hard farm labor. Born in Union Township, Elkhart County, Indiana, November 20, 1870, he was the son of Christian Z. and Fanny (Wenger,) Weaver. Both his father Christian and his grandfather John B. Weaver had arrived two and one-half years earlier from Lancaster County, Pennsylvania, and are remembered as Mennonite preachers at Yellow Creek.

Menno completed eight grades at the Good School with a desire for school teaching, but farm work became his portion. Beginning in the spring of 1887 he worked on the farm of his uncle, also named John B. Weaver, near Foraker, then on the Henry Freed farm southwest of Wakarusa, and in 1893 he began working for Cyrus and Margaret (Holdeman) Flickinger on the Joseph Holdeman farm a mile west of Wakarusa. His wages were sixteen or seventeen dollars per month for eight months, and ten dollars per month through the winter when he cut wood and hauled logs. One year he earned $160.00 and another $165.00. In 1899 he operated a wagon buying eggs and selling groceries for Claud B. Nettrour northwest of town, then did several months of farm work for Eli Yoder to the southeast, and on October 22 was married to Catharine V. Flickinger. Then he returned to employment for the Flickingers.

Several more years brought him to the decision to begin farming on shares. This he did one year with his family on the Ephraim Musser farm in Harrison Township, a second year on the Samuel Witmer farm in Olive Township, and then six years on the Flickinger farm in Madison Township, St. Joseph County. Here finally for the first time he had the use of a telephone. Now financial resources were sufficient for buying the farm in Locke Township with help from Stanford Willard of the Citizen's Bank in Wakarusa.

It was on this Locke Township farm that Harley C. Weaver later developed a dairy herd and became widely known in the milk producing industry. He is the youngest son of Menno W. and Catharine V. (Flickinger) Weaver. Of three other sons Edwin L., Mahlon A., and Willis W., the latter died at the age of twelve. There is one daughter Inez V., married to Philip E. Baum.

Although prosperous, Menno was moderate in adding houses and lands. By urgent request he bought in the depression years of the 1930's the Peter Hartman farm of eighty acres, and his wife Catharine V. bought a house at 412 East Waterford Street in Wakarusa to which they moved in 1936. He developed interest for the extension of an electric power line southwest of Wakarusa, which was constructed by Hawks Electric Co. of Goshen and came to be called the Weaver Line. He was long active in the Holdeman Mennonite Church near Wakarusa, and also derived pleasure and profit from travel.

Harley began operating the farm in 1936 and bought it in 1950. Promptly he acquired purebred Holstein cattle. His herd slowly increased until he usually had forty milk cows. He met modern requirements for taking care of milk, but was disappointed with the small profit producers were making. Concerned with what could be done through the associations, he was in 1961 elected president of District 17 of the Pure Milk Association and was re-elected annually, holding the office eight or ten years or until the Pure Milk Association merged with the Association of Milk Producers, Inc. Since he has been annually elected a delegate to both the regional and the national meetings. The Association of Milk Producers, Inc., has 40,000 members, and Harley is also on the resolutions committee. In this year of 1974 he has attended meetings in Madison, Wisconsin; Chicago, Illinois; and Minneapolis, Minnesota. He is also active in the Holdeman Mennonite Church, having served as trustee, Sunday school teacher and superintendent, member of the board of elders, and lay moderator of the congregation.

Married February 15, 1936, Harley and Romaine (Brumbaugh) Weaver have a daughter Frances, who was active in the Holstein 4-H Club until she entered Goshen College as a student. October 17, 1959, she married Ray S. Landis of Blooming Glen, Pennsylvania, and convinced him that he could make it as a dairy farmer. In 1963 they moved to the former Brumbaugh farm south of Goshen, earlier known as the Ecklebarger farm and acquired by Harley and Romaine in 1940. Here Ray, Frances, and their three boys continue the dairy business. Their layout includes a 20 by 60 feet sealed bottom unloading silo, a milking house and parlor built in 1973, a 96,000 gallon manure pit, and a herd of seventy Holsteins. Corn and alfalfa for the dairy operation are their main farm crops. Ray has been president of the Elkhart County Holstein Association, and is general Sunday School superintendent at the Holdeman Mennonite Church.

Mahlon A. Weaver in early years was employed by Holdeman & Son, Elkhart. He and Della Mae Loucks were married October 6,

1923, and purchased the Samuel S. Wenger farm one and one-half miles northeast of Wakarusa April 2, 1929. They have been engaged in general farming, but also had a dairy herd of Holsteins. They owned other farms in Elkhart County, and a winter home near Sarasota, Florida. They had two daughters: Mildred Marie married Lester Shriner and had four sons and three daughters; Gloria Louise married Merl Tyson and had a daughter and two sons.

Edwin L. Weaver began teaching at the age of nineteen in the public schools of Elkhart County, Indiana, and continued later in West Allis, Wisconsin. Then he prepared for and pursued teaching in Christian colleges - Huntington College, Huntington, Indiana; Kletzing (now Vennard) College, University Park, Iowa; Tougaloo College, Tougaloo, Mississippi; and Biola College, LaMirada, California. He also taught in government schools in Ethiopia, and served in Europe as director of an international youth training program.

On May 12, 1974, Lois Ann Baum Schreck graduated from Indiana State University, Terre Haute, Indiana, where her husband Raymond A. Schreck, Jr., is also a student, with the B.S. degree in Elementary Education, and her brother Philip Richard Baum graduated with the B.S. degree in Broadcasting. They are the daughter and son of Philip E. and Inez V. (Weaver) Baum who lives in Wakarusa, Indiana. Phil has been a salesman and owns Phil's Appliance Service. Their son Bradford is a student in Northwood High School.

Our neighbors built a water tank for Amos Weldy across the road in 1909. Mahlon's name is still on the tank beside that of Homer Lehman. Like yesterday!

OSCAR R. WEAVER

Henry Weaver, Oscar's grandfather, bought a purebred Guernsey bull from Levi Ressler, a Whisler Mennonite farmer about the time of World War I.

The upgrading of Henry's herd became the first impact of the Weaver story.

Mahlon, his son, carried on in the same idea and his first son Virgil, now on County Road 32 bought some purebreds in Ohio.

Oscar bought his first registered Guernsey calf from Loren and Maude Truex south of Wakarusa in 1927, for $75.00.

In 1931 Oscar was married to Bessie Hoover and they rented the

Sam Hoover farm, 89 acres, west of old Harrison Center. The next year he went to Berrien County, Michigan with his brother, Virgil, and bought Nancy Hanks of Silver Maples, for $100, and she became the foundation and cornerstone cow of what was to become Oscar's famous herd.

She was the first Guernsey in the State of Indiana to produce over 1000 lbs. of fat. At age 7 she produced 20,074 lbs. of milk, 1087 lbs. of fat in 365 days, milking three times a day.

Yellow Creek Meadow King became the foundation sire.

Truman was born in 1936 and took the Vo. Ag. course in Wakarusa High School and the first showing of cattle from Yellow Creek was by him in 4-H at Rice Field.

Oscar had his first champion cow at the Elkhart Co. Fair in 1951. He has always said production and classification were more important than Fair exhibit. From 1948 to 1956 he received 6 Premier Breeder Awards. In 1944 he bought 44 more acres and later 60 acres, now totaling 244 acres.

In 1947 he built his first barn of 20 stanchions and 8 box stalls, and when Truman was married in 1959, his 2nd barn with 27 free stalls and Truman became a 50-50 partner. They now milk 60 cows and have 130 total Guernseys. They have sold more bulls to artificial breeding groups than any other breeder in America.

They had the first gutter mechanical cleaner in the area.

In 1959, the Indiana Dairy Association gave him a special citation "Master Breeder, Dairyman, Farmer and Leader".

They have held consignment sales on the farm every other year since 1965 and this year, 1973, the average sale per animal was $1015.40. Any breeder may consign any animal which is related to the Yellow Creek lines.

The family was awarded "The Outstanding Family of the Year" in 1963.

Oscar says "There are easier ways to make a living, I'm sure, and dairying is hard work, and means on the job work, 7 days a week, but nevertheless, dairy farming is a very good way of life, breeding better cattle to help other people improve their herds. It has been fun and is challenging and rewarding for me, my wife, and family."

The Weaver family has, indeed, contributed much to Michiana Agriculture.

DOC WELDY — Magic Vet.

George Weldy was born in the Weldy Settlement, a mile west and two and one half miles south of Wakarusa in 1870. He went to the Lockwood one-room rural school to the north and when he grew up he married Lucretia Witmer in 1890. Then they bought the little 40 acre farm just east of Olive Center School on Road 36. The house still stands.

Nelson was born in 1892, the same year as the writer. Samuel was born in 1894, and Mary, Edna, and Glen were born after the turn of the century. Sam went to the Olive Center school as far as the 8th grade, and helped his father with the painting and paper-hanging. They made brooms in the winter. Sam was married in 1915 to Alva Loucks, daughter of Melvin and Fannie Loucks, who lived on the same road on the north west corner of what is now Indiana State Road 19. They settled down on the farm where Nelson Weldy has been living, and in 1919 he rented the Loucks farm on shares, later buying it in 1947. (120 acres). There they built up quite a nice Guernsey Herd of cattle.

Maurice (Doc) was born on this farm in 1916, Miriam after him, Dale in 1928, and Keith in 1933. Keith was in the writers Vo. Ag. Department in Wakarusa, a brilliant student, and we remember the Jimmy Drill with which we presented him as a graduating present in May 1950. Miriam is teaching at Concord, Dale is co-owner of the Ford outfit at Archibald, Ohio, and Keith is in Grand Rapids, Michigan.

Maurice went to Olive Center school 5 years, and when the consolidation came, was transferred to the Wakarusa school. He graduated from High School in 1933, studied at Goshen College one year, transferred his credits to Michigan State College at Lansing, and graduated from the Vet college in 1941. While he was still in college he was married in 1935 to Irene Grabill who had also attended Goshen College. After college, they set up a vet practice at Wakarusa, and soon Doc became the best cow man in the area. Any farmer knows how a vet's wife can help, and we know from experience that Irene deserves some of the credit.

Alice came in 1940, and graduated from Waky High in 1958, and studied at St. Francis in Ft. Wayne (Home Economics). She married Gary Lehman and they live at Archibald, Ohio.

Charlotte was born in 1943, was married in 1965 to Gerald

Mast, a student at Goshen College, and received her degree the next year.

Maurice and Irene split their name syllables to name their famous farm MAURENE, just east of SOUTHWEST which is 4 miles east of Wakarusa. It was set up in 1943, 120 acres. Here have been bred some famous heifers. Doc likes to show cattle and has won many, many ribbons at Local State and National Dairy shows. Last year ('72) he had the Grand Champion Guernsey female at the National Dairy Show at Madison.

He is active in organized Vet Medicine. He is a Past-Pres. of the American Association of Bovine Practitioners. At present he is a member of the House of Delegates of American Vet Medicine Association. He is also a member of the Council of Veterinary Service. Dr. Weldy is a recognized authority in the field of Veterinary Medicine, having given many papers at Local, State, National and International meetings and seminars. His herdsman is Clayton Haver, Jr.

Doc set up the Veterinary Animal Clinic south of Goshen in 1959. He has just completed a new re-planning job including three new examination rooms, the last word in Vet Clinics.

Doc says, "After 33 years, I would say a Vet's job is not an easy one, but it has its rewards from a service viewpoint and it is a source of joy and satisfaction to see the sick animal recover. Also it is interesting to note the great improvement in animal care, in which I hope I have had a small part."

THE WELDY PEOPLE — Locke Twp.

Abraham Weldy was the great-grandson of John Weldy, a native of Switzerland, and married Nancy Yoder, in Tuscarawas County, Ohio in 1849, had a daughter, Elizabeth and in 1951 came to Elkhart, Indiana, walked south of Jimtown with his wife and daughter, stayed overnight with Abe Holdeman on his homestead, and the next day made it to the farm by Letherman's Grove and bought the 138 acres for $872.

They gradually cleared the land and had a real struggle. He became quite a community leader and somebody in the Holdeman church. Gradually he bought other land and ended up with 816 acres.

They had 12 other children, including 6 boys we remember well, Jacob, who later bought the Mill at Waky, John, Evelyn Wyman's grandfather, Henry, Anna Louck's father, Joe, who spent his years to the west in St. Joe County, Levi, the father of Orin, Orville and Allen (Aden is gone) and Amos our good neighbor in the butcher ring days. Wayne showed me the tank we built for Amos with our names scrawled over the top surface.

Henry and Levi were both ordained ministers, Henry in the Funk Mennonite (Holdeman), and Levi in the M.B.C., now the Missionary.

The Weldy story would fill a book, but as the book is full, already, I had better stop before I start. All Nice People!

MENNO WENGER FAMILY

Christian Wenger came from Ontario, Canada (1853) when Russell's grandfather Eli was 7 years old, taking the farm (100 acres) from the government. They built a log cabin and a barn.

Menno was born 1879 and married Amanda Reed in 1904, renting the 100 acres on shares. The barn was struck by lightning and burned in 1906. His father-in-law, Aaron Reed, rebuilt the barn (frame with mangers).

Later Menno bought the 60 acres including the buildings. General farming was practiced.

Russell was born April 26, 1909. His mother died in 1912. Later in 1917 Menno married Ada Reed.

Russell attended the Old Harrison Center School and graduated from Goshen High School in 1927. He worked some with Harold Goldsteins Gladiola farm and became his right hand man.

In the meantime, at age 20, he bought 4 registered Guernsey calves from Dr. D.K. Buzzard, the Glenwood farm (now the Blazer farm) (two for himself and two for his father). These calves became the foundation cows for the famous Wenger Guernsey herd. At that time they had some hogs.

In 1932, Russell married Esther Eby, daughter of Mervin Eby and got 2 cows in the bargain.

In 1935 they bought 2 farms, 70 acres, and by that time were milking about 10 cows.

Carlton was born in 1936 and Ronald in 1937. That year, he seeded the first large field of alfalfa on heavy soil. Langwater-Timothy became the first famous Guernsey bull to be owned jointly by the

Eby's and Wenger's.

In 1948 Russell bought the first hay conditioner (John Deere) in the area.

Later Russell bought Willgorlam King's star bull which did a great deal to increase production and type in the herd.

In 1954, at the Walter Blaser dispersal sale they purchased Yankee Girl and her daughter which has proved to have played a tremendous influence on their herd to the extent almost all the animals on the farm can be traced back to her. Ronald graduated from Purdue in 1960 and received his MS in Nebraska in 1962. He was married in 1959 to Mary Arlene Yoder, daughter of Jerry and Anna Yoder. Carlton lives at home, single and teaches science at Northwood.

The first county Guernsey show was held at the County Fairgrounds in 1938. Animals from the herd have been shown every year since. In 1944 they won their first Premier Breeder Award, and have won a total of 17 including the last straight 10 years. During this time they won Premier Breeder Award at the State Fair the last nine years and 4 of the last 5 years won Premier Breeders Award at the National Dairy Show (Columbus, Ohio and Madison, Wisconsin). The above mentioned achievements contributed to their winning the Dairyman of the Year Award in the State of Indiana in 1971. Russell and Ronald have been in partnership together since 1965.

The losses of the Palm Sunday Tornado in which they lost 3 barns and 2 sheds, necessitated rebuilding.

The other farm boy, Clifford Wenger, married Lucille Pletcher in 1942. They moved into their new home west of her father Sam Pletcher. Later they bought the Parcell farm ½ mile east, 80 acres, and also bought the first location, 40 acres.

They now own 120 acres and farm her fathers place, 120 acres, total 240 acres.

Their family with 3 children was selected as the Outstanding Farm Family for 1972.

The 3 children are in 4-H and Clifford is proud of his Guernsey herd of 75 cattle, milking around 50 cows. Theirs is truly an outStanding farm family.

Menno's third son is an oil man with Abshires, Paul Devon Wenger, often nicknamed "Zeke".

Since this writing Russell has passed on to the "Good Dairyland".

THE WHITEHEADS

On September 23, 1742 Stoffel Weisskopft (Christophel White-head) landed in Philadelphia from Germany. With him was his wife Margretia, daughter Magdelina, and a son Valentine, born enroute to America. He was the first Valentine of seven to date (1974). Since 1742 there has been at least one Valentine living. At present there are two.

The father died soon after arriving in America, and the widow married Christian Rodebaugh and settled near Irwin, Pa.

Valentine the 1st, raised a family of 12 children. His son, Valentine Jr. moved to Montgomery Co., Ohio in 1815 and raised a family of 7 sons and 5 daughters and to their families were born 91 children. Of these 6 sons and 3 daughters came to Elkhart County, Indiana from 1836 to 1842 and they all settled in Jackson Township. They purchased a total of 42,784 acres of land from the U.S. Government. Today, only one direct descendant owns any of this land.

Samuel, the third son, settled just south of the Maple Grove Church, west of New Paris. He was married to Sarah Frantz and they had 5 sons and 3 daughters. Valentine, the second, father of the above children purchased the entire Section 17 from the U.S. Later Samuel acquired 240 acres, Valentine the third 160 acres, Peter 80 acres, and Lewis 160 acres.

Merl stayed on the farm until 1916. In 1918 he married Edna Berkey, daughter of Hugh and Amanda Berkey, and they moved into the house east of Samuel's homestead and started working as an electrician for the I.&M. He was in the trucking business from 1921 to 1937, worked at Penn Switch up to 1940, then purchased the Elias Lutz farm on County Road 38 east of the Lincoln Highway. He went into the broiler business, capacity 15 to 18,000, converting the barn into a broiler house, and a 30 x 50 bldg, and a 2 story cement block building 36 x 80.

After Valentine the 3rd died, Valentine Whitehead the 4th and Henry Whitehead bought the 160 acres from his estate. Later Valentine bought Henry's 80 acres. Henry was the grandfather of Carlyle Pickering, then Valentine the 4th moved south of New Paris. After teaching school a while, he married Christine Smith, and after living a while in his father's log cabin, built a new house in which he lived until he died in 1898. He had 2 sons, Samuel E. and Frank J. Then in

1890 he bought the Samuel Ott farm of 160 acres ½ mile west of the Solomon's Creek Church. Then that November, he, Samuel married Susan Peters and they moved on the Ott farm. Valentine's brother-in-law Samuel Smith had bought the Prickett farm a few years earlier. Eventually Samuel and Susan owned the entire farm.

Samuel and Susan had 3 sons, Merl, Russell and Harold and Cecil, a daughter. In 1920 Samuel died and Susan too, in 1940. Then after Samuel died, Russell and Harold farmed the farm for a while and after Susan died Russell bought it.

Russell had a daughter, Phyllis, and a son Richard. Richard now owns the farm, and lives there, married Doris Lehman of New Paris and they have 3 sons, Barry, Craig, and Brett. Harold bought the Jesse Metz farm a mile east of the intersection of U.S. 6 and State Road 15, and last year sold it and moved to New Paris. He married Alta Frey, and they have 2 daughters, Marylin married to Robert Guiver and live in Denver and have 3 boys, and Esther who married Robert Musselman, and they are in Bloomington with a son and a daughter. Cecil, Samuel's daughter married Clem Bowers and they now live in Sebring, Florida.

By 1850 Elkhart County was much interested in the promotion of the Broiler Industry, and Merl was instrumental in setting up the AUCTION, became a Director of the Poultry Association. The Poultry Association was very much interested in the art of Barbecuing and that led to Merl's interest in the field. As a labor-saver, he developed the Rotisserie and set up a factory on the farm in the first broiler building, to manufacture the barbecue equipment. That led to the catering he did at the County Fairs for many years, 12 to be exact, and then his whole family quit the business in 1968.

Merl says "The Poultry business was mighty good to us".

They enjoy their retirement years on Egbert Road in Waterford and their trips to Florida.

Merl gets in this book, because of his outstanding contribution to the Poultry and Broiler business. Some Contribution!

THE J. ORBIE WEYBRIGHTS

J. Orbie Weybright was born in 1878 on his father's farm and at school age went to Hardscrabble School on the Huntington Road, across from Ralph Smith. Later he started farming on what is now known as the Emerson and Robert Neff farm, then married a daughter of James Berry in Goshen.

Bill Weybright was born there in 1901 and went to the same school, and Orbie later bought the farm on U.S. 6, which we now call the Bill Weybright farm, Orbie's first wife died at an early age, and then he was re-married, to Bertha Culler and from that union came Mary Weybright, who later married Fred Gall.

When Bill grew up he married Bessie Wagner, who lived on the County Line Road. Later they bought a little place to the east on 6, and Gerald was born there in 1920. Later he bought 80 acres of his fathers 160 on U.S. 6. Then in 1922 Evelyn was born and Opal came 2 years later.

In 1927 Bessie died and for the time the children were farmed out to the grandparents, both sides. In several years Bill was re-married to Elsie Gall.

By 1930 Gerald joined the 4-H pig club at New Paris, and bought a registered gilt at the Indiana State Fair from one of the exhibitors, and that started them into the purebred Chester White business, him and his father Bill. Thereafter they would breed around 20 or 25 sows and gilts, and through the years sold many registered gilts and boars to 4-H, F.F.A. and also to individual breeders. To bring in new blood they would occassionally buy a new boar for improved breeding.

Then they bought the other 80 acres to the west and through these years 5 children were born by the second wife, Joan, Dorothy, Robert, Julia, and Bill. They also started with Holsteins, like 40 animals, milking 20 to 25. Then Gerald was married to Lola Stouder of the Union Center Church of the Brethren, and they rented the Sam Dillon farm, 100 acres, on the County Line Road, also renting other ground until they were farming 450 acres, general farming. This went on for years with Karen coming in 1942, Philip in 1945, and David in 1950.

In 1954 they bought the Glen Byler Farm on County Road 25, just north of U.S. 6. Gary was born there soon after they moved.

Later they bought 100 acres of the Rodibaugh farm to the south.

They went to Registered cattle up to 30 milkers, Grade A. This is when Gerald's children went into the 4-H pig club, Registered Chester Whites. They won many ribbons at the Elkhart County Fair. They also rented the Sheffield farm, put up quite a large silo, and when everyone else was going to bulk milk, they went out of cows, because the children were going off to North Manchester to College. For the last 10 years, Gerald has had Co-op gas for the south east quarter of the county, and the last 4 years he has been the county President of Farm Bureau.

Gerald and Lola have always told their children, if they would work hard on the farm, they would see them through college, and it has been so.

Now Karen is married to Jerry Snyder, son of Paul and Dorcas Snyder, and they live in Dunlap, and he is a probation officer; and she is a nurse in the Goshen Hospital. They have 2 children; Jeffrey 8 and Michelle 6. Philip was just married to Cynthia Hazen, they live in Argos and he is teacher and coach. David finished Manchester in '72, and works in Boston and Gary will be a Junior in Manchester.

ROBERT WILSON

Robert Wilson was born west of Milford Junction April 30, 1910 on a farm. His folks did general farming and later his father Marion set up a feed mill in the old Reddens flour mill on the mill race in Baintertown, south of Waterford Mills, after competition from National Flour brands had forced the flour mill to close. Bob worked in the Baintertown Mill as a boy.

In 1924, Marion and Irvin Darkwood set up a feed mill in a a building in Millersburg built by the Millersburg welfare association as an incentive for Marion to move his family there to serve the community.

Move there they did the next year, 1925, and even though Bob was going to Millersburg High School, he started to work in the mill from that time. He soon became the office boy keeping records and also handling transactions. Mr. Darkwood soon dropped out of the partnership, leaving Marion the sole owner. They had set in one of the first hammer mills in the area.

Bob graduated from high school and they secured a franchise with the Wayne Feed Mill of Ft. Wayne, so the Wilson outfit has the reputation of being the oldest Wayne Feed dealer in the county.

Right in the middle of the depression, Bob married Lottie Long, daughter of Ray Long. George was born in 1933 and Loretta in 1935.

Marion bought a coal business from another dealer and that helped some. In 1945, Marion bought the old opera house and moved it onto his property, and put in new grinding and mixing equipment. But the next year Marion died, and the following year Bob bought out the heirs of the estate.

Later he added farm supplies for the accomodation of customers. Nearly all their business is within 5 miles of town. Bob knows his business and is known as an authority in the feed business.

From the first he has supported 4-H giving beautiful canes to showmanship champions for many years.

Bob's motto from the start has been "Live, and let live".

WALTER WOGOMON'S BROILERS

Ben Wogomon was born in 1893, the son of James and Lisa Wogomon on a farm on Oakland Ave. south of Elkhart, north of the Cable Line Road.

They did general farming and Ben went to a little country school on the corner of the Fink farm. When he grew up he was married to Bessie Billman and moved in with her folks, and took over the farming. Walter was born there in 1916. Several years after that Mr. Billman was killed and the son John continued with the Threshing Machine. That was in 1918. Ben continued with the farming. The next two years, Mabel and Clara came. Sometimes in the busy threshing season, Ben would go with the outfit.

Walter went to the Olive Center School. Kenneth was born in 1927. Then Ben bought an eighty acre farm (the Burkett farm) east of State Road 19 and rented it out.

Ralph Metzler was the son of Solomon and Catherine Metzler, who lived 1½ miles north of Wakarusa on the east side in a lane. Then in 1917 Ralph married Viola Hoover a daughter of Sam and Lucinda Hoover just west of Harrison Center. At first he worked with the Hoovers, then bought the 80 acres (now the Raymond Pfeiffer farm.) There, during the next 12 years 5 girls were born. The first born died of T.B. at age 2, Lois in infancy, Rosalene, owner of the Credit Bureau, and Norma wife of Raymond Pfieffer, Wakarusa feed center, and Berdine, our Queen, who now becomes the wife of Walter Wogomon in 1937. They moved on Ben's Burkett farm on County Road

38. Walter did general farming there, also hauled milk several years for Silver Cup in Nappanee.

James was born in 1941 and Connie in 1943. Then is when he started filling silos, McCormick silage cutter, 60 silos a year, bought a 2 row mounted picker, picking about 400 acres per year, $2. per acre.

This extra money helped buy the 72 acre Jesse Christophel farm on County Road 15, and they farmed that also, resold it after 2 years, and a couple years after that bought the 145 acre farm west of Waterford on Road 138 (The Burt Uline farm), just a stone's throw from County Road 19. That is when the rainbow touched down.

At first they built up a commercial herd of dairy cattle like 40 head, milking 30, selling milk to Wambaugh's. This went on until 1950 when they went into the BROILER BUSINESS. They converted the barn into a broiler house and the first year produced 3 batches of 20,000 each, total 60,000 broilers or fryers. They sold the finished birds to J & J Poultry, of Middlebury, and a Mr. Miller on Indiana 13 just south of U.S. 20. It took 130 to 140 tons of feed per batch.

After 6 years they switched to roasters. Also they raised about 1500 Leghorn pullets, twice a year for flock replacement. In 1964 they bought the Albert Fisher farm of 70 acres and farmed that also.

Walter was on the Board of Directors of the Elkhart County Poultry Association for 15 years. Also, the Wogomon Swimming was a boon for the chicken catchers, probably the first farm swimming pool in the county. Then in 1973 they sold everything and moved to a home they enjoy at 2609 Martin Manor Drive. Also they spend some time on Key Largo.

They are both, still, on the Project Committee of the Elkhart County Agricultural Society, and he and Berdine put over the first big Agricultural Day for the Ag. Society last Thursday afternoon at our Elkhart County Fair.

After all these years Walter says "I surely miss working on my machinery". They are still very busy, even though retired.

YEATER'S EXCHANGE

THE FARMER'S EXCHANGE has been published weekly at New Paris, Indiana since January 1, 1928. It was founded in November, 1926 in Nappanee, Indiana by Vernon L. Stump, Waldo E. Yeater, Clarence V. Boyer and C.L. Thomas. It was a tabloid, the same as now, and was printed by the E.V. Publishing House, of which V.L. Stump was manager at that time (he died many years ago). Mr. Boyer was bookkeeper at the same plant. Mr. Yeater became the first editor of the Farmer's Exchange and served from November 5, 1926 to May 25, 1961 - about 35 years. In December of 1927 the Exchange moved from Nappanee to New Paris and the issue of January 6, 1928 was the first to be published there. On July 10, 1928 the Exchange Publishing Corporation was formed by W.E. Yeater and Charles F. Lamberg who had become partners at the start in New Paris. A number of New Paris businessmen gave financial support to the corporation and Mr. Lamberg sold out by end of that year. Mr. Yeater has remained a stockholder and a member of the board of directors up to the present (1974).

In 1961 following the retirement of Mr. Yeater his son Lawrence E. assumed the position of editor-publisher which he still holds.

Soon after World War II the Exchange grew with the general economy and now covers some nine counties in northern Indiana and southern Michigan with a circulation of over 12,000.

YELLOW CREEK FEED MILL AND ELEVATOR

Anson Witmer married Fern Weaver August 17, 1947 and in 1950 settled and rented the Harold Schrock farm and started a mill to grind feed for their laying flock of 2000 laying hens, and later 8000 broilers.

In the 1950's they secured a contract with Napiana for supplement and feed supply, securing several bulk trucks to deliver feed to dairy farms, cattle feeder and hog farms, as far as Herman Schrocks dairy on Beech Road, St. Joseph Co., south to Milford and north and east close to Middlebury.

They bought the farm (78 acres) and the mill in 1962.

Donald was born in 1952, Terry in 1954, and was killed in an accident, Marion in 1957, Betty in 1958, and Carl in 1960. All of them were in the 4-H program.

Donald and Devon live on the farm and both work at the mill, Devon full time. The others go to Wakarusa and Northwood High School.

In 1964 they put up a fertilizer building and started selling bulk fertilizer. The Palm Sunday Tornado took down the straw shed and they built a new 40 x 60.

In 1969 they built a new implement shed and hog house. They have 15 sows and gilts and feed out 250 hogs per year. In 1972 they remodeled the mill and installed two 2-ton mixers. They now have 5000 roasters (meat chickens twice a year 10,000 for the year).

They do considerable custom work with a new applicator truck (weed and feed mixture it is called). They do custom combining and have 2 grain dryers to do custom drying.

They are all members of the Olive Mennonite Church, where he has been a trustee for many years and also sponsors the annual C.R. O.P. kickoff dinners.

THE CLARENCE YODER FAMILY

Clarence Yoder was born in Midland, Michigan in 1921 on his fathers farm and his father died when he was 6 years old. At age 9 his mother married a man she knew as a child in Illinois and owned a farm in Kokomo, Indiana where family moved at that time. At age 17 Clarence rented 120 acres and went into general farming. At age 20 he bought a small farm still living with his mother and when he was drafted, 1942, he chose civilian public service and worked 3½ years on a large dairy farm near his home. Thereafter he rented 4 other farms (general farming) and then in 1948 he married Leona Hostetler in his church in his community and lived on his 25 acre farm. The first year on his 10 acres of tomatoes, the produce netted $3500.00. Glen Dale Yoder was the first child born in 1949.

In 1950 he bought 140 acres, remodeled the buildings and started in the Holsteins. He got his start buying some cows at the Elkhart County Holstein sale.

In 1951 Arlene was born and by 1953 he was milking 23 cows and he bought an additional 60 acres. Clint was born in 1955 and then Clarence sold the dairy herd at a dispersal and fed 70 head of Herefords followed by feeder pigs from 50 sows, finishing 6 to 700 hogs per year (2 litter basis). In 1956 he bought another 80 acre farm. The he owned 280 acres. In 1958 he sold out and the Pine Manor (Martin) farm was for sale and he bought the 267 acres, a beautiful layout with one of the most ample rural homes in the area.

He started in turkey business with 36,000 poults. The next year he bought the 160 acre Wiggins Farm. He increased the turkey a little each year, up to 150,000 now 92,000, also he remodeled the barn for 10,000 Leghorn layers. Selling eggs to different people but now to Kroger's.

Joyce Marie was born in 1960.

In 1961 he bought the Allem Smoker farm (144 acres).

In 1965 he started building homes on Kercher Road (East) and there are at least 20 homes there now.

Also he started a breeding herd of Angus beef cattle and in that year Joyce Marie went into 4-H Beef Club.

The Purina Mill was purchased in 1967 and he switched his feed line to Nutrena.

In 1970 he bought the Roman Gingerich farm (74 acres) bringing his total acreage of land owned to 645 acres.

Joyce Marie had the Grand Champion calf at the Elkhart Co. Fair and at the annual sale, sold for $4988.

The Yoders are members of the Waterford Mennonite Church, very active in church and communtiy and have a host of friends.

MANASSES — Rev. Allen — Leonard Yoder Family

Manasses Yoder was born in Logan County, Ohio, in 1848. With his parents he walked to Elkhart County and settled on the prairie southeast of Goshen. On Christmas Day, 1873, he married Lydia Smoker at the house of her parents, Mr. and Mrs. Jacob Smoker.

Manasses and Lydia spent the rest of their life farming on the Elkhart Prairie. They lived until 1933 and 1936, respectively, and had 6 children namely: Allen, Emma, Cassie, Irena, Arvilla, and Willis.

The eldest son, Allen Yoder, was born in 1874 and helped his father farm until he married Laura McConaughy in 1896. They had 7 children: Paul, Joseph, Esther, Thomas, Harry, Leonard, and William the latter died at the age of 9 years.

Allen and Laura started house-keeping on a farm by the six-span bridge near Bristol. Two years later they purchased a farm by the

198

Clinton-Elkhart township line on the Silver Street Road, now County Road 34. Nine years later they traded for a 150 acre farm on the College Road across from the Union Chapel Cemetery.

In 1911 the Allen Yoder family moved to the Weaver farm one and one-half miles west of the Silver Street Church, where Allen lived for 40 years.

April 16, 1920 Mother Laura died and was buried in the Rock Run Cemetery. Father Allen, Esther, and the boys managed the farming and household duties for 1½ years until Sophia Vercler and her 10 year old daughter, Lucille, came to help them. This second marriage was blessed with 3 children: Ruth, Allen Jr., and Dale.

In the spring of 1951 Allen and Sophia retired from farming. All 10 children were by that time married and had established homes of their own. Allen Jr. and Marie rented the home place.

Allen and Sophia's retirement home was a 37 acre farm just west of the Yoder homestead. He spent his spare time raising broilers.

Church work was very important to Allen. He was baptized into the Clinton Frame Mennonite Church in June 1890 by Rev. D.J. Johns. Not many years later he changed his membership to the Silver Street Mennonite Church and was called to the ministry by that congregation in 1913. He then attended Moody Bible Institute and toured the Holy Land. He served the Silver Street Church as minister for 22 years, at which time his son, Harry, became its pastor, Allen was very active in the General Conference of Mennonites. He became a member of Congo Inland Mission Board in 1914 and sent financial aid for mission work in what is now named Zaire, Africa.

Sophia died in 1955 and Allen then spent several years with Dale and Norma. He died at the age of 93 years and 11 months at Froh Retirement House, Sturgis, Michigan.

At the time of his death Allen had 30 grandchildren, 82 great grandchildren, and 2 great, great grandchildren.

The only member of Allen's family who does nothing but farming is Leonard. After 2 years at Bluffton College he married a neighbor gal, Pauline Phillips, who at that time was teaching at the Clinton Community School.

Leonard and Pauline started farming together in the spring of 1937 in LaPorte County. After 4 years they moved to Benton County for one year, and then purchased the Fred Yoder farm at the intersection of County Roads 36 and 31. Here they still reside on a 273 acre farm. In addition to this they have a 171 acre cattle ranch 2 miles north of Middlebury where Leonard tends a beef cow herd which furnishes approximately as much exercise as playing in weekly golf tournaments.

In this family are 7 children: Jay, Ray, Max, Sue, Lou, Zoe, and Pat. Also there are 3 daughters-in-law, 2 sons-in-law (the third one will join the family in August) and 10 grandchildren.

Len and Pauline have a very enticing hobby - that is travelling. They enjoy comparing cultures and geographical features in different areas - snow capped mountains is their speciality. Thus far they have seen a bit of each of Uncle Sam's states and four continents. Indiana is not the most beautiful but the most appreciated.

The community of this area is made up largely of people whose lives are guided by Christian principles set forth in the New Testament. This creates an ideal climate for all aspects of life - economically, mentally, socially, and spiritually. In an environment like this it is an easy task to have "high yields" in these 4 aspects of life. Therefore, if a person has the strength to "stand up", these good winds will blow us to an enjoyable life - this is what some people refer to as being successful. Therefore, Leonard says, "Stand up and be blown and success will be yours."

LOLA YODER AND HER SHEEP

Leland (Bud) Yoder; son of Marion Yoder; was in the navy in Hawaii in 1946 and met and married Lola Kehr in Honolulu; and they returned to the States in 1951, coming back to Goshen, Indiana where Kim was born. With a baby girl, Randi, born in 1950, they felt it would be best to buy a piece of ground out in the country where the children could grow up on a farm.

So they bought a 29 acre place on County Road 40, ½ mile east of U.S. 33.

Bud was well established in Real Estate and felt the family should play around with beef cattle and sheep until they knew what they wanted to do. When Randi became 10 they had to decide and the sheep won. They had grade sheep, so it was felt she should start with a registered animal and they went to Ray Mishler's sale and bought a registered Suffolk ewe lamb and also a ram lamb. That was their start in the sheep business. Then they bought part of the old Hess farm (91 acres).

Kim did not wait until he was 10 to get into 4-H. He started showing about 8 years old in the open class.

Lola has often said "It is good for youngsters to be brought up on a farm where they learn hard work and disappointments as well as achievements". Lola, herself, and with Bud, her husband got into the game and before they knew it were winning prizes at the Elkhart County Fair.

The sheep breeders had tried to organize a county association in the sixties but it did not succeed.

Tom Miller, Perry Miller's son and Lola wrote letters to all sheep breeders in the county to invite them to come to a meeting in the extension office. There an association was formed in 1962 (July 6). Tom Miller was elected President and Lola was made secretary-treasurer. Lola was secretary until 1972, when she was made President.

In the meantime, through the 4-H Lamb Club, she was able to have set up a 4-H Lamb Club food booth, featuring lamburgers.

Working away from fat cover toward lean meat type carcass, the breeders voted to set up the first carcass show in 1963, and have had one every year since. (The only show of its kind in Indiana).

In the meantime, Lola and the family were showing Suffolk sheep at Elkhart Co., Kosciusko Co., Centreville, and Indiana State Fairs, walking off usually in the County Fairs with firsts, reserve and grand champions, and high placings in the State Fairs.

To top it all off on September 6, 1973, Lola was appointed to the State Fair Board by Gov. Otis Bowen.

Both children are in Western Michigan University, Randi to graduate December 1973. The Yoders have contributed much to agriculture. Lola is now President of the Indiana Sheep Breeders and a director in the State Association of County Fairs.

Bud passed away on June 23, 1974.

MILO J. YODER AND MURIEL

Jonas Yoder was born in 1895, the son of Sam and Amanda Yoder of Yoder Corners, south of Shipshewana. At age 22 he married Delilah Borkholder (1917) and the next year our star was born, Milo J.

Soon they moved to Nappanee, and took over a 120 acre farm with peppermint as the main crop. They were there 4 years and then they moved to the little community called Little Pine near Pine Creek (the Church of the Brethren is just across the road from the Elcona Golf Club on U.S. 20). McCudney was the first farm, and then Ray Messick had a cattle farm there too. Milo went to the Little Red School House right there on the south east corner for several years.

After working a number of farms, Jonas finally moved to New Paris and ended up hauling milk for the New Paris Creamery for 20 years. It was during this time that Milo as a teen-ager worked for farmers by the day and month, dairyman for Mr. Dan Snider's herd of Jerseys for several years. Funny thing how fate takes a hand in our affairs. Milo wanted to practice with the basketball team in New Paris, but the long evening milk chores forbid it, and determined to participate in athletics, Milo left there and made expenses in high school by shovelling snow for the residents of the town, 10¢ per hr. Then he got the job at Rohrer's Funeral Home, and that is where he got the idea of the business. He graduated from New Paris High in 1937.

Muriel Kring was born in St. Joseph County, on the Burr Oak farm, west on Kern Road to the bend, and attended Greene Twp, the first consolidated school in 1929, and graduated from the high school in 1942. Greene Twp. was named after her great grandfather Jackson Greene. One of her teachers introduced her to Milo.

To some, World War II days might be a poor time to get married, but to Milo and Muriel it was a challenge to serve. Milo up and married her and then enlisted in Alternate Service in Michigan and Maryland, and together they had a great experience. Then in 1946 they went to Indianapolis and Milo took the year in Mortuary school, and while there, Muriel helped pay expenses, with a job for the Soil Conservation Service, right there in the city.

The next act begins with Milo and Muriel in North Manchester, trying for a college education, but after a while Nancy Jeanne came and that ran up the expenses, so after two years they decided Milo had to get a job and some experience in Undertaking more than a sheepskin, so they went into a funeral home in Hammond, then a turn in a set up in South Bend and in 1949 they took the plunge, moved to Middlebury, bought out Owen Ott and Mel Haines Funeral

Parlor, and set up their own business. These were the years of building, Richard Miller of Middlebury took training and worked for them and in the meantime Milo's brother John went through mortuary training, spent 5 years with Culp's in Goshen, and that is when they took the bull by the tail, borrowed a thousand here from a friend, and $5000 from another and built the grand set up south of the College, selling the Middlebury location to Richard Miller.

By June, 1958, Elmer Culp had died, and Floyd and Elmer's son Bob were willing to sell Ephraim Culp and Sons to them and for Floyd to go in with them, which he did a year until he died.

Then in 1962 Rieth Rohrer and Ehret were formed and Milo and John, sold them the buildings at 311 South Main as a place to start from scratch, Milo and John, retaining rights to the name Yoder-Culp.

Carl Yoder a brother in Nappanee, has the old Wright Funeral Home but there is no connection with Yoder-Culp.

Milo was elected to the Board of Directors of Heifer Project International in July of 1973, after serving as a volunteer for 25 years. These years he has been serving to raise funds for the program, then helping to deliver animals to numerous countries around the world, including India, Russia, Ecuador, Dominica, and our own states of Miss., and South Dakota, to start herds for milk production to feed hungry babies.

N.B: Brother John, is married to Elizabeth Hostetter. They have 3 children. Tim has just graduated from Purdue, and helping; Margaret, married to a farmer in Pa. with 600 steers; Robin, doing a year, volunteer, Retirement Home, Sebring, Florida. Nice People!

STUFF AND THINGS ABOUT MICHIANA FARMERS

When you accidentally step in a pile of fresh manure, you hurt your foot, then as you approach the house, you had better do the Barnyard Dance before you go inside, or get a cuff on the head by the old lady, wiping it all off on the grass or the snow, sideways, backwards and every way. Many farmers have scrapers to make the job easy.

These days early farm programs over the cow barn radio help raise the spirits, farm news, crop reports, farm pointers and all.

All our old cook stoves used to have reservoirs for hot water, heated while the cookin' was going on. A big dipper hung near by, and it took only about 4 big dippers to fill the dish pan to wash the dishes.

Every farm had a SLOP BARREL and the dishwater would be dumped in that as they figured it contained lots o' goodies for the hogs. The big barrel was half sunk in the ground half way to the barn, fair to both the gals who had to dump the dish water, and to the boys who had to carry the big 5 gallon slop pail to the barnyard to the hogs.

The MEDICINE CABINET in the barn had lots of uses and lots of smells, including the strong smell of Spohn's Distemper cure, with a smell of tar, salves for animal injuries, carbolic acid, and turpentine.

The SMOKE HOUSE was an institution of its own, with hams, shoulders, and ribs, hanging high out of reach of the fox. When you opened the door to fetch a ham in for supper, your saliva would start to drip.

The CELLAR in winter was heaven-on-earth, bushels of apples of a dozen varieties, potatoes and other vegetables by the bin, a score of gallon crocks of apple butter, but you would always come out smelling the turnips, or the cider, or the wine, or the peppermint.

When the corn crib was about empty, there would always be a RAT DAY, every dog and cat on the place and every kid armed with a stick or club. It was fun comparing the "kill" of your own rat days with the neighbors.

Everyone had a kick out of the "SNIPE HUNT", take the least suspecting dumb-bell in the crowd and let him or her "hold the sack" while the rest chased the snipe around the tree, way out in the woods, and then slip home and wait till late for the erstwhile sackholder to catch on and start the long trek home.

The BUTCHERING RING. It was the natural thing for a few close neighbors to plan a butcher ring, say like 4 families come to your place at 7 in the morning on a set day, help kill your 3 or 4 butcher hogs, scald them in barrels of scalding water, use hog scrapers to get the hair off, hang up on a scaffold, gut the thing, saw down the back, and on with the different stages, always hog liver with salt for dinner, and the last thing in the afternoon, frying out the lard, and running the cracklings through the lard press.

When I was ready to butcher I would notify the rest of you to come, with all your tools, special shaped butcher knives especially. No suppers, everybody had to dig for home to start chores.

THRESHING RINGS the same. When you were notified you had to go, whether or not. If you were sick, you had to hire a man to go in your place. No one who ever lived through it, will forget the wonderful threshing dinners, as well as the practical jokes, or tricks.

APPLE BUTTER DAY was an experience never to forget, the bushels of apples, the peeling, sometimes with a newly invented device, the shining copper kettle, the fire, the long fabricated handle for stirring, every helper with a different idea when "it was done".

Question please, how do you cover the crock so the top will not mold?

BLACK RASPBERRIES. Every gal over 50 knows what it means to don a pair of overalls, take a gallon pail and start around the 20 acre field making all the patches of old fashioned black raspberries, the insufferable hot sun, mosquitoes, and flies, and above all the old fashioned stink bug, which invariably fell into the pail, and the suffering of it all, but when dad would rave about the delicious pie or cobbler at night, the pain would be forgotten, and the loving smile, paid you off BIG. BLACKBERRIES, were the same, only worse, as the jaggers were longer and sharper and even through several pairs of trousers, and dad's jackets, they would still stick you to the quick, and the long high stalks, hard to reach, and then the bumble bee nest in August would be the last straw. Well they say the more you suffer, the more you enjoy the payoff.

THE LITERARY SOCIETY. Every community has gone through that. A group of do-gooders want to elevate the community so they get the thing started. Then somebody asks you to perform, entertain, give a reading or take a place on the program. You take a whack at it and every time you do you do it over 3 times, first how you think you will do it, secondly, how you actually do your thing, and thirdly when you get to bed how you wish you "had done it".

THE BOX SOCIAL. Did you ever make a box of goodies and take it to a BOX SOCIAL? and did you ever see a city slicker outbid you for your best girl's box, after your pocket book said STOP?, and then not to be humiliated you had to bid off another girl's box, and it was rough!

THE LAST DAY OF SCHOOL. Younger people have missed a circus, who have not lived through it. The Program, the Photo of Pupils and Teacher, the many visitors and parents for the first time ever, and the tearful farewells. These are just a few of the mountain top experiences that will live in our hearts FOREVER.

SUGAR TIME. When February comes, then you know its time to get fixin' to get ready for the tapping of the sugar trees. The trees must be hard sugar maple. You have to sharpen the bit, clean up the spiles, pails and all the equipment, for when it starts to melt in the day and freeze in the night, that's when the sap runs good. There had to be a central shack or sugar camp, a place in which to set the big tank in which we would boil down the sugar water to a syrup. Probably less than a dozen sugar camps left in the county. Too Bad!, how can you beat pancakes with the heavenly maple syrup?

COON HUNTIN'. Women have to put up with it. Two or 3 neighbors comin' to the farmstead about 10 o'clock when every honest man should be in bed, with their coon dogs yelping, anxious for the hunt. There has to be a big sack lunch, and plenty of coffee, for who knows, we may not be back til' mornin'. Then a cat nap, and the distant bellowing is the sign that they have a coon treed. But the trouble is, there is a big hole in the top of the tree where the coon sought shelter, and a noise in the shed says the boys came back for cross-cut saw, aimin' to cut the tree down to get the coon. What men won't do when they get started?

ASAFETIDA. That's a salve-like stuff mother puts in a bag and hangs around daughter's neck, she says to keep away whooping cough diptheria, and scarlet fever, but I have often wondered if she doesn't do it to keep the boys at a safe distance, as it stinks to the high heavens. At a party of young people, the moment some gal would enter with the stuff around her neck, everybody would start to sniff.

At spelling bees many years ago, the dictionary held it must be spelled asafoetida; now the "o" is dropped.

COUNTRY ODORS I HAVE KNOWN. Calamus, is something'. When you dig up the bulbous root, you realize it is merely Blue Flag, or Wild Iris; Mice, when you open the corn crib door; rotting wood when you bust up an old stump, fresh sliced peaches, and real ripe strawberries in a pan, ready for cobbler; turpentine, when sniffing the uncorked bottle; Spohn's Distemper cure; meat in the smoke house; a horse stable with MARSH HAY as the bedding; the fertilizer box in the planter or drill; skunk on a foggy morning; cinnamon in the spice cupboard; lather on a sweated horse; the "still" on a peppermint farm; the breath of the ferret, after a long stay in the rabbit hole; harness leather, long in use; a score of odors from the fruit cellar; fresh-mown hay; powder in the gun after discharge creosoted posts; the pig-sty; axle grease; fresh window pane putty; Venetian Red; bees wax, and a hundred others, each one a smell of its own. My! My!, if you cannot close your eyes and recall those pungent odors, you haven't lived!

THE OLD FASHIONED HUSKIN' BEE. In most cases it would be when a farmer or his oldest son, or his right-hand-man was injured or laid up, and help was needed, badly, with winter comin' on. Word would be sent around through the grapevine that a date was set. It took a close friend of the family to do the invitin'. At sunrise that morning the folks would start to gather, some wagons, all kinds of huskin' pegs, wooden or metal, with a piece of whang to go round the index finger and you were in business. In good weather it was in the field and in winter with snow, the shocks would be brought into the barn - the Threshing Floor of the bank barn would be a wonderful setting for a night huskin' Bee, some huskin', some cribbing the corn, and some of the young men hurrying to find the first "RED" ear of corn which always entitled him to a kiss from the "Farmer's Daughter". Cider, popcorn balls, and just nice big red apples couldn't be beat. Such nights will never be forgotten!

THE MAIL ORDER CATALOGUES. You can order a new catalogue every year so when you get the new one make the best use of the old one. The heavy sheets when torn out carefully are just right in size for tying over crocks of Apple Butter and many other uses. Of course, once somebody drags it out to the little house, it can never be used for anything else. Even today, after the many changes, folks cherish the memory of happy hours spent leafing through the old thing dreaming of how they would enjoy the thousand things pictured therein. For many, that time is gone forever!

MOTHER'S OLD FLOWER GARDEN. Dozens of varieties and colors, tall spindley stems, short fleshy stems, fragrance of all kinds, beds, rows and rings. No doubt she got ideas of arrangement from grandmother. The mere memory of the gorgeous show make us love her the more; canterbury bells, ageratum, phlox, dahlias, larkspur and a score of others.

BARN RAISINGS. They were numerous the last ten years of the past century and the first two decades of this century. A few farmer-carpenters did their own framing, like Elias Fisher of Locke township. But there were barn framers who made a business of it like the Culps and the Moyers, and last but not least Ollie McDowell State Road 19, north of Wakarusa. The timbers would be squared out right on the ground, measured to the sixty-fourth inch, mortise joints chiseled out the tenon ends sawed accurately and trimmed with the chisel, to slide freely into the mortise, and holes to match to accommodate the lock pin after the frame would be raised in place, likewise the cross beams and braces, as well as the purloins half way up the roof to accommodate the rafters for the sheeting and shingles, and when sides were an engineer's masterpiece, the approximate day would be confirmed, and on the set day, 50 to 100 men would come for the "barn-raising". Then the signal, "take hold", then "heave", and "a little more", every barn framer with his own vocabulary, until the beautiful frame would stand erect, and when the last brace would be in place, allowing for a little sway, to allow for sliding the tenons in place, Ollie McDowell would invariably end the last tense moment with a deep groan, followed with a dramatic cry of Joy and exaltation "Safe in the arms of Jesus".

The number of men would depend somewhat on the size of the barn. Many of those same barns were later raised to bank barn height and a stone wall built for the bank. Now the era is over, and when a barn burns, a Borkholder pole goes up in a few weeks. Anthony Lechlitner had the barn moving outfit until 1910, my brother Lloyd and I had it until 1930, and we sold it to Ollie McDowell. Very dangerous business! Occassionally some would be killed by a falling timber out of control.

Farm People have a great PHILOSOPHY, a farmer in this county who has not had a drop of water since June, said his wheat crop was good and his oats were great, 72 bushels per acre, even though his corn cannot come out with more than half a crop, even if it should rain every day from now on. He knows that because of his diversification he can count on something.

He has learned to "Live with it", even though sometimes it looks rough. He has learned to sell the hams and shoulders, and eat the "sow belly," Shaken up the potatoes to get the big ones on top, sold them as selects, and cut up the little ones for German fries, picked out the big apples for a good price, and cut up the knarley ones and rotten ones, and schnitzed them up and dried them for snits pies. When he did not have the money for something, he has done without.

In Uncle Elmer's humble opinion he is the salt of the earth.

INDEX